Northwest Vista College
Learning Resource Center
3535 North Ellison Drive
San Antonio, Texas 78251

The Missing Corpse

The Missing Corpse
Grave Robbing a Gilded Age Tycoon

WAYNE FANEBUST

Foreword by John Ellis Kordes

PRAEGER

Westport, Connecticut
London

Library of Congress Cataloging-in-Publication Data

Fanebust, Wayne.
  The missing corpse: grave robbing a gilded age tycoon / Wayne Fanebust; foreword by John Ellis Kordes.
     p. cm.
  Includes bibliographical references and index.
  ISBN 0-275-98762-0 (alk. paper)
  1. Robbery investigation—New York (State)—New York—History—19th century. 2. Stewart, Alexander Turney, 1803–1876—Death and burial. 3. Grave robbing—New York (State)—New York—History—19th century. 4. Body snatching—New York (State)—New York—History—19th century. 5. Merchants—New York (State)—New York—Biography. 6. Rich people—New York (State)—New York—Social life and customs—19th century.   I. Title: Grave robbing a gilded age tycoon.   II. Title.
  HV8079.R62F36   2005
  364.16'2—dc22   2005016848

British Library Cataloguing in Publication Data is available.

Copyright © 2005 by Wayne Fanebust

All rights reserved. No portion of this book may be reproduced, by any process or technique, without the express written consent of the publisher.

Library of Congress Catalog Card Number: 2005016848
ISBN: 0-275-98762-0

First published in 2005

Praeger Publishers, 88 Post Road West, Westport, CT 06881
An imprint of Greenwood Publishing Group, Inc.
www.praeger.com

Printed in the United States of America

The paper used in this book complies with the
Permanent Paper Standard issued by the National
Information Standards Organization (Z39.48–1984).

10 9 8 7 6 5 4 3 2 1

Contents

Foreword *by John Ellis Kordes*		vii
Acknowledgments		ix
1	The Life of a Merchant Prince	1
2	The Death of a Merchant Prince	19
3	Violation of the Tomb	31
4	The Resurrectionists	51
5	Middleton, Allekton, Dr. Christian, and Other "Clews"	69
6	In Search of the Ghouls	87
7	Hackman Kelly	105
8	Closing In on the Ghouls	115
9	The Mystery Deepens	133
10	Grave Robber Christian Again	147

11	The Investigation Winds Down	163
12	First Contact with the Ghouls	173
13	The Dream of Mr. Bryson	191
14	A Footnote to a Grave Robbery	209
15	Was Stewart's Body Recovered?	223
Notes		249
Index		265

Foreword

"The man who amassed the largest fortune ever accumulated within the span of a single life was simply a hardworking, careful merchant with a decided talent for organization and a somewhat rare faculty for taking as firm a grasp of petty details as of broad and general principles." This was the way the *New York Times* described Alexander T. Stewart the day after he died in April 1876.

Stewart was, indeed, along with Vanderbilt and Astor, one of the wealthiest men in the world. His accomplishments as a merchant were unparalleled in the nineteenth century, and his death was mourned on two continents. He was a commercial genius and is credited with creating the concept of the department store. "A. T. Stewart and Company" was one of the best-known business names throughout the world.

By the dawn of the twentieth century, however, Stewart had already faded into history. He and his wife Cornelia were childless, and his commercial empire collapsed after his death. Despite all his accomplishments and fame, it was an incident that occurred after his death that kept his name in the public mind. Two and a half years after he died, Stewart's remains were stolen from their resting place in the St. Mark's churchyard in New York City. It was one of the most bizarre crimes in American history.

Here, for the very first time, is an extraordinary look at the A. T. Stewart body-snatching case. Author Wayne Fanebust has done the most extensive research to date into the crime. What is revealed is nothing short of proof that fact is often stranger than fiction. This crime, which shocked the nation in 1878, struck at the very heart of society, begging the question: "Is nothing sacred?"

The Stewart case was never solved and remains an intriguing mystery to this day. The facts surrounding the case are laid out and examined in this book. It is a fascinating look at grave robbery, an episode of American history that many people have forgotten.

The decades following the Civil War were marked by rapid growth and industrialization. While America was experiencing rebirth as a nation, A. T. Stewart was planning and building Garden City on Long Island in New York. Founded in 1869, Garden City is a place where Stewart is remembered. The Cathedral of the Incarnation, built by his widow, stands as a monument to his memory. It was intended to be his final resting place. The body snatching disrupted those plans, but the village he created flourished and became his legacy. In the city of New York, however, where he earned fame and fortune, the name Alexander T. Stewart lost all meaning long ago. Such can be the cruel irony of history.

John Ellis Kordes
Village Historian
Village of Garden City, New York

Acknowledgments

The idea for this book came to life when my sister Connie Lilla and I were involved in family-history research. We were reviewing some old newspaper microfilm at the Omaha Public Library when we came across an article about the theft and ransom of the body of Alexander T. Stewart, a self-made multimillionaire from New York. I was just then considering a book about the dark side of American history and thought about including the mysterious Stewart "resurrection" among the chapters. My sister said, "No, it's a book in itself," and so it has become a book.

Researching a celebrity grave robbing was a long and fascinating project, and I met some interesting people while pursuing the dark mystery. All of them contributed in some way, and all deserve my thanks. I want to thank the late Ted Goldstein and Sallie Williams for taking a stranger into their Long Island homes while I worked at the New York Public Library. Sallie has become a special friend and steadfast supporter.

I want to thank the people at the Cathedral of the Incarnation of Garden City for patiently answering my letter inquiries when I could have been dismissed as a crank. The Very Reverend James J. Cardone introduced me to John Ellis Kordes, a Garden City historian. John immediately took an interest in the project and gave me a personal tour of Garden City, Stewart's creation, including the cathedral and the crypt that was the focus of so much controversy and speculation. John has been a very important link to valuable sources of information for the book, including several photographs from the Garden City Archives. Thank you, John.

I want to thank the Garden City Archives; the public libraries of New York, Garden City, and Omaha; and especially the Sioux Falls public library, where most of my research was conducted by way of interlibrary loans. Tina Irvine of the Sioux Falls library assisted admirably and patiently, and I greatly appreciate her friendly effort. I became a member of the New York Historical Society and was able to spend a day doing research at that outstanding facility, and I am grateful for that opportunity.

A very special thank-you is due to my friend and fellow writer, David Swan, for spending many an hour reviewing and editing the drafts of my chapters. Thanks to his thoughtful and careful editing, my manuscript was improved and eventually accepted by Authentic Creations Literary Agency. Through the efforts of Ron Laitsch, I was able to find a publisher. Thank you, Ron. I want to thank my friends and fellow history buffs Alice Marquis, Bruce Blake, Byron Schmidt, Aaron Munson, Tom Kilian, and John Timm for listening to me talk about ghouls who robbed graves for a living and the Stewart mystery, while never questioning my sanity.

My family has always believed in me and cheered on my writing projects. I thank my mother, Dorothy Fanebust, along with my sisters, brothers, and other family members for their love and support. Finally, I thank my daughter, Danae, for without her love and cheerful encouragement, my creative output would be greatly diminished. She is my inspiration and the joy of my life.

Wayne Fanebust
Sioux Falls, SD

CHAPTER 1

The Life of a Merchant Prince

> More than any one else in America probably Alexander T. Stewart is the very embodiment of business. He is emphatically a man of money.
>
> Junius Henri Browne, 1869

Alexander Turney Stewart rose from obscurity to fame and power in New York, turning a small inheritance into a great fortune. The very embodiment of America's Gilded Age, he was the celebrated "Merchant Prince" of Manhattan, the founder and ruler of the greatest dry goods business empire the world had known.

Although he wasn't striking in his appearance and could easily get lost in a crowd, A. T. Stewart—as he was usually called—was a public figure. He was one of the first self-made multimillionaires in America. While he made enemies, he was widely known and admired for his success and wealth. Long before America ascribed celebrity status to artists, entertainers, and sports figures, ordinary people looked at the wealthy with both admiration and contempt—but always as fortune's favorites. Over time, Stewart became an almost mythical figure, symbolic of all the good that a creator of wealth could bring to the world.

Those close to Stewart remembered him as a plain man in most respects, not the mythical giant that existed in the public mind. Simple and carefully unostentatious in his dress and manner, A. T. Stewart was a short, slightly built, sandy-haired man with large, cold, and discerning blue eyes. His bearded and dour countenance—backed by his millions—commanded respect. Although his voice was soft and slightly effeminate, he was terse, direct, and convincing in his verbal presentations. The *New York Times* remembered him as "austere" although not "morose" and a man who "could not appreciate a joke, and was not gifted with a sense of humor."[1] Having spent many years bent over his books under lamplight, he was far too practical for jokes.

Stewart used his rare marketing genius to gather unto himself what many believed was the greatest fortune ever earned by one man in a lifetime. He had business connections in many American cities, nine factories in Europe, and mills throughout New England. He owned the Grand Union Hotel in the resort community of Saratoga Springs, New York, and the Globe Theatre, Niblo's Garden Theatre, and the Metropolitan Hotel in New York City. His reach went as far west as Dakota Territory, where he endorsed a scheme to establish an Irish colony in the wilds of Brule County, by the Missouri River.[2]

However, the lure of faraway places had no hold over him. He was a New Yorker first, last, and always, and it was there that he used his consummate business skills, the commercial advantage of New York, and the freedom and opportunity offered by America to make his life an overwhelming financial success. If Horatio Alger was looking for a poster-boy to advertise his gospel of wealth, he could do no better than Alexander T. Stewart. A contemporary declared he was the very "embodiment of business," a man who "thinks money; makes money; lives money."[3]

During the 1870s, New York boasted having the three richest families in America. In addition to A. T. Stewart, there was Cornelius Vanderbilt (commonly referred to as "Commodore"), who made a fortune in the stock market, railroads, and shipping after years of ruthless competition. The third in this triumvirate of wealth was William B. Astor. He inherited a fortune from his father, John Jacob Astor, the fur-trading and real estate magnate. William more than doubled the fortune in his lifetime. The Astor family was "old money," and it was known as the "landlord of New York" and the unchallenged social ruler of New York high society.

Information about A. T. Stewart's early life varies among available sources. Conflicting stories were circulated freely, attempting to explain just how, when, and where he started his business career. It was as if

A. T. Stewart, 1803–1876. 1860 portrait by T. P. Rossiter. Image courtesy of Garden City Archives.

no one was willing to believe that a mere immigrant could set his own rules and be successful as a merchant.

Stewart was born in Lisburn, Ireland, on October 12, 1803, to a Scotch-Irish family of some means. His father died when he was three. His mother remarried a man named David Bell and moved with him to the United States. Young Alexander stayed in Ireland and looked to his maternal grandfather John Turney for guidance. He was expected to become a member of the clergy and, to that end, was engaged in a classical education.

Alexander was in his second year at Trinity College in Dublin when his grandfather died. He was a levelheaded sixteen-year-old when he was suddenly on his own. He accepted this change as if only good could come from it and booked passage for America, arriving in New York in 1818.[4] He may not have known exactly what he wanted to do, but he decided he would not be a minister.

The *New York World*, a newspaper with a keen, posthumous interest in Stewart, had a slightly different slant on his early days. A reporter sent to Ireland in 1890 to scout out his past concluded that Stewart was born just two months before his father, a poor but ambitious farmer, died of overwork. Stewart's mother and her second husband, David Bell, were the parents of two children: a boy, James, and a girl, Mary. The Bells moved to America intending to buy a farm somewhere in the West, leaving Alexander with his grandfather.[5]

An article in *Harper's New Monthly Magazine* stated that Stewart was left an orphan at age eight. It also had him a graduate of Trinity College who came to America with letters of introduction from the Society of Friends in Ireland—letters directed to prominent New York merchants.[6] Such inconsistencies in the written record lead one to believe Stewart purposely allowed conflicting stories about his origins to be spread around, taking comfort in the mystery.

What everyone agrees upon, however, is that, after the death of his grandfather, A. T. Stewart left his native Ireland and came to America. He landed in New York, a growing, energetic city that cast a rustic and rural appearance as livestock still roamed at large on its unpaved streets. Young immigrant Stewart was a "stranger in a strange land," as the saying went, but he had some money from his grandfather's estate and letters of introduction. He stayed with his mother and stepfather and spent some time teaching. It wasn't long before he found his true calling: dry goods merchandising.

Stewart returned to Ireland, and with his inheritance (or money he earned in New York), he invested about $5,000 in a stock of dry goods that he took back to New York. Most sources state that Stewart launched his merchandising career in 1823 in a small rented store at 283 Broadway. However, one writer uncovered evidence that Stewart's first store was actually on Greenwich Street, a place he occupied sometime between 1819 and 1823.[7]

Whatever the truth, from the very outset Stewart displayed a flair for merchandising; he had a shopkeeper's mentality and a seller's instinct. Taking advantage of a new trend in dresses, Stewart invested all his available funds in cotton trimmings, and by buying low and selling high, he made his first killing.[8] Early on, he found out what the ladies liked and was thereafter a ladies' man first, last, and always.

Giving every aspect of his business personal attention, Stewart prospered, thanks to his matchless faculty for detail and his eye for finding a saleable, popular product. His formula for success was simple and sound: buy in large quantities for a fair, cash price and sell at a cash price sufficient to reap a reasonable profit. To implement his plan, he put into play certain basic business practices that he never relinquished. First and foremost, Stewart was committed to complete honesty toward his customers and those from whom he purchased goods. Second, he sold his goods at a fixed price that assured a reasonable profit. This way his customers were freed from the hazards of haggling and came to understand the value of their purchases. He only lowered his prices when the market was depressed and liquidation was the wisest course. His third principle was cash on delivery; credit was barely in his vocabulary. He believed its place in business was very limited, if at all.[9]

Using these three rules, Stewart's business was enormously successful. His radical, "one-price-for-all-customers" rule astounded the merchandising world—and it worked. The ladies of New York became his faithful customers, and he served them faithfully, bringing in the latest styles and fabrics. He also benefited from the amount of clothing women wore. The layers of constricting garments that wrapped a woman tightly in a cloak of respectability were extra profit.

Stewart's advertising was modest, plain, and limited to straightforward newspaper ads, and he never placed a sign or used his name on his stores. Yet his stores grew larger as he rolled over his competition, and he was barely slowed down by the financial panics of 1837, 1857, and 1873. While he was called ruthless and was feared and hated by his competitors,[10] he operated quite like other successful capitalists of his day; he recognized an opportunity and acted without undue delay. He is credited with creating the modern American department store in the galleria style.

Often thought of as a cold, greedy man who "clutched at all the gold he saw,"[11] Stewart worked very hard, usually into the evening hours. He rarely celebrated holidays and had little or no time for leisure or recreation. So devoted was he to the day-to-day details of his business that an assistant screened every caller, regardless of each caller's relative importance.

One day in 1862, a man from President Lincoln's administration called at Stewart's office, requesting a meeting. Though the man displayed an air of importance, the assistant insisted that the visitor first explain the nature of his business. When the man retorted with indignation that he represented Lincoln, the assistant said, "Sir, if Mr. Lincoln himself were to come here, he would not see Mr. Stewart until he should have first told me his business."[12] Like everything else that worked, Stewart stayed with this procedure.

His enormous success notwithstanding, there was really no mystery about the man at all, except for one unusual feature. Stewart was said to be superstitious, and his superstitions were well-known in New York. For example, he avoided the number thirteen and would shy away from a business transaction if that number appeared. He preferred ridicule to tempting fate. Also, he would never sit and eat at a table that had thirteen diners. After many years, he struggled to overcome this superstition and finally sat down at a table of thirteen. Within a few weeks he was dead.[13]

Once when Stewart changed business locations, he brought with him an eccentric old woman, who for many years sold apples outside his former store. Stewart, who regularly ate her apples, believed the old woman brought him good luck and insisted that she move, rickety stand and all, to his new location. His new store was a success, of course, and he believed it was because of the old woman's presence.[14] His superstitious nature was odd indeed, for such a practical man, and one that he did not rise to dispute.

While he epitomized the self-made man, Stewart owed something to his marriage. In fact he married well. His wife, Cornelia Mitchell Clinch, was the daughter of a well-connected New York family. Her parents were Jacob and Susanna (Banker) Clinch. Jacob Clinch was a successful ship chandler with the firm of Jones and Clinch. Cornelia was one of nine children who survived out of twenty-four births. Stewart met her in 1818 when both were members of the St. Mark's Episcopal congregation. They were married on October 16, 1823.[15] The Stewarts had two children: a boy, John Turney Stewart, born in 1834 and who died within a few weeks, and a girl, May, stillborn in 1838.

In 1823 Stewart opened the first of his Broadway stores at 283 Broadway, a modest place that lived on in the memory of New Yorkers as "Stewart's little store."[16] In 1827 Stewart moved to a larger facility at

262 Broadway. In 1830 he again acquired a bigger store at 257 Broadway, in a building constructed by John Jacob Astor. He stayed there until he was ready to branch out in a style that amazed all of New York and fairly exhausted his breathless competitors.

By 1837 Stewart was eager for more.[17] He had a plan to get more. Beginning in 1844 Stewart methodically and carefully purchased the lots on Broadway between Reade and Chambers streets for the construction of a new store. Then on September 21, 1846, Stewart opened up a huge new store that became known as the "Marble Palace."[18] He was 41 years old, a multimillionaire, and justifiably proud of his success and standing. The grand opening of this store was the defining moment of his life. The doors were opened, the first sale was made (for good luck) to a lady friend who requested to be the first customer, and Stewart was moved to tears.

With this state-of-the-art store, Stewart stood alone among dry goods merchants of New York. It was four stories of cast-iron and marble magnificence at Broadway and Reade Street[19] that went soaring into the vacant skyline. The building site was originally a burial ground and later the site of Washington Hall, once one of New York's leading hotels. Washington Hall burned to the ground in 1844, luckily saving Stewart from having to tear it down.[20]

In 1842 Charles Dickens described New York City as "low, dull, straggling and ill built."[21] Stewart attacked this negative image of his city. Constructed in the new and daring Anglo-Italianate style, faced with Tuckahoe marble, rich in detail that included mahogany and maple shelves, fresco decorations and brilliant chandeliers, and built around a central well that terminated in a massive dome, the Marble Palace intrigued and dazzled New Yorkers. It was a spare-no-expense extravaganza that seemed out of character for so plain a man.

His envious critics called it an outlandish "pile," and as it was on the "shilling" side of Broadway, many believed it would fail, yet Stewart proved them wrong. It was so successful that Stewart enlarged and restructured the Marble Palace, also called his "downtown" store.[22] Ultimately, the store was extended to Chamber Street, occupying an entire city block. The building is still standing.

On November 10, 1862, Stewart opened yet another huge and opulent store on Broadway between Ninth and Tenth streets in the Astor Place area.[23] This store, five stories of cast iron and stone with a central atrium;

A. T. Stewart's Dry Goods store, Broadway, NY, 1851,
engraving by J. A. Bogert; negative #41435.
Collection of The New York Historical Society.

was devoted entirely to retail trade. It was in the Renaissance style and was considered the largest retail store in the world. It became known as his "uptown" or "Great Iron" store.[24] Stewart spent the next six years enlarging the Great Iron store until it took up an entire block. After this new store was opened, the Marble Palace became Stewart's wholesale establishment.

At his peak Stewart employed more than 5,000 people, mostly women and girls, many of whom toiled over rows of sewing machines on the fourth floor of the Marble Palace. He also had his pick from among his many failed competitors, and he added these men to his staff as managers. While these losers lacked Stewart's genius and luck, they were experienced. Their boss—known as "The Autocrat of Trade"—harnessed their

Stewart's Great Iron store on Broadway between Ninth and Tenth streets. Image courtesy of Garden City Archives.

ability and used it to his advantage. Still it was said "no man in the concern works harder than its owner."[25]

As he maintained high standards for himself, it should be no surprise to learn he was very demanding of his workers. The workday began at 7 a.m. and ended at 7 p.m., with a half hour off for lunch. Among his many rules, employees were not permitted to sit down during business hours. He once flew into a rage and fired an employee who was caught reading a newspaper during a quiet moment. Drinking was forbidden, although Stewart was known to overlook this if he really liked the offender. It was impermissible to stay out late, go to the theater, and patronize brothels.

Stewart even monopolized his employees' time off, as they were required to go to church twice every Sunday.[26] Workers who were late for work were fined twenty-five cents per act of tardiness, the money going to charity.[27] There were other fines for various infractions, all rigidly enforced. Every employee was subject to a search by a detective upon leaving the store at the end of the day.

Stewart was very fussy about appearance, especially his own. His suits and linens were the finest, although very plain in style. His personal valet, William P. Smith, was kept busy brushing, pressing, and folding the Stewart wardrobe. It was an edgy, nervous occupation for Smith. Yet despite this ritual devotion to detail, it was said that Stewart often exuded a foul body odor that his perfumed hankie could not overcome and, as such, kept people at a discreet distance.[28]

It was his rules, not body odor, that caused Stewart's workers concern. The boss would not allow his female employees to wear jewelry. Strangely, men were permitted to wear "tasteful" jewelry. Stewart would explode when angered and chew out a clerk in a shrill voice that left no doubt about who was the boss. He was their master, and they were his servants. In an era when employers were, for all practical purposes, rulers, he controlled their lives with a rigid, paternalistic hand that was unique to nineteenth-century America.

Throughout much of the 1870s America was caught in the grip of a severe depression set off by the Panic of 1873. The national unemployment rate was high, and in cities like New York, masses of poor families lived without hope in the most abject of conditions. Charities barely had any ameliorative effect. People fortunate to have work seldom complained, even when wages were cut by as much as one-half. The worker and his family were utterly dependent on good relations with his employer, for there was no governmental "safety net" to catch them should they fall.

Those who were in good standing with A. T. Stewart and Company were blessed by comparison to the unemployed. Although his employees were underpaid and exploited, a job with Stewart could mean a lifetime of security. His workers had good reason to toe the line. In the age of big business, workers were forced to sacrifice their pride and dignity to receive whatever pittance was offered.

The female customer, however, was another matter. Giving up nothing, the customer was queen at Stewart's, and his employees had to know it or seek work elsewhere. Be they rural or urban, the richest of the rich or women of modest means, ladies entering his store were often greeted with a courteous bow from the owner himself. It was a gesture executed without the slightest indication of snobbery. After that a legion of ushers provided direction, answering questions with precision and politeness as if they were extensions of Stewart himself.

The ladies loved Stewart's because they could shop leisurely, for hours, knowing they would not be forced to buy anything. His store became a meeting place, a sort of New York club for women. Stewart was the first to provide revolving stools for his customers' comfort while

A. T. Stewart, "The Modern Un-Pharaoh" (anonymous) from *The Arcadian*, ca. 1875. Print Collection, Miriam and Ira D. Wallach Division of Art, Prints, and Photographs, The New York Public Library, Astor, Lenox, and Tilden Foundations.

they examined the goods including luxurious silk gowns, Belfast lace, and camel hair shawls costing $1,000 each.[29]

The popularity of Stewart's store and the great diversity of women it attracted led to at least one incident of violence between two women. It happened when Elvira N. Spinola, wife of General Frank B. Spinola, encountered another shopper, Mary Gill, on a staircase. Apparently there had been some bad blood between the women for Gill casually said to her companion, but loud enough for the general's wife to hear: "There goes a deserted wife; her husband has got his trunk at my house, and I have just come from breakfast with him." Hurt, embarrassed, and angered, Spinola lunged forward and struck Gill several times on the head with her parasol. She was pulled away from her screaming victim and placed under arrest for assault and battery. Understandably, the scene caused quite an uproar.[30]

Stewart's skill at the art of display and visual seduction was peerless; shoppers were overcome by a materialistic desire in his store. Shopping at Stewart's became a pleasure to be enjoyed over and over again. The wise and witty Henry James said Stewart's store was "fatal to feminine nerves."[31] Another source suggested Stewart created the "right to shop."[32]

Stewart knew exactly what he was doing, and hiring the best-looking young men available to wait on the ladies was part of the seduction. Women freely admitted they came to Stewart's store to buy from his "nice young men."[33] They came, they saw, they spent. After all, the rich had to do something with their money. The culture of consumption that blossomed in the 1890s under Stewart's successors took root in the Marble Palace. John Wanamaker, Henry Siegel, Marshall Field, and others paid homage to Alexander T. Stewart, the original merchant prince. He had the vision.

While Stewart had some understanding of the female psyche, he developed few close friendships among men and had limited use for business partners. Of the thousands of people he employed, some went on to prominence in other fields. Among them, Cyrus W. Field of Atlantic Cable fame started with Stewart as an errand boy. Mathew Brady, who was employed by Stewart as a clerk from 1838 to 1845, later achieved success and fame for his Civil War photographs.[34]

When the Civil War broke out, Stewart was worth about $8 million. By the time it ended, he was a great deal richer. The Civil War is known for its waste, devastation, and terrible loss of life, but for a handful of capitalists, the war brought a harvest of wealth from a general expansion of business and the military requirements of the Union. As Stewart had many connections in the South, he abhorred the idea of a war between the North and South. Still, while the war disrupted these lines of business, it opened up others. Stewart turned his attention to government contracts, selling uniforms and blankets to the Union army.

Before the war was a year old, a newspaper article declared that no one in America was "coining money at so rushing a rate as Alexander T. Stewart." While his competitors failed or sputtered, Stewart's sales, it was reported, ranged to a million dollars per week as people considered it "impossible to pass any number of days" without visiting his Marble Palace. More important than retail sales was his monopoly on supplying the government with dry goods. For a time he was alone in the field. Having foreseen that the demand would be huge, he cornered the market on materials and was able to set his price, and Uncle Sam was "compelled to pay tribute to the Marble Palace or go without goods." Who wouldn't, a journalist inquired with a hint of envy, "be a member of the Union Defense Committee under such interesting circumstances?"[35]

To his credit, however, Stewart did not engage in pure profiteering, as did many of his peers. Cornelius Vanderbilt, for example, shamelessly leased a beat-up old steamer to the government at $800 to $900 per day. Stewart, on the other hand, sold good merchandise at a fair price, while members of the "shoddy aristocracy"[36] cheated the government by supplying uniforms that fell apart not long after the soldiers put them on. Stewart's strict sense of business honesty would not permit him to cheat a customer, not even the federal government.

Like many other merchants, Stewart was a Democrat. While he never joined the Republican Party, he was an ardent supporter of the Union and believed it had to be preserved at all costs. He was a patriot. He understood that he owed his great wealth to the American way, and he pledged his life and fortune to the Union cause.[37] He and other likeminded men became known as "war Democrats."

In 1860 Stewart favored the presidential candidacy of Senator Stephen O. Douglas of Illinois but soon shifted his support to Abraham Lincoln. The two men met in the late 1850s and, as a result of the war, they became friends and allies. They had a common goal: preserving the Union and saving the U.S. Constitution. After he was elected, Lincoln sought the counsel and support of the New York rich. Lincoln and Stewart breakfasted together in New York just before the president took office.

The president's wife, Mary Todd Lincoln, also had a connection with Stewart: she loved to shop in his store. After he threw a dinner party in her honor, she promptly ordered $2000 worth of rugs for the White House.[38] Mrs. Lincoln was a mad, compulsive buyer who spent extravagant sums of money wherever she went. She bought gloves the way Imelda Marcos bought shoes, at one time ordering 84 pairs of gloves.

In 1864 Mrs. Lincoln went on a summer-long shopping spree in New York.[39] Stewart and other merchants allowed her to charge—a big mistake. She drove the president deep into debt with her uncontrolled spending. Stewart considered suing her over the $27,000 owed him but did not, most likely out of his respect for President Lincoln.[40] Mrs. Lincoln's debt was a pittance to Stewart, who could easily spare it and avoid an embarrassment to the president, who he admired.

Stewart, along with other eastern and northern merchants, lost heavily because of southern debtors' repudiation of debts, proving war was not always good for business. In April 1861 he took a Tennessee debtor to task for defaulting. The debtor refused to pay because of Stewart's open support for the Union. Stewart answered this charge saying, "All that I have of position and wealth I owe to the free institutions of the United States." It was too bad, he added, that Tennessee turned its back on the Constitution. Stewart, however, pledged loyalty to the Union, saying, "I shall be with them, supporting the flag."[41]

Stewart voted for Lincoln in 1864. After the president was assassinated, he supported Andrew Johnson's controversial Reconstruction policy for rebuilding the South. Next, he turned his attention to General Ulysses S. Grant. Stewart admired Grant for his military success in the Civil War. In 1866 Stewart led an effort to raise $100,000 to pay Grant for his wartime services, contributing $5,000 of his own money.[42]

Stewart supported Grant's presidential candidacy in 1868, although he was still a Democrat and Grant was running as a Republican. Soon, he became a full-fledged Grant insider, hosting lavish dinner parties and organizing campaign events. It was said that in the city of New York, "no man contributed more than Stewart in turning the tide in favor of Grant."[43]

In March 1869, immediately after he was sworn in as president, Grant surprised everyone by naming Stewart his secretary of the treasury. The *New York Times* heartily approved of Grant's choice because of Stewart's proven business acumen and sound reputation. Stewart, the *Times* said, was already rich and, therefore, would not be tempted to use the office for personal gain. On the other hand, he would "touch the dead corpse of public credit" and cause it to breathe healthily again. The public should be so lucky to have a man of his sense of frugality and practical ability running the Treasury Department.[44]

Not everyone felt that way. The selection caused a storm of criticism from many sources. Some disliked the appointment because Stewart supported the rapid reconstruction of the war-ravaged South. Others resented it because he was not a Republican. One highly placed Republican accused Stewart of seeking the post to elevate his stature among the rich elite, since wealth alone did not admit him into the "first circles."[45] Those who emitted the loudest howl of protest were the "protectionists," who feared his "free trade" beliefs might result in reduced tariffs on imports.

Despite the backlash, the Senate unanimously confirmed Stewart. He attended one cabinet meeting, but suddenly it was revealed that a 1789 law prohibited a man from acting as Secretary of the Treasury who at the same time was in the business of commerce. High tariff advocates breathed a sigh of relief. Grant was crushed and Stewart was perplexed. Grant wanted the old law modified or suspended so Stewart could serve.

Stewart met with Grant, and the two drank tea and discussed the dilemma. Stewart expressed great concern over the prospect of having to ignore his business for the next four years or more, but he had to avoid a conflict of interest. He considered placing all his business interests in trust or transferring them to trusted individuals, namely Henry Hilton, William B. Astor, James Brown, William E. Dodge, and James T. Roosevelt. These men would run A. T. Stewart and Company and turn the profit over to preselected New York charities. It was estimated that had Stewart served four years as secretary of the treasury, the lofty sum of $8 million or $9 million would have poured into the designated charities.[46]

It was a terrible dilemma for Stewart. In order to take the coveted cabinet post, he would have to part with his business empire. He would be forced to separate himself from his creation, from everything that was important and dear to him. How great an irony to deal with—to see his beloved global enterprise rise up and present an insurmountable barrier to furthering his political ambitions.

The cabinet position represented a high point in his life, and Stewart very much wanted to serve. However, he changed his mind in view of the opposition and the obstacles, and on March 9, 1869, he resigned. With thanks, he said, "I cannot consent to enter upon the administration of law by any act or course that may be construed into a disregard or violation of law." His admiration for Grant was undiminished, however, and it was reported that Stewart sent an agent to Kentucky with instructions to purchase a $5,000 horse and ship it to Washington as a gift for the president.[47]

Stewart never again dabbled in politics,[48] although he ignored Grant and supported the candidacy of his friend and fellow New Yorker Horace Greeley in the 1872 presidential campaign.[49] Greeley, an original Republican, ran for president as a "liberal" in opposition to the corrupt Grant administration. He was the able editor of the *New York Tribune* and was popular with the masses, but he was brutalized by his political enemies, was defeated, and died not long after Grant was reelected.

It is probably just as well that Stewart quit the quest for public office, for quite likely he would have found the politics of his time too distasteful. The year 1869 ushered in an era of unparalleled political dishonesty and corruption. The Grant administration was rife with incompetent and corrupt officials who used office openly and shamelessly for personal gain. While the South was suffering from postwar pains, the rest of America bore witness to a mad scramble for wealth and power marked by graft, bribery, and blackmail.

A sense of cynicism prevailed among the people, especially in New York where the city was caught up in the coils of ultracorrupt machine politics. It seemed no one, high or low, had a proper motive. Political offices were openly sold. Politics could be described as a joke, were it not for the great detriment to the public good. A thoughtful Henry Adams quipped: "Society laughed a vacant and meaningless derision at its own failure."[50] It was a scathing, well-deserved indictment.

In New York financiers Jay Gould and Jim Fisk were clawing their way to the top by cheating partners, investors, the government, and the public at large. While their fortunes were approaching those of the "big three," Stewart would have nothing to do with Fisk or Gould. Yet it was the sinister and friendless Gould and the jovial and hedonistic Fisk who stole the financial show and earned more historic recognition than the quiet and clerkish Stewart. Fisk and Gould quickly and inevitably evolved into the products of a corrupt time, making Stewart look like a saint.

If that were not enough, the swimmingly corrupt William "Boss" Tweed held the reins of power in New York City and throughout the state from 1866 to 1871. A man utterly without morals, his influence was so complete and his organization so strong that he controlled every facet of political life. He controlled or manipulated elections, sold offices, issued phony warrants, and accepted and paid bribes. Judges, police, legislators, and other officials were beholden to him. All answered to the gregarious, gaudy, and gluttonous "Boss" Tweed. He had his own man—the erratic, flamboyant, and openly corrupt "Elegant" Abraham Oakey Hall—elected mayor, and in 1871, he announced that his organization would nominate and back Stewart for mayor, an "honor" Stewart wisely refused.[51] Tweed and his gang raked in millions at public and private expense until he was finally brought down in 1871 by reformers under the leadership of the *New York Times*.

Meanwhile, Stewart thrived, staying by his business standards. Ever the Merchant Prince, he kept his focus on matters of commerce. However, politics had placed him in the public eye whether he liked it or not, and for the rest of his life he was a public figure. While he was not thought of as a particularly charitable man, he was, nonetheless, subjected to requests from the public for money or favors. After he made a generous donation to the burned-out city of Chicago in 1871, Stewart was hit with a flood of letters from desperate people who wanted to take advantage of what many perceived to be a philanthropic attitude.

Late in life Stewart adopted a genuine public-spirited stance and made plans accordingly. One such project was the construction of a hotel for working women in the heart of New York. It was to be a facility to diminish the number of filthy tenement houses where thousands lived in poverty. Like his rich contemporaries, Stewart was suspicious of the poor. He distrusted their ideas and feared their raw power. Yet he saw in those who were working hard to escape poverty something that deserved respect and support, especially the women who worked for him in the "needle trade."

He once said, "I owe my fortune to the working women."[52] In so saying, he decided to help the workingwomen of New York and threw himself into the hotel project with dedication and purpose. Like other Stewart projects, this was to be an exceptional hotel, with great attention to detail and comfort and to be operated within strictly enforced guidelines.

Even more lavish and ambitious was his plan to create and develop an entire community, a place for "upscale" working and professional people to live. For this he chose the Hempstead plains of Long Island, which up to the late 1860s was for the most part a sea of grass used for grazing livestock. By 1871 Stewart had acquired more than 9,000 acres of Hempstead land.[53] His city, named Garden City, would have parks, streets, comfortable homes, and a commuter railroad. It was meant for people of "moderate circumstances" who had "refined or cultivated tastes"[54] and were willing to live a disciplined life. Included in this group were undoubtedly many of his best and most loyal employees. Stewart was widely praised for his plan to raise a city out of a "wasteland."

Garden City was to be well-planned and orderly, like Stewart himself. In fact it could be argued that the city was to be his legacy, as he had no heirs to carry his memory forward. While he may have felt there could be no substitute for children, Stewart would at least leave behind a creation that would live on into perpetuity, a reflection of himself, like the human offspring he never had.

The centerpiece of Garden City was to be an inspiring but "modest" church, named the Cathedral of the Incarnation.[55] Plans for building the church were barely underway, the workingwomen's hotel was partially built, and several structures were completed in Garden City when Stewart died. As with most ambitious and perpetually busy people, his life ended before he could complete his most cherished projects. He simply ran out of time. Like all of the great doers throughout time, he left things undone.

CHAPTER 2

The Death of a Merchant Prince

> His death ... touched the hearts ... of the people among whom and in whose eye he had lived for fifty-four years.
>
> *New York Times*, April 11, 1876

Alexander Turney Stewart was pronounced dead in the afternoon of April 10, 1876, just as America, his adopted country, was planning its centennial celebration. Stewart loved America and would have visited the great centennial exhibitions at Philadelphia had he lived a bit longer—but only if he could have pulled himself away from his work. No, Stewart did not work himself to death, but work—tending to every aspect of his business—was at the very center of his life for as long as he lived.

At the time of his death his personal worth was estimated to be $40 million to $50 million, including more than $10 million in real estate. According to *American Heritage* magazine, the value of Stewart's fortune in 1998 dollars was $46.9 billion, making the Merchant Prince the seventh all-time richest person in the history of the United States.[1]

Death was a frequent and casual visitor in New York City, and most folks were simply consigned to eternity with a few lines, if any at all. Stewart was one of the wealthiest and best-known men in America, so his demise in the year of the centennial celebration brought forth a rush of memories and praise. Antipathies were muttered in stony silence and would have to wait for another day to be heard. His obituary was written with painstaking care, and his funeral—planned to the hilt and described in minute detail—became the social event of the season. It was a send-off worthy of a prince, presented by people who believed death was not simply a quiet exit into dark nothingness.

Stewart was in the seventy-third year of his life when he died in the famed "lace room" of his palatial, four-story residence at Thirty-fourth Street and Fifth Avenue in the heart of New York. His illness was of short duration, and as he was known as a man with a strong constitution who looked much younger than his years, his death came as a surprise to New Yorkers.

With him at the end were his doctors who had attended his sick bed the ten days previous. Also at his side was his wife, his faithful Cornelia, along with some in-laws. For those gathered at his beside, death was not unexpected. It was a sad good-bye nonetheless, and the beginning of one of the strangest and most enthralling mysteries in the history of New York.

His death set off the usual forms of consternation among his family, friends, and business associates, but there was more. He was missed as people of wealth, power, and prestige were missed. The loss of Stewart signaled the loss of those blessings and meant that a grand fixture was taken away from New York. William B. Astor had died the year before leaving only Cornelius Vanderbilt outside the grasp of death. New York's "big three" was down to one.

Stewart's death was the cause of excited speculation. What would become of Garden City, Stewart's planned community? Would there be money to continue the ambitious and visionary project? Who would sit at Stewart's table at Del Monico's, where the Merchant Prince regularly lunched? Wouldn't it seem strange not to see Mr. and Mrs. Stewart seated in their box at Niblo's Garden Theatre every Monday night? Who would occupy his stateroom on the trans-Atlantic ocean liner that took him to Europe on business? Most assuredly, his European associates would miss his annual visits. While he was no colorful knight in shining armor, he was a prince among merchants, which was enough to make him respected and envied by many and missed by all.

He died in a house that can hardly be called a house. Begun in 1862, it was a magnificent mansion, huge and imposing, that dominated an entire city block on Fifth Avenue at Thirty-fourth Street. After he decided to build on a grand scale, Stewart bought and demolished the large brownstone home of Dr. Samuel P. Townsend, the patentee of sarsaparilla. In 1854 Townsend spent $100,000 to build a luxurious and impressive mansion that was rather plain and block-like on the outside.

The Stewart "palazzo" made everyone forget about the boxy brownstone. Fit for royalty, the Stewart house looked out and down on mortal humanity, as if designed to be a permanent reminder of nineteenth-century wealth and domineering, capitalistic power. Done in the new, modern French style, faced with Tuckahoe marble and topped with a mansard roof, the cost of construction was $2 million. Most of the artists and artisans who worked on the house were European, causing some criticism from those who thought Stewart "toadies on foreigners" to the exclusion of American products and workers.[2]

Because of its great size and shortages brought about by the Civil War, construction proceeded slowly, and the mansion was not ready for occupancy until 1872.[3] It was regarded as the finest in America, overshadowing the house of the nearest neighbors: the Astors. The location was no accident, of course, as Stewart was sending a message to that aristocratic family.

While the Stewart mansion was luxurious in every detail, it cast a certain cold, forbidding appearance, dwarfing everyone who came near. And come they did—by invitation of course—for the Stewarts often socialized in their home. Dinner parties with selected guests were legendary at the Stewart house. One night his guests might consist of snooty diplomats; the next one might find struggling artists or poor musicians at his table.[4]

Since Stewart was engaged in "trade," he and his wife were snubbed by the Astors and the rest of New York high society. While he no doubt built next to the Astors to impress them, they and their fellow elitists heaped undue criticism on the Stewart home, calling it an "ice palace" while barely concealing their envy of his success and just dying to get a look inside the house. Their scorn did not matter, for the lord of the Stewart manor was his own man. He proudly served as a convivial host to those who would come, engaging in high-toned conversation at the side of his small, nicely figured wife.

One notable feature of his house was Stewart's personal library. It was well stocked with the classics, and although Stewart was as busy as a man could be, he still took time to read in the evenings. His library was his sanctuary from the madhouse world of business transactions, and his knowledge of Greek and Latin was said to be the envy of college professors.[5]

Another outstanding feature of the Stewart house was the great proliferation of paintings and sculptures. Stewart, as did other business barons in his time, developed a deep and abiding interest in art, especially paintings. It seems he could not go to Europe without bringing back paintings to adorn his seventy-five-foot-long art gallery. At his death his art collection was valued at more than $600,000. It was rated the best in the United States and was the envy of the society of wealth that rejected the Merchant Prince.

Included in this rich legacy was a picture of George Washington by Gilbert Stuart[6] and an 1853 painting titled "The Horse Fair" by Rosa Bonheur, which Stewart bought in 1866. While he had no particular expertise in the field, his house was dominated by art, including his bathroom, which featured an "allegorical representation of the Union" by Yvon.[7] Renowned American landscape painter Albert Bierstadt was one of Stewart's friends.[8]

All of this and much more was suddenly the property of the estate of A. T. Stewart, making his will the subject of juicy speculation. Would his artwork go to a museum? Would his house be donated to the city for a museum? In addition to his wife, who would inherit money? Who would carry on his business affairs? These were tantalizing questions, but anxious New Yorkers would have to wait to see the will, for Stewart's funeral came first. It was to be a grand affair, befitting a man of his stature. A giant had fallen and everyone had cause to stop and reflect. The city of New York went into mourning, and most conversation was focused on Alexander T. Stewart.

All day on April 11, the body of A. T. Stewart lay in the lace room while funeral arrangements were being made. As he wasn't embalmed, his body was placed on ice to preserve it. His face was photographed by Gustavus Pach, a well-known photographer, and a plaster cast was taken by a sculptor. He probably would have disapproved of this because in life he disdained being photographed or sketched, fearing people would "lose faith in my prestige if they became familiar with my insignificant face."[9] For the first time, Stewart was not in control of his affairs.

Nor was Mrs. Stewart. She was overwhelmed by grief, and funeral plans were in the hands of Henry Hilton, who for many years previous had been the confidant, lawyer, business associate, and constant companion of A. T. Stewart. Hilton willingly took charge and arranged a showy, spectacular funeral, befitting the stature of his friend and benefactor. The pallbearers and guest list had to be arranged with great care, and as St. Mark's Episcopal Church was old and small, seating would be limited and by invitation only. The Stewart family vault in the St. Mark's churchyard was situated near that of the Fishers, the Livingstons, the Winthrops, the Beekmans, and other famous "old stock" New Yorkers, including the Dutch colonial Governor Peter Stuyvesant.

The vault was marked by a small, plain slab, flush with the ground, that simply said:

No. 112
Alexr T. Stewart's
Family Vault.

On April 12, Fifth Avenue outside the Stewart mansion was awash with the curious and the mourning. As people lingered or passed by, all turned their eyes to the upstairs window, hoping to get a glimpse of something beyond the curtains. All that day, two police officers and two

Interior of St. Mark's Church—A. T. Stewart's funeral. Image courtesy of Garden City Archives.

porters stood at the door, carefully scrutinizing the cards of everyone who came to call. Flowers costing thousands of dollars were brought to the house.

At 8 a.m. the next morning, a group of A. T. Stewart and Company employees arrived at the mansion to begin their duties for the day. While an estimated 15,000 people arrived and wanted to be a part of the funeral proceedings, admission to the house, as with the funeral, was strictly limited and by invitation only.

Police cordoned off the house and cleared the street of stragglers. At 9 a.m., the doors of the house were opened for the invited guests, which included much of New York's rich and famous. For an hour, important people streamed in. The *New York Times* called the procession "the most select that ever gathered in New York." It included "nearly every prominent man in this City," along with many wives and daughters.[10]

It was said that among his personal goals, Stewart desired, above all else, to be accepted by the New York aristocracy. He hoped the old stock bluebloods like the Beekmans, Livingstons, Stuyvesants, DePeysters, and Schermerhorns would, at long last, overlook his humble origins and his life as a working merchant to accept him and his wife into their exclusive group. However, they would not, and his last years were spent in bitterness, a childless man with few friends, shut up inside his "marble mausoleum."

A coarse man like Commodore Vanderbilt could casually thumb his nose at the knickerbocker aristocracy for rejecting him and his family. After all, he had many descendants who added to the family fortune. The next generation of Vanderbilts not only forced their way into society, they also became its leaders.

Stewart, for all his wealth and power, had no heirs and therefore lacked the ability to keep pace with the onrushing Vanderbilts. Strangely, his only chance to entertain high society came after he died. How pleased he would have been then, if he could have seen the aristocracy flock to his funeral, *by invitation*, finally getting inside his mansion for the look they had so long denied themselves out of their shallow sense of superiority.[11]

On that unforgettable day, a "thoroughly representative body" of the wealthy and powerful paid their respects. The body of A. T. Stewart was placed in the hall amid a lavish floral display that was called "the most elaborate and expensive ever prepared by New York florists." His coffin was costly although not as extravagant as some might have expected. It was rectangular in shape, made of solid English oak, covered with the finest black velvet from Lyon, France, and lined with white satin. At the edges were four-inch fringes of gold bullion. The handles and rods were gold plated. The coffin lid was hinged, and on its underside was a plate bearing the simple inscription:

ALEXANDER T. STEWART
Born Oct. 12th, 1803
Died April 10th, 1876.

Many of the invited mourners brought their own floral tributes, including one small basket of violets from "Little Nellie Hurd" to her "friend."

The doors closed at 10 a.m. sharp, and the prayer service started. After it concluded, the doors were reopened, and Stewart's servants were allowed to pass by his coffin for one last look at their master. As in life, rules concerning Stewart and his servants were strictly enforced. The line had to keep moving, and each person was permitted one glance at his pinched and pallid face. One woman, who had been his

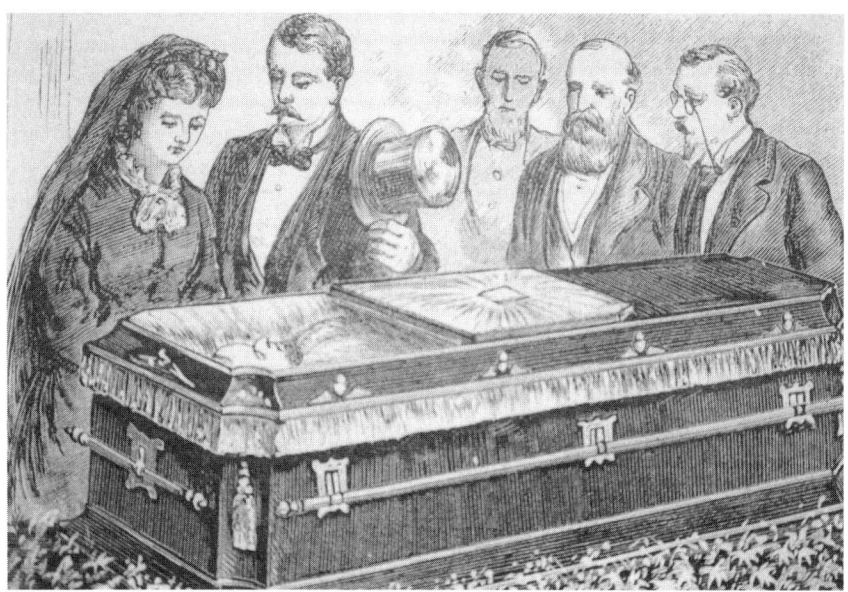

Mourners at A. T. Stewart's funeral. Image courtesy of Garden City Archives.

employee for twenty-five years, stopped and kissed Stewart's face. At this, Hilton intervened, and there were no further overt demonstrations of affection.

At 11:20 the undertaker closed the coffin. This was a signal to everyone that it was time to proceed to St. Mark's Church. The coffin was carried from the house by four assistant undertakers and followed closely by the pallbearers. Among the pallbearers were Stewart's old friends and associates, including New York governor and Democratic candidate for president Samuel J. Tilden; William M. Evarts, lawyer, future U.S. senator, and the husband of one of Mrs. Stewart's sisters; industrialist and philanthropist Peter Cooper; C. H. Russell; and Royal Phelps. It was all sad and solemn, all under the awful spell of death.

In those days the dead were often referred to as "corpses," now a rather impolite reference. With no disrespect toward the remains of A. T. Stewart, the *New York Times* made liberal use of the word when describing the opulent funeral ceremony. Every detail was attended to in a manner that best reflected the high status of the deceased and was well within the standards for taste and style that he set for himself in life. His body was

Carrying Stewart's casket from his mansion. Image courtesy of Garden City Archives.

carried to the church in a fine black hearse, drawn by two fine black horses. The hearse was "highly gilded," but had no "superfluous ornaments of any kind." Stewart was that kind of man. Still his funeral was quite a show.

Funerals in the last half of the nineteenth century were remarkable for a prolonged public display of grief and a heavy emphasis on sorrow and mourning, much in the manner of the early Renaissance era of Europe. Symbols of grief were everywhere, as mourners and other participants made a dramatic, colorful show of death. A person may have passed quietly and unnoticed through life, but in death he or she took center stage and commanded attention and respect.

This sort of beautification of death did nothing, however, to disguise the tragic nature of the event. In a time when people accepted suffering as an inevitable part of life, death was there to inflict additional pain and a sense of desperation. All was black, formal, and somber, from the gloomy, mask-like expressions on the faces of the servants to the darkened and veiled widow. So it was with A. T. Stewart's funeral—solemn, sad, and processional.

Then there were the flowers. At the church, everyone was greeted by another lavish floral display intended to beautify death and offset the pain and feelings of hopelessness. There were flowers in columns, flowers in wreaths. There were flowers arranged into crosses, and one display designed as a harp complete with violet strings. There were many violets. It was said that it was almost impossible to buy a flower in New York, as Hilton had ordered so many.[12]

Once again, "the most rigid care was exercised in the scrutiny of all applicants for admission" into the church,[13] which had room for 800 people. Clearly, Hilton and the Stewart family wanted to prevent any type of disruption. Among those with tickets were New York Mayor William H. Wickham, Secretary of State John Bigelow, William H. Vanderbilt, banker August Belmont, and assorted "honorables," judges, and generals. It was said that former president Grant was invited but was unable to attend.

Yet a multitude of the curious and uninvited crowded the square outside the churchyard, while countless others stood on balconies, porches, trees, lampposts, and rooftops, observing as best they could. It was as if everyone had a sense that this was a milestone event and all wanted a piece of the memory.

After the service, the coffin was carried outside to the churchyard. With Mrs. Stewart swooning and wracked with grief, it was lowered into the subterranean vault, beyond the view of man and in the moldering company of his two infant children, his mother, and a niece. The vault was closed and covered with fresh sod, and suddenly—like a good omen— the sun broke through on what had been an overcast day.[14]

With that, the solemn and spectacular event was ended, and people slowly drifted away, thinking some final thoughts of A. T. Stewart before turning their attention to more mundane matters. Yet for some weeks after, people with time to spare would gather outside of St. Mark's and, with extraordinary curiosity, peer through the iron fence at the mound of dirt covering the vault.[15]

He was consigned to the grave and to history, and no one considered for a moment that Alexander T. Stewart would reemerge as one of the great newsmakers of New York. Aside from his brush with politics and fame as a merchant, Stewart had lived a relatively quiet life, growing, expanding, and making money without trying to draw undue attention to himself. No era or place on earth had produced a merchant such as A. T. Stewart—not London, Venice, Tyre, or Alexandria in the nineteenth or any other century.

Lowering Stewart's body into the St. Mark vault. Image courtesy of Garden City Archives.

While he was not always secretive (except about his family), Alexander Turney Stewart had no desire to conform himself to the personality that was created by his enormous success. He was not an Astor, a Fisk, or a Vanderbilt, and he would have been content to become the forgotten Merchant Prince. He even expected his business empire to break up into dissolution after he died. How ironic then, that in death he became a sort of cult object, the high-profile subject of relentless inquiry and morbid curiosity.

CHAPTER 3

Violation of the Tomb

> A more exposed and difficult position for a grave robbery it would be difficult to imagine.
>
> *New York Times*, November 8, 1878

The press and publicity surrounding the death and burial of A. T. Stewart were dim and dull by comparison with the horrifying news that followed the violation of his tomb. The grave of one of the most famous men in New York history had been robbed of its sacred contents, and the city was suddenly thrown into an unprecedented state of excitement.

Most men and women of greatness are taken in by death and left sinking into the past, gradually disappearing until authors write their biographies and ease them back into public view. Not so for the Merchant Prince. His reemergence was far more spectacular. The startling news that body snatchers took his body from the family vault at St. Mark's Episcopal Church exploded from the presses and then came crashing down on New York and America in gruesome and nauseating detail. No biographer need apply.

Grave robbing in the 1870s was a familiar crime, and reports of this peculiar activity hardly surprised anyone. Newspapers usually dispensed with these dirty little crimes in a few paragraphs. Then sometime before or after midnight of November 7, 1878, a team of grave robbers pulled off what many believed was impossible: the theft of A. T. Stewart's entombed body. This placed the dark business of grave robbery in a new light, forcing it to the front pages of newspapers all over America. To steal the body of an ordinary citizen was "sick," but it was an "outrage" to disturb the remains of a multimillionaire.

The remains of a celebrity who died poor were disturbed not long before the Stewart outrage occurred, although the incident drew only minor attention. The Baltimore grave of famed poet and mystery writer Edgar Allan Poe was exhumed and his bones reburied beneath a new monument, prompting some small mention of the master of the macabre in the *New York Evening Post*.[1] The brief article was like an unintended preface to the New York horror story about to unfold, Poe-like, before a mass audience.

New Yorkers were busy adding up the score from the most recent election when the outrage was pulled off in a most skillful and daring manner. On a dark, wet night, the thieves—or "ghouls" as the *New York Times* and other newspapers preferred to call them—gained entrance to the small, well-illuminated graveyard at St. Mark's. They located the Stewart vault, which was completely underground, dug down, removed the cover slab, and entered. The interior of the vault was fifteen feet long and ten feet wide with an arched, twelve-foot-high ceiling. After descending the

St. Mark's Church showing the theft of Stewart's body. Image courtesy of Garden City Archives.

twelve stairs, they located the thick cedar box containing Stewart's casket and unscrewed the cover. Next they cut through the hermetically sealed lead encasement, revealing the lid of the casket.

They forced the lid open, and then—in what must have been an awful moment of truth—they removed Stewart's unembalmed body, slipped it into a bag, and exited the vault. The thieves made their escape, leaving behind a small, galvanized coal shovel, a "bulls-eye" lantern, a piece of rope, a strip cut from a woman's stocking, and a copy of the *New York Herald*, dated September 24, 1878. It was believed the thieves used the newspaper to wipe their hands after handling the body.

Along with the body, they took a silver nameplate—valued at about $30—from inside the casket lid, some screws, and a piece of the velvet lining cut from the inside of the casket. Once outside they replaced the cover slab and made their escape without leaving a single traceable footprint on the ground. All this was accomplished without drawing suspicion from the neighbors, police, passersby, or church personnel.

Aside from the shocking nature of the crime itself, the nerve and skill of the thieves impressed the authorities and challenged the investigative mettle of a large team of detectives. The New York City Police Department threw itself into the tangled web of facts with vigor, determination, and no little concern for the macabre aspect of their work. At the outset a sense of disbelief plagued both police and public alike. When news of the grave robbery began circulating around the city, most people laughed it off as nonsense. Then, after the awful truth set in, comic disbelief was replaced by outrage and indignation.

The theft was discovered shortly after 8 a.m. the morning after the crime. The cemetery was opened at that time, as was customary, and the assistant sexton, Francis Parker, immediately noticed a suspicious pile of dirt near the Stewart vault. Struck with fear, Parker surmised that someone had been up to some ghoulish business during the night. Without further examination he immediately located the sexton, George W. Hamill, and reported his findings. The two men went back to the disturbed earth, where they opened and entered the vault. Surrounded by the foulest stench imaginable, they saw for themselves that the tomb had been violated and Stewart's body removed.

Hamill instructed Parker to stay in the cemetery. Then, instead of immediately informing the police, Hamill returned to his office and remained there until he was visited by a real estate agent, who convinced him the awful event should be reported. Still, Hamill was reluctant to inform the authorities. Rather than go directly to the police, Hamill rushed off to the residence of Henry Hilton and related the shocking facts.

That Hamill went first to Henry Hilton would have surprised no one. Hilton had long been identified with Stewart, first as his personal attorney and then as a close friend. During the great merchant's later years, Hilton enjoyed a relationship so close and uncanny that those who knew them seldom saw one without the other. Under the circumstances, Hamill no doubt concluded there was simply no other place to start. It was, of course, what Hilton would have expected.

Upon learning of the dreadful crime, an alarmed and angry Hilton called for his coach and was off to police headquarters. When he arrived, the wild-eyed Hilton charged inside and said loudly, "Someone has robbed the Stewart vault!" Upon hearing this, Police Commissioner Sidney P. Nichols said, with no little nonchalance, "Well, they've made a good haul then."[2] When he was informed that the robbers stole Stewart's body and not his money, Nichols' mind quickly shifted gears. After a moment's hesitation to fully grasp the awful reality, he listened to Hilton's story and was quickly drawn into the intrigue.

Clearly a man who commanded attention, Hilton had an investigating party in full swing within minutes after reporting the crime. Commissioner Nichols himself took charge of the investigation, assisted by

Detectives examining the scene of the grave robbery. Image courtesy of Garden City Archives.

Inspector William Murray and Inspector George W. Dilks, two veteran police officers with favorable credentials.

Murray and Dilks were known for their investigative skills and toughness in the trenches. Murray joined the department in 1866 after serving in the Civil War, where he was wounded in the first battle of Bull Run. He was appreciated for his ability to hunt down thieves, burglars, and gamblers. Dilks entered the force in 1848 and earned praise for his courage under fire during the longshoremen's riots of 1857 and the Civil War draft riot of 1863.[3] The commissioner chose two of his best to launch the investigation of the Stewart grave robbery.

Commissioner Nichols immediately went to the churchyard, along with the coroner and several detectives. Meantime, Dilks issued the following police bulletin:

FROM THE CENTRAL OFFICE, Nov. 7, 1878, TO ALL:

The remains of A. T. Stewart were last night stolen from the family vault, St. Mark's churchyard. The casket was found broken and the body removed. The decomposition of the remains is so offensive that they cannot be concealed. This is apparent from standing at the opening of the vault this morning, consequently the body cannot be taken across the ferries or placed anywhere above the ground without discovery. Cause diligent search to be made in your precinct, as the remains were evidently stolen in hope of reward.

Inspector Dilks.[4]

After the initial shock wore away, the police expressed the belief that the investigation would be short and the results sure and swift. They would track the criminals to their lair by following the malodorous trail left by the rotting corpse. It would be impossible to travel with it and not arouse suspicion. It would attract attention and, therefore, witnesses. People would come forth with hard evidence. After sizing up the scene and asking a few questions, the police had suspects in mind.

After a thorough investigation of the churchyard, however, they were less confident. In fact, they were baffled. Other than the presumption that the body was taken for ransom, the police were faced with several questions. How did the thieves enter the graveyard, and how did they know the exact location of the unmarked, subterranean vault, which was one among many? Why were they able to dig down to the slab without being seen from the sidewalk or from a number of houses that looked out over the churchyard? What explanation could be offered for their ability to dig down to the exact dimensions of the opening slab? How did they get the body out of the graveyard? Hardest of all, how could any sane human being take hold of a corpse that had been entombed for more than two and one-half years?

The church grounds were bounded on the north by East Eleventh Street, on the south by Stuyvesant Street, and on the east by Second Avenue. St. Mark's "in-the-Bouwerie," as it was often called with affection, was a very old church. It was considered ancient by 1878, having been organized in 1791 and built in the years 1795–1799, in the colonial style.[5]

Its beginning was actually much earlier, going back to 1660, when colonial Governor Peter Stuyvesant, famous for his hot temper and wooden leg, built a small chapel on his farm, next to his manor house. Upon his death in 1672, he was interred in a crypt in the churchyard.

One night in the mid-1860s, the unforgettable old Dutchman reappeared at St. Mark's in ghostly form. The sexton was attending to his duties when he heard footsteps following him. Turning around he saw the ghost of the long-dead governor clumping down the street with his unmistakable, peg-leg gait, brandishing his walking stick as if on a mission. This sent the sexton screaming into the night, fearful that a dead man had risen from his grave. Next, the bell in the St. Mark's tower began to ring, arousing nearby sleepers. Soon the street was filled with curious onlookers, all willing to support the sexton's ghost story.

The next morning, the cemetery was examined and, to the relief of everyone, there was no evidence that the Stuyvesant grave had been disturbed.[6] However, there was no doubt in the minds of those involved that the old Dutchman had returned, perhaps to express his disapproval of the city he helped to create, or was it a foreboding of things to come?

Whatever the reason, the story became part of the charm of St. Mark's in-the-Bouwerie and its old knickerbocker graveyard. The small church remained a popular and fashionable place, insuring its survival in the midst of a fast-growing city. By the 1870s St. Mark's found itself in the very heart of the city, an area dominated by large and luxurious homes and a mere three blocks away from Stewart's Great Iron store. It was surrounded by a ten-foot-high iron fence topped by a row of sharp spikes. Not long before the theft of Stewart's body, a small boy died after he was impaled on the fence while trying to retrieve a ball from inside the churchyard.

There were visitors in the churchyard during the day preceding the horrible crime, and at 9:30 that evening, a couple was married in the church by the rector, Reverend Dr. J. H. Rylance. The reverend and his wife left the church at about 10 p.m. It was a cold, dark night and raining hard, but the area was well illuminated. He recalled seeing no suspicious activity. As usual, the exterior gates were locked before the last man left the premises.

At about midnight, a dentist who lived nearby saw four or five men standing by the cemetery fence, but he thought nothing of it. Another man recalled seeing a covered, two-horse carriage parked near the church entrance. As it was sitting directly beneath a lighted gas lamp, he was not suspicious.[7] Yet another told police and reporters that he saw six men carrying a six-foot-long box on their shoulders while walking down Ninth Street at about 2:30 a.m. He noticed that all the men were wearing "ulsters" and "high hats" as they passed by slowly with a "merry" disposition. One of the men asked jocularly, "Can't you give us a lift?" The witness merely passed this off as nothing until the next morning when he learned about the grave robbery.[8] These were among the many clues that both tantalized and mystified the authorities.

Six large French willow trees adorned the grounds, but the foliage had fallen away with the coming of autumn, therefore the trees would not conceal someone digging atop the Stewart vault during the night. There were no standing tombstones to hide behind, as all the vault markers were flush with the ground. With streetlamps on each of the street corners and one on each side of the church, it was reasoned that any number of people could have looked out an upstairs window and seen any activity in the churchyard that night. According to the *New York Herald*, the balloon gas lamps created a light so bright that "one might read a newspaper on the opposite side of the street."[9]

Three police officers patrolling the streets bounding the churchyard saw nothing unusual that wet and rainy night. So for all the reasons stated above, the crime took on an occult aspect, as if the body was snatched by some malevolent beings that first bewitched all those who would have detected their presence. It was estimated that thousands of people passed by the churchyard between the time of the break-in and the time the crime was discovered.

The Stewart family vault was near the center of the churchyard, quite close to Second Avenue, where the ground sloped down toward the street. From Second Avenue, the view was almost unobstructed. The vault was covered by approximately two and one-half to three feet of soft earth. It was one of a number of underground vaults where many of New York's prominent people were interred in the old-time fashion. The Stewart family vault, number 112, was flanked by the family vaults of Benjamin Winthrop and Thomas Bibby.

Several gates were located on the outside and inside of the cemetery premises. The police believed that the thieves had a key to the Eleventh Street gate and used it to enter and exit. They also believed the digging must have been done by men lying on their stomachs to avoid detection. Furthermore, the shovel discovered at the scene was too small for a man to use while standing up and was not believed to be the type normally used by grave robbers. Even if one of the thieves did stand up in the light, those on the outside of the cemetery could have concluded that he was a night watchman and there was no cause for concern.

Police estimated it would have taken about one hour to dig down to the tomb opening. Physicians estimated that Stewart's body weighed about 100 pounds and stated that, although not embalmed, it would have been in a "tolerable state of preservation" until exposed to the air, at which time it would begin to liquefy.

Seasoned detectives were mystified at the daring and expertise of the thieves, more so because they had to withstand the foul odor given off by the corpse. During their lengthy investigation that morning, officers were sickened by the stench that emanated from the open tomb. The men who committed this crime were, indeed, made of strange and stern stuff. In no time at all, New York was wondering: Who were they? Who were these daring, evil giants? It was seen as an impossible, unnatural crime, fit only for the supernatural company of witches, ghouls, and vampires. This sort of thing was remarkable, even for New York.

The *New York Times* expressed the shock and sentiment of the moment, saying, "How the robbers carried it [the body] off without attracting attention by its bulk or by the smell, is one of the strangest parts of the entire business."[10] It was a hard-to-swallow revulsion no doubt shared by readers as well.

It was a morning like no other morning for the police, too. When they left the churchyard to begin their search for suspects, the police were faced with an unspeakable crime and too few substantial clues. They knew that an aroused and curious public would eagerly follow the progress of the investigation and scrutinize every move. They knew the nation's press would be equally, if not more, inquisitive and demanding. Moreover, great pressure would be brought to bear from every quarter because of the wealth and stature of A. T. Stewart.

Despite examples from Ohio and other states, New York police considered grave robbery a crime out of fashion and therefore wholly unexpected. Yet it happened, and it was imperative that this mystery be solved and silenced with no undue delay.

While grave robberies were commonplace events in the 1870s, the New York authorities had no precedent to rely on. It was believed that the theft of Stewart's body was the first grave robbery in New York, or at least the first in recent memory. So said the *New York Times*, once again leaving Stewart in a class by himself and a celebrity whether he would have liked it or not.

The *New York Herald* had a different slant on this subject, dredging up details of a grave robbery that made headline news on a distant day, well beyond the memory of any living person. It happened in 1788, in post-Revolutionary War New York, and set off a brief but bloody altercation—the doctor's riot—that claimed many lives.

It started, like spring itself, innocently enough. In May 1788 a group of young boys were playing in the backyard of the Columbia College Hospital, where medical students were hard at work on the second floor. The future doctors were studying anatomy, cutting up freshly procured corpses, when an impetuous student, looking down at the boys, encouraged one of the lads to climb a ladder to the window of the classroom. He was going to have some fun. The curious innocent did as requested, and when he reached the top of the ladder, the student suddenly thrust a disembodied arm at the boy, saying in a loud, jovial voice, "Look at your mother's arm, sonny!" Little did he know that a casual attempt to scare a boy would erupt into hours of terrible and deadly violence.

As it turned out, the boy's mother had just died. Imagining the worst, he immediately went to his father's place of employment and explained the horrifying experience. His father at once set out for the cemetery where his wife had just been buried, opened the grave and beheld an empty coffin. The body of his wife had, indeed, been stolen by body snatchers.

This was, of course, not proof that the Columbia students were learning anatomy from his wife's body, but the man was convinced of their guilt. Determined to have his pound of flesh, the saddened and outraged widower gathered several of his fellow workers, and in a group, they descended upon the medical college, shouting "death to body snatchers" and "out with the doctors."

The cries alerted the authorities, but before they could arrive, the angry mob had reached the college, entering and ransacking the dissecting room. They found bodies, and their rage was out of control. While they were busy attacking the college collections, a group of peacemakers, headed by the mayor and the sheriff, arrived at the school. After some effort the mob was convinced to cease its mission of destruction. The arrest of a number of medical students also helped to end the riot, but only for a little while.

As evening approached, groups of angry men once again gathered near the college, expressing their indignation. Urged on by their leaders, the men decided to invade the college for another round of mayhem. Since they could find no more bodies, they ransacked the homes of the physicians attached to the medical department of the college. The renewed riot attracted the attention of the authorities, and the rioters were soon confronted by the governor of New York, the mayor, and the college chancellor, all of whom begged the mob to cease and desist.

Some of the men were convinced and left the scene. Others would not depart and instead marched upon the jail where the medical students were incarcerated. The mob laid siege to the jail and threw rocks and other dangerous projectiles at the authorities who dared to confront them. A troop of twenty-five or thirty soldiers marched to the jail intending to put an end to the riot. It was the rioters, however, who triumphed. In a matter of minutes, the soldiers were disarmed and sent scattering.

Soon after, a larger contingent of troops arrived at the jail with fixed bayonets. The emboldened mob, however, felt itself up to the challenge, and instead of retreating, stood its ground, yelling insults and tossing rocks and other lethal objects, seriously wounding some of the soldiers. Their anger was fueled by the mayor's lukewarm approach to the problem, interpreted by the mob as a sign of weakness. The mob was winning the battle, or so it seemed, until without warning, the order to open fire was quietly given by the troop commander. The volley left several men dead and wounded, but amazingly failed to drive away surviving members of the mob. Another order to fire had the desired effect, and amid a mass of dead and bleeding bodies, the remaining rioters fled. It was a very costly revenge.

The students, exhausted from fright, were released. Thanks to the troops, they were not dragged into the streets and murdered. However, the mob instilled a high degree of fear into the medical community, and not long after the violence subsided, many doctors left the city, believing they were not safe at the college. Columbia's medical college was closed down for a considerable period of time; New York was no place for those who wanted to study dissection. It was believed that this tragic incident was so indelibly impressed upon the public that New York was safe from grave robbers until the Stewart incident.[11]

Ninety years after the doctor's riot, public reaction to the ghastly crime of grave robbery was no less indignant. Fortunately, however, there was no motivation for mob-like retaliation against the authorities or any other target. New York was no longer a small town and had developed tastes that were jaded and sophisticated. This was a spectacle to be savored with gross curiosity, not attacked and consumed in the streets. While there was no apparent confidence in the police, the public was, nonetheless, content to follow the progress of the case in the press, in stylish parlors, on street corners, and in saloons. For a time, at least, the police were given center stage and allowed to perform.

It was a performance handled rather clumsily, with no small degree of regret for having been left out of an important loop. The police were very upset when they learned that about a month previous to the grave robbery, Hamill, the sexton, noticed someone had tampered with the name slab covering the Stewart vault. It appeared as if someone had tried to raise it with a bar. Instead of reporting this to the police, he informed Henry Hilton, who also failed to notify the police. Acting entirely on his own, Hilton concocted a deception, as he suspected someone was after Stewart's body. He had the name slab moved about thirty feet away from the vault and hired a night watchman, telling him nothing more than that he was guarding the churchyard. Hilton explained to the police that there were only four people who knew the exact location of the vault: himself, Hamill, Assistant Sexton Parker, and William Libbey, one of Stewart's most trusted business partners.

Hilton, of course, spent a great deal of time at the crime scene on the first day of the investigation. He huffed and puffed like a man who was accustomed to pushing across his point of view and winning the argument. Hilton was indignant and overwhelmed with anger and insisted he would not pay a penny in ransom. Of course the police listened to Hilton, and the press quoted him because he was important and was the handpicked successor to handle and wind down the affairs of the A. T. Stewart dry goods empire.

It had been widely rumored about the city that Stewart was buried with a large amount of silver and gold, possibly even diamonds, in his casket. Anyone who knew Stewart understood this to be absurd, as he was far too plain and practical a man for an ostentatious display of wealth, dead or alive. When asked whether Stewart wore three pearl studs on his grave shirt, an angry Hilton said no. "Why, Mr. Stewart would have turned over in his grave if he had any idea that three pearl studs were to be wasted in that manner."[12] Lamenting the loss of his friend, Hilton said, "Mr. Stewart was buried with the same simplicity that characterized his life."[13]

On this point Hilton was correct. Stewart's public persona was bland and businesslike, matching his cold and frugal disposition. Aside from the fine horses that pulled his carriage to and from work, he was so thrift-conscious that he once wore a string instead of a watch chain and was known to pick up pins from the floor of his store and save them. He once fired a carpenter for throwing away a single nail.[14] A man such as this would not appreciate having his dead body adorned with valuables only to be wasted in a grave. Hilton understood this, and it angered him to think that his friend and mentor was torn from the tomb because some fools thought they would find riches in the casket.

Hilton easily cast aside all forms of wild speculation and focused his thoughts on the gang of thieves. In an interview with the *New York Times*, he suggested that at least six men were involved, a group that included some "professional undertakers." Two acted as "crows" or lookouts, two went into the vault, and the other two waited on the outside to receive the body.[15]

The *New York Evening Post* snagged an interview with William Libbey, who, next to Hilton, was Stewart's most trusted ally. Libbey (also spelled Libby), who joined with Stewart in 1837,[16] was an astute manager and partner placed in charge of hiring and firing employees. His own company, Hastings, Libbey and Forbey, failed, but his mercantile skills were not lost on Stewart.

Stewart hired Libbey from among the many broken-down merchants of New York, some of whom were crushed by the heavy hand of the Merchant Prince himself.[17] Libbey—whose ancestors came to America in 1630[18]—fit in and worked his way up. While Libbey didn't socialize with Stewart, he understood the company business completely. After Stewart's death, Hilton relied on Libbey's management capability, and the two men became partners in A. T. Stewart and Company.

Libbey expressed anger and disbelief to the *Post* reporter when asked for an explanation about the terrible crime. "I am at a loss to understand it, unless money was at the bottom of it," Libbey said. He was quick to add that the Stewart estate was prepared to spend $100,000 for the capture of the "outlaws," but "not one cent to them for the return of what they have taken." He paused and then added with emphasis, "Not a single cent," as if trying to convey a message to the body snatchers. Although he was upset and saddened by the shocking turn of events, Libbey was a lifelong businessman, and he spoke like a man who was accustomed to having an eye for the bottom line and a good grip on the purse strings.

The *Post* reporter asked Libbey if he thought that, in connection with money, jealousy might also be a motive. He questioned whether there might be some people who so resented Stewart's great wealth that they stole his body to deny his wish to rest in the Garden City mausoleum that was under construction. Libbey dodged this question, saying only, "Human nature at its worst, you know, is pretty bad."[19] As a talker Libbey was no match for Hilton, and the reporter didn't pursue the matter any further.

The press and public put forth a variety of reasons for the grave robbery. There was the inclination to believe the crime was the natural outgrowth of body stealing for profit that plagued Ohio and the Midwest. Because of the advanced state of decomposition, it was readily conceded that Stewart's body was not stolen for sale to a medical school. Furthermore, morgues and hospitals kept dissecting rooms well supplied with cadavers. The urban resurrectionists who took Stewart's body, while no less skilled and daring than rural body snatchers, were of a different sort. According to the dominant initial theories, the theft was committed for revenge, to make a political statement, or for ransom money, with greatest emphasis on the latter.

Indeed, most people connected with the investigation immediately suspected the thieves' motive was money, meaning ransom or blackmail. The Stewart estate had been in the news on and off following the death of the Merchant Prince because of an onslaught of inheritance claimants coming forth with their theories, genealogy charts, and lawyers. Just a few days before the break-in, a lawyer for the Stewart estate, Ira Shafer, remarked that "things have arrived at such a pitch that it is not safe for a rich man to die in New York City." At the time he had no idea his words contained prophetic import. After the crime broke, a reporter from the Herald sought out Shafer, who was constrained to admit that in New York there are "men who are capable of doing almost anything for money."[20]

Hilton—a man many believed was capable of doing anything for money—was fully in accord. He rattled off his indignation in an interview with the New York Weekly Tribune. Talking as if Stewart's money was his money, Hilton said, "It [the grave-robbery] is an infamous attempt to extort money from me—one of thousands. It was my intention to have the body removed shortly to the crypt preparing for it in the Garden City Cathedral, and I had made my plans accordingly. It is a beautiful crypt, octagonal in shape, inlaid with solid marble, ornamented with statuary and stained plate glass."[21] The plans included a life-size angel of the resurrection placed on a white marble pedestal.[22]

Stewart's original concept was to build a stylish but modest church as the centerpiece of his Garden City. However, two weeks after his death, his widow announced plans for a more ambitious church—a great cathedral that would stand as a memorial to her late husband.[23] A cornerstone bearing the year "1876" was laid on June 28, 1877. Henry G. Harrison of New York City was the architect. Mrs. Stewart made regular visits to Long Island to inspect the slow, steady progress of the cathedral.

The contractor was scheduled to have the $80,000 crypt completed and ready for Stewart's remains by the first week of November 1878. Accordingly, plans were in the works for the transfer of Stewart's body to its magnificent and final resting place beneath the sanctuary of the Garden City cathedral. However, the contractor was unable to stay on schedule, and plans for the transfer were put off until April of 1879.[24]

If plans like this were floated about or leaked out, it is not unreasonable to think that a group of clever and daring thieves might come up with a plan of their own. If Mrs. Stewart, Hilton, and Libbey were going to

Interior of the crypt in the Cathedral of the Incarnation. Henry Hilton is on the left and Cornelia Stewart is standing beside an unidentified man. Image courtesy of Garden City Archives.

such great expense to build a lavish mausoleum, they might be willing to pay a large ransom to be sure Stewart's body could be deposited into it. What good would an expensive tomb be if there were no body to lie therein? Thinking thusly, the clever thieves intervened, or so some people believed.

Hilton made no secret about whom he suspected: Sexton Hamill. He was the logical suspect. Hamill knew of the marker deception, and just the night before the theft, he casually discharged the night watchman (without first notifying Hilton), believing the man had served for as long as Hilton required. If the thieves had a key, it must have been obtained from Hamill. Where else? It was not that Hilton believed Hamill participated in the actual theft, but that he could have been an accomplice.

This explanation, however, lacked motive, and it was refuted and weakened, in large part, by the insistence of Rylance, the rector. He insisted that Hamill—and Parker as well—was a decent man of integrity who had served the church long and faithfully. Members of the St. Mark's congregation were openly indignant over the accusation. Hamill was deemed to be beyond temptation, for he was paid a good salary to look after the dead in the churchyard. Even Hilton was forced to admit that

Hamill was a man of good reputation. Both Parker and Hamill cooperated fully with the police and gave written, exculpatory statements, causing attention to shift away from them.

Henry Nicholas Hilton was the central figure in the mystery, although never suspected of involvement in the break-in. Usually referred to as "Judge" Hilton, he—more than anyone including Mrs. Stewart—benefited from the millionaire's will. Stewart appointed Hilton to wind up the affairs of A. T. Stewart and Company, and for this service, he received $1 million. This largess only fueled speculation about the close and unusual relationship Hilton enjoyed with the older Merchant Prince.

Little is known of Hilton's background, as he was as secretive about his past, as was his benefactor. It was something that he refused to discuss, and his closest friends were mum on the subject. According to reports he was born in October 1824 in Newburg, New York, the son of Scottish immigrants. It was said his father was a cartman, a somewhat humble line of work. Henry was the youngest of four boys, all of whom became educated professionals, including a brother, James, who was a judge in Iowa.

Henry Hilton married Ellen Banker, daughter of a wealthy ship chandler and sister of James H. Banker, the president of the Bank of New York. Ellen was a second cousin of Cornelia Stewart. As a result of the marriage, Hilton became related to A. T. Stewart. Over time he became Stewart's most trusted ally and confidant, a protégé of sorts, the one man Stewart couldn't do without. The man who lived by good connections forged several more with his marriage.

Before that the young Hilton was an attorney employed by the law firm of Campbell and Cleveland. While there he earned a reputation as a hard worker and a shrewd, skillful lawyer. In 1857 he was elected judge of the Court of Common Pleas in New York and served until 1863. He was a Democrat, connected with the infamous Tweed ring in the 1860s, a part of the "silk hat brigade." William "Boss" Tweed's gang of crooks held him out to be a gentleman, "proof" of their honorable motives and practices.

In 1863, the Tweed ring refused to back Hilton's candidacy for reelection as judge because Hilton had joined Stewart in opposition to the ring's fight to install a streetcar line on Broadway. Without Tweed's backing, he lost.

In 1870 Hilton was back in the good graces of Tweed, serving on the park commission, which was in charge of Central Park. At that time, Waterhouse Hawkins, a well-known naturalist, was creating a special exhibit for the ark, consisting of several large, plaster models of extinct animals. After two years, with two models completed and $12,000 of public money spent, Commissioner Hilton intervened, ordering Hawkins to stop his work and, after that, seeing to it that the models were destroyed. Showing a total lack of knowledge of art and science as well as no tact, Hilton chided the naturalist, saying it was useless to bother with "dead animals" when there were "so many live ones to care for." Taking insult to art and taste even further into disrepute, an insensitive Hilton ordered a bronze statue of a whale, which had been donated to the public by the popular philanthropist Peter Cooper, painted an ugly white.[25]

Despite his insensitivity to the public good and his arrogant nature, Hilton moved onward and upward, escaping the legal snares that caught Tweed and some of his henchmen. By the early 1870s he was thoroughly caught up in the life and finances of A. T. Stewart. They met when Hilton worked for Campbell and Cleveland. Stewart was impressed with Hilton's expertise, ability, and hard work and made the young lawyer his private counsel on a modest salary. From 1866 to 1874, Hilton went to Stewart's office on a daily basis at four in the afternoon, staying until the merchant went home to dinner.

Hilton once told a reporter that he and Stewart were "just like brothers."[26] By 1874 Hilton's shingle and fate were linked permanently to Stewart's office. Two years later he was fully in charge of handling Stewart's great fortune.[27] It was a move that astonished and angered many observers.

Hilton was artful in the social graces whereas Stewart was not, and he played the master of ceremonies on many auspicious occasions hosted by Mr. and Mrs. Stewart. It galled New York's elite that Hilton came out of relative obscurity to become the millionaire's sole advisor and trusted confidant. Those who had to endure Hilton's haughty manner and shallow, self-serving theatrics thought they brought humiliation on the great A. T. Stewart. Even though New York society snubbed Stewart, it thought even less of the upstart Henry Hilton.

Hilton could take that in stride, however, and he took full advantage of his good fortune, dismissing criticism as mere jealousy. He had the "king's ear" and used it to his advantage, to the utter terror of anyone who crossed his path. He understood Stewart's dark moods and could divine the very words needed to deal with the torment of the moment. He met, screened, and cross-examined, without exception, all those who came to talk to his boss. His job was to find ways to prevent callers from making their way to Stewart's cold, closed-mouthed presence. In his later years, Stewart seemed utterly dependent on the domineering Hilton for advice.

Stewart believed in symbols of good luck. He was especially pleased if a hunchback or a cross-eyed person came into the store, as he viewed human oddities as indicators of success, but the portly Hilton was his ultimate talisman. They went everywhere together, including Europe. Hilton was treated like family, sharing fully in the great wealth of the Stewart financial empire. It was even speculated by Stewart's biographer that Hilton—said to have had a fat, blank-looking face—was the illegitimate son of A. T. Stewart. A state department official said Hilton was Stewart's "counsel and reputed son-out-of-law."[28]

This suggestion was drawn from an article in Joseph Pulitzer's *New York World*, a daily newspaper of great popularity and wide circulation.[29] As will be seen in Chapter 14, Pulitzer lambasted Hilton in a series of articles that characterized the ex-judge as a grasping and devious nonentity who had knowledge of some deep, dark secret tied to A. T. Stewart like a weighted chain. Buried deep in one of the articles, Pulitzer indelicately stated that the "secret, on the authority of one of the best known and most reputable citizens of New York," involved the birth of a child, presumably Stewart's illegitimate progeny. According to the *World*, Hilton—never one to scruple over ethics—used this to leverage his way into Stewart's empire. Pulitzer's newspaper said Hilton kept quiet while becoming indispensable, keeping secret the small particle of truth that would have taken away every respectable customer and caused the ruin of the Merchant Prince.

While Hilton's parentage is probably beyond absolute proof, Stewart could be described as a father figure to him, and Hilton served as the dutiful son who never let his father down. It was said that on his deathbed Stewart told his wife that he owed his enormous success to Hilton's guidance and assistance.[30] To a disapproving (and envious) public, Hilton was known as the scheming "man who got all of old Stewart's money."[31]

After Stewart's death Hilton vainly and unsuccessfully tried to run the business empire, even to the point of manipulating Mrs. Stewart, who apparently trusted him as much as did her husband. So it was no surprise to anyone that Hilton tried to shield the widow as much as possible from outside influences and called the shots during the turbulent investigation that followed the violation of the tomb.

Cornelia Stewart was said to be 75 years old when the bizarre crime was committed, and she had been ill for some time. Learning the awful truth about the theft and disappearance of her late husband's remains caused her to be prostrated by indescribable grief and anxiety. At a time when 75 was considered aged, she was suddenly thrust into the deepest nightmare imaginable. The body of her beloved husband, whom in life she always called "Honey," was cruelly taken away in the night by grave robbers. There was immediate concern that the shock and stress, coupled with the illness, threatened her very life.

The responsibility for telling her about the grave robbery, of course, fell to Hilton. He was reluctant to do such a painful thing, and he came to her weighted down by a dread burden. Late in the afternoon Mrs. Stewart noticed the newsboys in front of the mansion as they cried out the terrible news to stunned New Yorkers. The newsboys paced and shouted in front of her house longer than usual, arousing her curiosity. It was at this point that Hilton forced himself to tell her what had happened in the churchyard at St. Mark's, lest she venture outside and hear it shouted in the streets.

According to Hilton she bore the news bravely and better than he expected. In a short time, however, she weakened as the shock wore off and the full brunt of the awful truth settled upon her. Hilton tried to be positive, telling her that the fiends would be caught and her dead husband's remains returned.[32] In the meantime, Mrs. Stewart's household staff was given strict orders not to breathe a word about the awful crime in her presence.

About two years previous, Mrs. Stewart had received a letter from someone threatening to steal her husband's body unless she paid a demand for money. She gave the letter to Hilton, who tossed it away as he had done to "thousands of such hyena-like letters" from anonymous people who he said felt that Stewart had failed to earn the admiration and respect of his fellow man. The letter could have come from any number of such people who passed by the churchyard after Stewart's death and stopped to gaze upon his grave, daydreaming of buried treasure.

CHAPTER 4

The Resurrectionists

> There are men in every large city who are criminals, and yet are tolerated and encouraged by a certain (medical) profession simply because they are a necessary evil.
>
> *National Police Gazette*, January 3, 1880

Throughout the last half of the nineteenth century, grave robbers, or resurrectionists as they were more commonly called, supplied American medical schools with cadavers for dissection. As medical science advanced, the need to study anatomy and related courses became more apparent and critical. Still, there was strong public opposition to using the dead for medical purposes, even if it meant advancing treatment for the living. It was like playing God, yet in a devilish sort of way. Since man had been created in God's image, the argument went, there was nothing about man that God didn't know and nothing that man had any business learning.

While this was beyond question for the unsophisticated man of religion, it presented a terrible dilemma for scientists who were anxious to move beyond their antecedents. Since the Middle Ages, Christian authority had prohibited dissection, and for hundreds of years, anyone who studied anatomy by cutting up the dead risked dying for his crime. By the nineteenth century the penalties had been greatly reduced, and the physicians of Western world were ready, at long last, to cast off this most medieval of restraints.

Restless youth led the way. Schools, medical students, and young doctors—unwilling to wait for public approval—were all too willing to circumvent the archaic restrictions. They paid grave robbers to find fresh specimens to work on. One such young doctor was David L. Rogers of New York. During the antebellum years in New York, he honed his surgical skills on bodies stolen from graveyards, eventually becoming famous for his breakthrough work on treating ovaries and hernias.[1]

It was a time when some in medical science, well in advance of public opinion, preferred to take certain risks rather than retreat. The United States was at a crossroads and had to choose which way to turn. The current debate over the morality of stem cell research comes to mind. Medical scientists want to move forward with experimentation hoping to find cures for diseases like cancer, while religious conservatives are opposed. They believe stem cell research results in the taking of life, as if it interferes with God's control over human destiny. When faced with the unknown or untried, there are some who want to move forward and others who want to turn back.

The battle over the morality of dissection was a dilemma that benefited men of daring and nerve (and strong stomachs) who were willing to be labeled ghouls, or worse, so long as the pay was good. As such, grave robbing was commonplace in many parts of the United States, particularly in medium and large midwestern cities or nearby rural cemeteries. Ohio, where there was a concentration of medical schools, led the nation in grave robberies. A body that would sell for $5 in Iowa would fetch $30 in Ohio.[2]

By 1878 when A. T. Stewart's body was stolen, grave robbery was a cottage industry, and resurrectionists were seen as a "professional" class. It was not unusual to read about a gruesome grave robbery next to articles about Congress, the West, or world affairs. It was on the low end of the business hierarchy, but in that age of big business it was a market-driven concern nonetheless. The irony, however, seemed lost on market-driven people riding high in the Gilded Age, for each resurrection was a terrible outrage, and the elusive perpetrators were cause for blood-boiling anger.

The title "resurrectionist" was applied to these shadowy figures because they brought people back from the dead, so to speak, but the facetious name was the only humorous aspect of their work. This was a foul and damnable practice because it disturbed the blessed sleep of the departed, as people believed that the dead were more than a mass of lifeless tissue. Yet, their audacity, skill, and success earned the resurrectionists a certain, grudging respect. Some men who operated successfully for years acquired a reputation of sorts and were referred to as "noted" or "notorious" resurrectionists, proving that every occupation has its own sense of celebrity.

Digging up graves for bodies or bones and looting tombs for valuables is an old practice, not all of it unacceptable. Unearthing American Indian burial mounds and excavating Egyptian tombs are two examples of acceptable activity of this type. The older the grave, it seems, the less likely one will incur public wrath. Those who engage in "scientific" grave excavation have been called anthropologists or archeologists, not desecrators. Yet, there is always a certain unease about this sort of thing, as if there is something dangerous or disrespectful about interrupting the long sleep of the dead.

Throughout all civilized time, burial places have been treated with reverence and respect. Fenced off in all their rustic glory, cemeteries tend to survive unchanged, while on the outside the living world evolves at a hectic pace. Cemeteries are quiet, holy places where we tread lightly with somber thoughts and introspective gaze—where we lovingly place our dead, set aside for all time to come. In every era and in every religion, the living maintain strong ties to their dead kith and kin. Cursed be he who would surreptitiously dig and disturb the blessed sleep in "God's acre." It took a determined scientist or a hard, rudely practical (or desperate) man to ignore such a curse.

Throughout the nineteenth century, especially during the last half, many men willingly and freely accepted such risks. After all they could always say, with wry smiles, they were in their line of work to promote science and thus lay the dastardly mess at the feet of an institution that, by reputation, occasionally displayed motives that were not always pure or acceptable.

Penalties were relatively light, amounting in many jurisdictions to a few months or a year in jail and a small to moderate fine. The pay offered was reliable, and it was a means for a man to feed his family. Newspaper records abound with examples of the faceless Frankensteins of the night and their grim labor during the "witching hours" when "graveyards yawn."

This was, indeed, an "underground" occupation with a long and haunted history.

Grave robbers operated by stealth in the dark of night, using common, well-rehearsed techniques. Typically, a team of five or six operated together. A couple of men would act as lookouts, or crows, while the rest did the digging and removing. They favored dark, wet nights, when they were less likely to be detected. Cool autumn months were preferred over hot summer nights.

Cemeteries were usually selected in advance through connections with an undertaker or a doctor who had a need for certain cadaver. If a particular disease swept through a community leaving many dead, doctors would sometimes want a look at one of the victims. They would make their desires known to the right men, who would in turn contact the grave robbers. Rural cemeteries were preferred, usually within a thirty-mile radius of cities where medical schools operated.

Sometimes doctors went directly to the grave robbers to order a certain body. Both doctors and diggers watched the obituary columns for recent deaths and attended burials to locate fresh graves. Some doctors, particularly country doctors, actually participated in the digging and stealing, being strangely attracted to the ghoulish business. While many laymen were compelled by poverty to rob graves, a "most noted surgeon" in Cleveland told a reporter, "I would rather steal a 'stiff,' so far as real enjoyment is concerned, than eat the best meal of victuals I ever saw ... it has an almost irresistible fascination for me."[3] This indeed, was an interesting psychopathology.

Coffins were often located by using a thin, metal rod five or six feet long, which was forced into the ground until wood was struck. This was called "tasting." A good resurrectionist could tell the type of wood in the coffin by examining the end of the rod. If they were looking for an oak coffin and the rod "tasted" like walnut, they moved on. Once the desired grave was located, an inclined hole was dug starting about ten to fifteen feet from the edge of the grave. The hole was usually about two and one-half feet wide—just large enough for a live body to go down and drag out a dead one.

When the head of the coffin was reached, it was forced open using a strong bar. Next, one of the crew—undoubtedly one of the boldest—went back down in the hole with a hook attached to a rope. Then, face to face with a dead man or woman, he forced the hook into the corpse's mouth, and the body was pulled out of the hole. It was disrobed, placed in a sack, and loaded on the wagon. As the body was not considered property, it was not the subject of a theft. This was not so for the clothing, however, and it was invariably put back in the ground and reburied. All excess dirt was loaded into sacks and hauled away to be scattered along the road.

The grave robbers hauled the body to a location where it was concealed until it was handed over to parties who would, in turn, see that it reached a dissection table. According to the *National Police Gazette*, grave robbers were well paid, getting up to $100 for a few hours work.[4]

If the team was successful, no one would discover what took place. The living would visit the grave, leaving tears and prayers. All the flowers would still be in place, lilting on the grave with their comforting fragrance and reassuring beauty, masking the awful reality hidden in the dirt. For unbeknownst to the living, a broken, empty coffin would be all that lay beneath their feet. There can never be an accounting of the hundreds, perhaps thousands, of examples of this most awful deception. Loved ones were gone in more ways than one. Perhaps they were lucky, those who never knew the terrible truth.

A reporter for the *Cincinnati Enquirer* interviewed a veteran body snatcher in 1878 who talked freely about his trade. His name was Charles Keeton, and he admitted to having taken about 500 bodies over an eleven-year career. "I get my living by it in the winter time," he said, matter-of-factly, as if he thought of it as an ordinary trade.

Keeton acknowledged that people were revolted by the horrible nature of his work, but he pointed out that were it not for him and kindred spirits, doctors would be denied valuable learning experiences. He spoke earnestly, almost as if he expected people to understand and come to terms with a simple fact of life.

Preferring to exhume in the poor section of the cemetery where people without friends or family were often buried, Keeton and his colleagues would dig down, force open the coffin, place a rope around the neck of the corpse, and pull the body out. Often, though, Keeton went into the grave and lifted the body out. A knife was used to cut off the clothes, and the body was put into a sack with its knees flexed against its chest.

The reporter asked, "How do you enjoy your work?"

Keeton replied calmly, putting the best face on an ugly business: "Well, it wasn't very pleasant at first, of course, but anyone gets used to it. It is for the good of science, and I think it is just as right and honorable as for the man what does the dissecting."[5] While he stopped short of recommending it as a career, clearly, Keeton saw nothing disrespectable or evil about his chosen work.

A Cleveland resurrectionist also provided some unusual insight into the ghastly business. After reaching the body, his technique was to "try the ear." He would pull on the ear of the corpse, and if it pulled away from the head, the corpse was left in the ground. Such a body was too far gone and usually gave off a terrible stench. It was often too overpowering even for the stoutest of body snatchers, causing the entire group to abandon their search for a body and look, instead, for the nearest saloon.[6]

There was an uncanny casualness about these men that defies an easy explanation. Eager for excitement or desperate to earn money to feed their families, they were much like countless others who labored in obscurity. Yet they belonged entirely to their own time and peculiar circumstances, and their work and reputation took them far beyond the ordinary poor man. Unlike their powerless contemporaries, the horrifying image of the grave robber worried and tormented the conscience of the Americans. Crouched unsuspected in the shadows of night in some cemetery with his lantern, shovel, and bag at the ready, the grave robber loomed large on the late nineteenth-century horizon.

A bizarre occupation was bound to result in some bizarre experiences, such as the time a grave robber was caught in the act by two butchers from Pittsburgh. Appalled at what he saw, one of the men struck the grave robber with a board, splitting his skull. "He fell dead on the body he was stealing," was the way it was described. The butchers panicked after their rash act and hurriedly buried the would-be grave robber in the grave he had opened. In 1880, more than thirty years later, one of the butchers confessed to the killing.[7]

Even more weird, there are some recorded incidents where the grave robbers uncovered people who had been buried alive. In one such case in North Carolina, a wealthy woman was interred after falling into a state of "suspended animation." The doctors declared her dead, and she was buried with her favorite rings and a gold watch, just as she requested. A pair of adventurers learned of this and decided to retrieve the valuables.

Digging down, they located her coffin, opened it, and upon pulling off her rings, the "dead" woman suddenly "came back to life."

Needless to say the gravediggers were horrified and ran off at great speed. However, curiosity got the best of one of the men, and he returned to the grave. The revived woman asked to be taken home. Her husband greeted her at the door, and thinking he stood face to face with the ghost of his late wife, fainted on the spot. He recovered, however, and it was said the couple resumed their relationship.[8]

A similar incident occurred in the town of Manlius, near Syracuse, New York, but the "resurrected" person wasn't so fortunate. Grave robbers were after the body of a woman who had been buried just that morning, after seemingly dying of a heart attack. One of the thieves was attempting to force open the coffin lid when he jumped out of the hole in terror. The breathless man would only say that he saw something too horrible to explain. Angered at the delay, another man leaped down in the hole, and using a hatchet, broke through the glass over the lid. In so doing, he drove the hatchet into the head of the woman in the coffin, who had apparently been revived by the work of the first man. They concluded she had been buried alive because of the fresh blood on the hatchet blade.[9]

The body of a man buried alive in rural Pennsylvania was unearthed surreptitiously, not by grave robbers but by a group of his friends. This occurred in the spring of 1879, after the man died—or at least he gave out the appearance of death. His body was displayed for three days before interment. After burial a "curious person" recalled that the deceased's sister had fallen into a death-like trance and remained that way for several days before she "came back to life."

It was then that someone suggested that perhaps their friend had been buried alive. In all haste they went to the cemetery, where the deceased had been reposing for three days. Upon opening the coffin, "a horrible sight greeted the eyes of the resurrectionists." It was clear to all that sometime following the premature burial, the man had revived and put up a terrible struggle within the narrow confines of his coffin. "Imprints of his finger nails" were visible on the torn lining of the coffin. The body was turned over and the coffin was "strained and wrenched" at the joints, further evidence of a valiant fight by the horrified man. His face bore a "distorted countenance," showing the intensity of his suffering while in the constricting grip of slow death.[10]

Perhaps the strangest of all was a grave robbery that took place in the winter of 1859 near Cumminsville, Ohio. The thief—apparently working alone—successfully removed a body from the ground and placed it in a sack. Next, he strapped the sack to his back with a rope. He then attempted to climb over a "high board fence" to exit the cemetery. To accomplish his escape, he pulled the rope up around his shoulders to free his hands. When he swung his foot over the fence, he apparently lost his grip and fell, and in so doing, the rope slipped up around his neck while the weight of the body—still on the other side of the fence—caused the rope to tighten, like a noose. The next morning, both thief and corpse were discovered hanging lifelessly from the fence.[11]

Undoubtedly, no instance of these crimes was more shocking or sensational than the conspiracy and attempt to steal the body of President Abraham Lincoln. It happened on November 8, 1876, the very night of the most controversial presidential election in the history of American politics. Eleven years after Lincoln was assassinated and less than two years[12] after his remains were moved to the marble sarcophagus in a semicircular catacomb and monument at Oak Ridge Cemetery in Springfield, Illinois, the sacred vault was desecrated. That someone would do such a diabolical thing shocked the public into disbelief. Most of those who read the newspaper reports scoffed and concluded the story was untrue, that it was some awful hoax. This was not an ordinary body snatching; this was the attempted theft of the body of a dead president, and a martyred one at that.

The public determined that to do such a terrible thing placed a man far outside the realm of human decency. Such men surrendered all connection with their fellow humans and were beyond redemption, unfit even for animals. No one, people said, no matter how evil or desperate, could do such a thing. Yet the reports were true. The resting place of President Abraham Lincoln was broken into by men who escaped without their plunder.

As the story unfolded, disbelief was replaced by amazement and outrage. After reason began to supplant indignation, the prevailing theory pointed to an attempt to ransom the president's remains, but the U.S. Secret Service revealed a double motive. To make the case even more intriguing, a secret service agent was acting undercover with the conspirators from the beginning. While this infiltration did not result in apprehending the criminals in the act, it insured their speedy arrest.

When the story first broke in the *Chicago Tribune*, the public learned that the custodian of the Lincoln monument, John C. Power, had some kind of premonition that plans were afoot to steal the president's body. So concerned was Power that he went to Robert Lincoln, son of the late president, and Leonard Swett, a well-known Chicago attorney and lifelong friend of the president. After Power convinced Robert Lincoln and Swett of his sincerity, they alerted the secret service, and work was underway to investigate and prevent a possible break-in at the monument.

Agents sought out the low places frequented by unsavory men. One such place was a saloon called the Hub at 294 West Madison in Chicago, which featured a bust of the late President Lincoln above the bar. This infamous "resort of counterfeiters" was run by Terrence Mullen (also spelled Mullins), a man of low repute. The reasons for suspecting this as the site for the conspiracy to steal Lincoln's body are unclear. However, Detective Tyrrell of the secret service planted one of his men in the saloon with instructions to work his way into the confidence of Mullen and his friends and listen carefully for talk of criminal activity.[13] They were to get much more than they expected.

The agent was Lewis C. Swegles, a young man whose talents were especially adapted to infiltration and the gathering of information. After a short time, the affable Swegles was "one of the boys," having convinced the "boys" he was "the boss body-snatcher of Chicago."[14] He soon became the friend of Mullen and another man, Jack Hughes, a notorious counterfeiter who had thus far successfully evaded attempts to catch him printing and passing phony money.

In mid-October, Mullen and Hughes asked Swegles to join them in a grand plan that would net all three a great deal of money. They would rob the tomb of Lincoln, steal and ransom his body for $200,000 or $300,000, and secure the release from Joliet prison of Ben Boyd, their friend and a key member of the counterfeiting ring. Because of Lincoln's immense popularity in the North, Mullen and Hughes believed the authorities would willingly pay the money and agree to release Boyd.

Other than Swegles, Hughes, and Mullen, one other man, known only as "the contractor," was a party to the plot. He was said to be the brains behind the plan, as he was the "sharpest one of the crowd." The contractor wanted no part of the actual theft, however, and remained in the background, but he went to the cemetery, inspected the area, and was satisfied that the job could be pulled off. The secret service refused to release the name of the contractor because the evidence against him was deemed inconclusive.[15]

The contractor was probably "Big Jim" Kneally, said to be the leader of the Chicago counterfeiters, or "coney" men as they were commonly called. For some years Kneally (also spelled Kinealy) and his cohorts made huge sums circulating counterfeit five-dollar bills. After their supply of phony money was depleted, Kneally decided to obtain the release of his master engraver, Ben Boyd. He cooked up an elaborate plan that included stealing Lincoln's body, holding it for ransom, and offering to return it for a substantial sum of money and the release of Ben Boyd.[16]

Swegles, though shocked at the audacious and outrageous nature of the plan, remained calm, learned as much as he could, and reported back to his superiors. At first they refused to believe that anyone could conceive of such a horrible crime, but they were ultimately convinced by Swegles' earnest explanation. The secret service, with the assistance of Robert Lincoln and Swett, quickly adopted a plan of action to catch the conspirators in the act. For this they needed frequent updates from Swegles, who seemed to have no difficulty maintaining his ruse and keeping himself in the good graces of his bold but unsuspecting colleagues.

The conspirators decided to strike on election night. This was not for any symbolic reason, but because they felt that people would be preoccupied with the election, the monument would be unguarded, and the sight of a wagon with a covered box could pass through busy traffic without suspicion. It was decided that Mullen, Hughes, and Swegles would do the actual work of stealing the body. Another man had to be selected to hire a team of horses and park a wagon at a designated place so that the body could be carried away to some hiding place. For this job Swegles convinced his partners to use the services of a rogue named Billy Brown, a man who could handle a team and talk the language of thieves. Brown, who knew Swegles from a past adventure, was let in on the secret service plan and, after some urging, agreed to help out.

Before the conspirators left Chicago, Swegles tore a piece from a page of a London newspaper. He stuffed the torn piece into the bust of Lincoln that sat above the bar at the Hub. The remaining part of the newspaper page was to be left at the scene of the desecration. When it came time to return the body and claim the reward, the piece of newspaper hidden in the bust would be turned over to the authorities, who would then match it with the page found at the scene, thus proving they were dealing with the right parties.[17] Swegles was playing his role masterfully.

After Swegles planted the newspaper page, he, along with Brown, Mullen, and Hughes, traveled by train to Springfield. Once there, they split up, having carefully worked out their plan and each man's role. Acting on Swegles' instructions, Brown disappeared. He alerted the secret service, and a party of five agents was sent to the cemetery on election night. The Lincoln monument was part of a complex that included a memorial hall, a museum, and a dark, winding labyrinth. One of the men was stationed at the end of the labyrinth next to the wall of the monument, where he could hear any noise coming from within. In his hand he held a string that reached the hiding place of the other four secret service agents.

The sarcophagus that held Lincoln's casket rested on a pedestal inside the monument in full view of visitors. It was positioned in front of the crypts that held the bodies of his three sons, Tad, Willie, and Eddie. The thieves planned to break into the tomb, open the sarcophagus and then the casket, remove the body, double it over, stuff it inside a bag, and exit the cemetery.

It was a cold November night when the gang set out to pull off their ambitious crime. With Swegles standing by, Mullen and Hughes sawed through the padlock on the door of the tomb. Once inside, they found it surprisingly easy to remove the sarcophagus cover. While they were engaged in this work, the secret service man in the labyrinth—who had noiselessly braved three hours of cold—heard grating noses from within and pulled on the string as a signal for the others to approach.

The four other agents approached barefoot so as not to make a sound. With revolvers drawn and orders to "shoot to kill," they quickly made their way to the vault. Unfortunately, one of their guns discharged accidentally. The shot alerted the thieves, and Swegles, Mullen, and Hughes disappeared into the darkness of night. They left behind an ax, a chisel, and a pair of snippers. The conspirators had not broken into the casket but were in the act of pulling it from the sarcophagus when the errant shot was fired. While the actual damage was not great, the investigators and the press believed the break-in was "unparalleled in the history of crime."[18]

While Lincoln lived he was subjected to relentless ridicule, criticism, and outright hatred by a legion of political enemies. After his death, however, the process of deification began, and by 1876, Lincoln had achieved god-like status. Had the conspirators pulled it off, the theft of Lincoln's body would have challenged all other nineteenth-century misdeeds for the title "crime of the century."

However, they failed, and it wasn't long before the fiends were in custody. Within a few days after the crime, Hughes and Mullen were back in Chicago, making their arrest relatively easy to effect. At nine o'clock on November 17, 1876, the two were apprehended at the Hub and soon thereafter transported to Springfield to face charges. At midnight on June 1, 1877, a jury found Hughes and Mullen guilty of attempting to rob Lincoln's tomb and each was sentenced to one year in prison at Joliet, Illinois.[19]

The excitement surrounding the crime troubled the officials at Oak Ridge Cemetery. They concluded that Lincoln would not be safe in the monument. So in the dark of a November night in 1876—six days after the break-in—a select group of men led by Powers, the custodian, removed the president's casket from the sarcophagus. The men carried it through the memorial hall and into the labyrinth, where they planned to conceal it in a grave only they knew about. However, it was very hard to dig in the dirt, and they gave up after the hole filled up with water. Lincoln's casket was covered by "a heap of boards in a cellar." It stayed there for two years while tearful visitors from the world over gazed into the monument at the empty sarcophagus, believing they were standing in the presence of the dead president.[20]

The public was understandably shocked and outraged over the crime, which cut across political lines. Still it struck a partisan chord and added to the tension caused by a decade of post-Civil War Reconstruction politics. The recent presidential election had been more than just Samuel Tilden, the New York Democrat, against Rutherford B. Hayes, the Ohio Republican. It had pitted North against the South again, and old wounds were reopened. The attempt to steal Lincoln's body evoked memories of the president and the Civil War and played into the deadly sectional rivalry that threatened to renew the conflict.

While most men simply believed the crooks were motivated by a desire to cash in on a ransom, there were those who held different views, believing it was a politically motivated crime. It was generally believed among blacks that ex-rebels had at long last carried out their threat to exhume Lincoln and scattered his ashes "to the four winds of heaven." A story was circulated that a secret group called the Knights of the Golden Cross might have had some involvement. It was said that one of the group's more strident members vowed in 1868, "I shall live to see the bones of the tyrant Lincoln food for the vultures of the South."[21] In 1876 the North was still angry at the South, and vice versa. With the election results in doubt and dubious political machinations in the offing, the shocking events of November 8 were resented all the more.

Strangely, the Lincoln grave robbery conspiracy is rarely mentioned in the many books about the life of the illustrious president. Most writers chose to leave it alone, believing it better that such awful facts lie buried and forgotten in the pages of the newspapers that were forced to trumpet the story to a readership unprepared and unwilling to accept the news. President Lincoln freed the slaves, he gave the Gettysburg Address, and he preserved the Union. These are memories not to be marred by the designs of loathsome criminals whose wholly unsentimental and selfish motivations spoiled an otherwise storybook record. As it turned out, there were other high-profile grave robberies that diverted public attention from the Lincoln case.

In the spring of 1878, Ohio—which attracted more than its share of body snatchers—was again sent into shock over another big-name grave robbery. This time it was the theft of the body of John Scott Harrison, son of the late president William Henry Harrison and father of the prominent Republican politician and future president Benjamin Harrison. John Scott Harrison had served in Congress in the 1850s and had two other sons, John and Carter Harrison. With the exception of the attempt to steal Lincoln's body and the A. T. Stewart outrage, no other body snatching drew as much public revulsion and rebuke.

The facts were positively horrifying. John Scott Harrison passed away a respected old man, beloved by his family. During his burial in Congress Green Cemetery at North Bend on the Ohio River, it was discovered that a nearby grave had been robbed. The violated grave was that of a young man named Augustus Devin, a twenty-three-year-old nephew of John Scott Harrison, who died of consumption ten days previous. His family and friends were notified, and a search warrant was secured against the Medical College of Ohio in Cincinnati.

Strangely, one of those who conducted the search was John Harrison, who had buried his father just the day before. He was assisted in the search by a cousin, George Eaton; a constable; and a reluctant janitor, A. Q. Marshall. The latter did his best to hurry the searchers along, all the while insisting that they were wasting their time.[22]

The medical school was not in session, and only a few bodies were seen in the dissection room. The searchers were about to leave when Harrison "noticed a windlass with a rope reaching down into the lower story." He pulled on the rope and drew up a body. When a cloth was removed from the cadaver's head, young Harrison realized to his unspeakable horror that he was standing face to face with the body of his father, John Scott Harrison. The long, gray beard, which in life had been fondly stroked by grandchildren, had been cut off, and the corpse was in other ways disguised. Yet there was no doubt that he had inadvertently discovered the body of his father, which had been tenderly laid to rest the day before.

"My God, that's my father!" exclaimed young John Harrison.[23]

If he had any doubt that he had just discovered his father's body, it dissipated on the arrival of Carter Harrison with news that the grave had, indeed, been robbed. Within a short time news of the dastardly crime hit the streets, causing the public to seethe with anger and outrage, asking themselves a desperate question: what kind of fiends would take the body of a distinguished citizen and the son of an American president?

Moreover, people were perplexed at the speed and skill of the resurrectionists. Because of the prevalence of grave robbing, a guard had been hired to watch the grave by night, and a heavy stone slab was placed over it. Still, the thieves made away with their plunder with an efficiency that baffled all observers, delivering the body at 3 a.m. to the Ohio Medical College, about twelve miles from the cemetery. People immediately suspected that the college faculty—made up of respectable men—was involved.[24]

The body of John Scott Harrison was promptly reinterred in the Jacob Strader vault in Spring Grove Cemetery near Cincinnati, with plans for a permanent reburial in some other "silent city." The family even considered moving the president's ashes. This, of course, didn't end the matter, as the Harrison brothers, led by General Benjamin Harrison, went on the offensive, determined to bring to justice the ghouls who brought them so much horror and mental anguish. They openly accused the faculty, demanding a thorough and forthright explanation.

Under pressure because of the strong threat of mob violence, the police immediately arrested the college janitor, A. Q. Marshall, while staying away from the faculty for the time being. Not to be outdone, the entire faculty of the Ohio Medical College rallied to their janitor's defense, pooling their money and putting up a $5,000 bond to secure Marshall's release.

Next, the faculty put up a strong defense, issuing a statement denying any connection with the crime. Dr. Robert Bartholow, dean of the faculty, drafted and published a statement in the *Cincinnati Times* on June 1, 1878, setting forth the faculty's position. While the staff decried this activity and deeply regretted the sorrow experienced by the Harrison family, Bartholow said, "It is merely justice to the Faculty to state that they are ignorant of what transpired in the college building on the night in question." True, the college was utterly dependent on cadavers for teaching anatomy and the like, but it would never countenance the theft of such an honorable man. The doctor went on to defend the use of bodies for dissection, although the practice had given medical schools a bad reputation.

Bartholow's explanation served as a lecture as well, reminding the readers that however disgusting the public may find the practice of dissection, the schools had no choice but to teach it, if for no other reason than to combat the profusion of medical malpractice lawsuits that plagued the profession. The medical men understood that grave robbery was an outrage but stated that, instead of blaming the medical profession, the public should blame the archaic laws that forced the theft of bodies for legitimate scientific purposes.

Openly, almost defiantly, Bartholow called for understanding as if he believed he could single-handedly inject sufficient knowledge of science into the public so as to create, at least, a common ground for further discussion. He stated calmly that the bodies of those who died in "public institutions" should be turned over to medical schools for use by the students and faculty, for there simply were not enough bodies. "Under existing circumstances bodies necessary for the instruction of medical students must be stolen," he said. In other words, he was saying: if you want us to get you well, we first must determine what made you sick, and for that we need dead bodies.

Thus, with unabashed frankness and a little panache, Bartholow turned an apology into a plea for understanding while at the same time admitting that medical schools paid the hated resurrectionists—a secret that everyone knew. As for the body of John Scott Harrison, Bartholow blithely explained it away by saying some unknown resurrectionist, acting entirely on his own, brought the corpse to the college "to replenish his exchequer." He insisted no one connected to the college, including the "poor janitor," was in any way involved.

The Harrisons would have nothing to do with Bartholow's explanation of the body theft. General Benjamin Harrison issued his own public statement, thanking the people of Cincinnati for their outpouring of sympathy. He offered a prayer that "God keep your precious dead from the barbarous touch of the grave robber." Then with understandable emotion and profound indignation, Harrison demanded a thorough explanation from the medical college faculty and an outright admission that one or more of them were involved in the theft of his father's body.

Who paid the resurrectionist who delivered the body? Who hung the body from a hook by the neck like a side of beef? Who but a doctor could have made the incision in the neck? How could the faculty not know that the body—or any body—was brought in, received, and paid for? It is only logical to conclude that someone had to authorize the transaction. The arrangements, Harrison insisted, were made with more than a nod of the head and a wink of an eye. The faculty, Harrison conceded, may not have known the identity of his father's body, but it certainly was aware of its presence and was, therefore, covering up for the resurrectionists and those who hired them. While he acknowledged the faculty and students' need to study human anatomy, he chastised them for their insensitivity, vowing to see the matter to a just conclusion while confessing he lacked the composure to state his case with the desired clarity.[25]

Some relief for the Harrisons came on June 17, when Augustus Devin's body was discovered in a vat containing about forty naked, rotting corpses, at a medical college in Ann Arbor, Michigan. When it was returned to North Bend, Ohio, in the company of Devin's brother, a crowd of the curious and angry was gathered at the cemetery awaiting the reburial. To satisfy their morbid curiosity, the coffin was opened, and the badly decomposed body was positively identified. "That's Augustus," many proclaimed with confidence.

Citizens were further gratified by the arrest of Charles O. Morton, "the noted resurrectionist" from Toledo. It was believed that he and his wife, disguised as a man, stole Harrison's body pursuant to a contract with the Ohio Medical College. Morton—who used several aliases, including Dr. Christian—and A. Q. Marshall, the college's janitor, were the only parties charged in the theft of the bodies of Harrison and Devin. Morton was arrested after a fearful Marshall confessed that he was in league with the notorious professional grave robber.[26]

The Harrison family was bitterly disappointed with just two arrests. They had hoped that the grand jury would indict members of the college faculty,[27] but General Harrison understood that this was not likely to happen, as he knew there was a lack of convincing evidence. For this reason, the Harrison and Devin families filed civil suits for damages against the college. These, too, apparently did not produce results, as nothing emerges from the records to indicate that they succeeded in their lawsuits. The entire matter seemed to fade away without resolution or justice.

In 1880, the grave of the famous gunfighter Wild Bill Hickok was found disturbed in Deadwood, Dakota Territory. His body was not taken, but his friends feared there would be another attempt and took precautions. It was said they loaded his grave with "torpedoes."[28]

The torpedoes were probably a reference to the invention of Phil K. Clover, an artist. In 1878, he filed papers to obtain a patent on a "torpedo for grave robbers." It was similar to a "miniature needle-gun," about six inches long. It was, in essence, a trap or spring gun, installed inside the coffin. When the grave robber attempted to remove the body from the coffin, the trigger was sprung, sending a ball or buckshot upward and, hopefully, into the body of the thief. Several could be installed so that if one was tripped and failed to strike the thief, others might still hit their target.[29]

If anything, this clumsy reaction demonstrates the depth of public concern over the insidious crime of grave robbery. It was all too frequently left in the hands of the authorities only. This innovation, this "torpedo for grave robbers," was developed to defeat an evil practice. Once again, America's inventive proclivities emerged to meet a crisis.

Besides, the police needed help, as the crisis easily overwhelmed the use of torpedoes and other such deterrents. The police were unable to make arrests in most cases, often as a result of incompetence or internal corruption. Grave robbers were hard to catch anyway, because they operated under cover of darkness, and very few people other than grave robbers cared to venture into a cemetery at night.

As a result, grave robbery was a crime that usually went unsolved and unpunished. It lay hidden in the dark shadows of a complex social tapestry, almost too gruesome to be believed, let alone understood, except, perhaps, by the grave robbers themselves—a select few for whom stealing bodies was merely a means of augmenting their income. Strangely, the men who created this great, dark mystery seemed unable to grasp and appreciate the awful influence of their creation.

By 1878, after four years of economic depression, political corruption, cynicism, bloody strikes, and social upheaval, American society seemed hopelessly divided and chaotic. With poverty and crime moving hand in hand, fear and anger forced its way through the most optimistic rhetoric and religious fervor; democracy itself was threatened. In any age, hate and hunger drive people to deadly extremes. This is especially true of the 1870s. There was a sense that the dark side of the human condition was as unsettled and wild as any creature that stalked the night and capable of any outrageous act. Grave robbery fit into this desperate and macabre setting quite appropriately.

CHAPTER 5

Middleton, Allekton, Dr. Christian, and Other "Clews"

> It's called Allekton, and is a colorless fluid, with an odor not unlike that of creosote ... for use "on a badly decomposed body."
>
> *New York Herald*, November 9, 1878

Soon after A. T. Stewart's body disappeared, the letters poured in to the press and police from a variety of people who had some "indispensable" information. Many letters were morbid; some were written in red ink, as if to symbolize blood or to get extra attention. Some were demanding and angry in tone; some were desperate and pathetic. Some writers had seen Stewart in their dreams and claimed to know where he was hidden and how his body was taken. Other letters, far more lofty and detached, came from so-called spiritualists who claimed to be in touch with Stewart from beyond the grave.[1] The bottom line: everyone wanted a piece of the Stewart fortune, and they were willing to embrace the mystery.

Mrs. Stewart endured these barbs as best as she could, spending most of her time inside her lavish mansion, but nothing could ease the terrible pain caused by the grave robbers. When her husband's body was carried away that dark November night, it was as if his soul had been stolen from the rolls of paradise. For all her great wealth, she was reduced to a tormented and pitiable creature confined within the walls of a luxurious dungeon, waiting for the comfort of a Christian death.

Cornelia Stewart had long been a steady, faithful ally and helpmate to her husband. While he was busy constructing a business empire, he relied on her common sense and placed great credence in her taste, attitude, and conclusions about merchandise. She had simple tastes in her own wardrobe that she defended against those who thought she should have dressed with more flare. Once when a friend asked why she dressed so plainly, she said, "I can afford to do so."[2]

Having come so far together with her Alexander, rejoicing in his enormous success, she no doubt spent endless hours after his body disappeared retracing the steps of the long journey that were so firmly embedded in her memory.

Mrs. Stewart's sorrow aroused the profound sympathy of everyone, including the police, who promised a vigorous and thorough investigation. They were, however, soon to be upstaged by Henry Hilton. While at the outset he agreed to let the police handle the case their way, it was not long after that he assumed control of the investigation. Not officially, of course, but by brute force of personality backed by his wealth. He hired his own detectives and followed leads entirely on his own without bothering to consult the authorities. While this was bound to result in some duplication of effort, no one seemed to mind. Indeed, during the first few days following the crime, there was a sense in the community that everyone should pitch in and get the case wrapped up as soon as possible.

While Stewart's body was missing, New York was transfixed by an unseen and unholy presence. The city was accustomed to crime, scandal, chaos, political corruption, and unfavorable publicity, but it had seen nothing as evil and macabre as this crime. It was a crime beyond the comprehension of a people jaded by lawlessness and bizarre behavior. People were drawn to the dark crime's morbid aspects, and crowds of the curious gathered daily at the St. Mark's churchyard fence despite the cold, cheerless weather. Young and old, they came—women with their children, groups of giggling girls, and jostling boys. One enterprising man was seen with a bundle of advertising flyers, which he stuck in the interstices of the fence. Another man suggested Stewart's body was stolen by men who wanted to study the brain and learn how it was that Stewart made so much money.

The masses flocked to the fence, seeing very little but hoping for a glimpse at something unforgettable. Their sentiments could be summed up in the quotation of a bewildered New Yorker who said very plainly as he peered through the fence at St. Mark's, "Jes' think on't! Not known'n any more where the bones of the biggest millionaire do be!"[3] Since Stewart was world famous, the disappearance of his body was difficult to accept.

A terrible unease set in among the wealthy. A double guard was placed at the tomb of Cornelius Vanderbilt at New Dorp on Staten Island,[4] lest the dark team of resurrectionists strike and once again break the silence of the illustrious dead. People were repulsed by the gruesome nature of the crime but deeply concerned about the fearlessness and consummate skill of the criminals, who were seemingly guided by a malevolent power.

Somewhere in America—or possibly Canada—a small group of people in hiding followed the newspaper reports and plotted their next move, while others from all over the world waited for developments. One wonders if these anonymous culprits had any sense of their tenuous, worldwide celebrity, their ability to create fear among the public and to command the attention of the enraptured press.

Although it was unlikely the grave robbers would strike again until after the Stewart business was finished, having that kind of men on the loose was frightening to contemplate. Hilton shared those thoughts and wasted no time in posting a reward for the villains. Yet he was adamant that no money be spent in exchange for the recovery of the body, unless it was returned along with the thieves in chains. He placed the following notice in the *New York Times* and other newspapers on the day after the disappearance of Stewart's body:

> $25,000 REWARD!—Whereas, in the early morning of November 7, 1878, the vault of the late Alexander T. Stewart in St. Mark's Churchyard, in this city, was broken into, and his remains removed from there, the above reward is offered by direction of Mrs. A. T. Stewart, and will be paid for the return of the body and information which will convict the parties who were engaged in the outrage. Or a liberal reward will be paid for information which will lead to either of these results.
>
> HENRY HILTON

Hilton was questioned by a reporter about the amount of the reward. He replied that at first he decided on a $10,000 reward, then changed it to $20,000 and, just as quickly, wrote down $25,000.00. He said he was "desirous of doing what would meet public approval; not too little; not too much."[5] Most likely, however, Hilton was thinking about spending as little as possible to apprehend the criminals.

The police scoffed at Hilton's "reward," believing it to be puny and totally unacceptable to the thieves. They thought Hilton should be prepared to pay at least $100,000, possibly even $1 million, for the return of the body. They understood, however, that Hilton was not the kind of man to spread wealth around, but he had to make some overture for the sake of Mrs. Stewart's feelings, and do it without undue delay. All concerned were under pressure, with special demands placed on the detectives in charge of the investigation.

An early theory, probably developed by Hilton,[6] was that the vault had actually been robbed a month before, and the body then had been stored in one of the other vaults or at another cemetery. The second opening of the Stewart vault then was merely a ploy to throw off the police. This caused a bit of a stir, but a reporter for the *New York Evening Post* called it palpably erroneous. Had the thieves stolen the body beforehand, they could have simply sent Hilton a postcard informing him of this and thereby avoided a second, risky graveyard adventure.[7]

Still, the theory had support, and acting on this belief, a group of detectives headed by Inspector Dilks returned to the St. Mark's churchyard and began digging down to and opening some "receiving vaults" in the church basement. The first one contained two coffins and nothing else. The second, unused since 1830, had thirteen coffins but no trace of Stewart. Nearby cemeteries were searched for signs of fresh digging, to no avail. The idea was abandoned after another search of the St. Mark's grounds was undertaken without results.[8]

The *New York Sun* came forth with another lead. The publisher of the *Sun* sent word to Hilton that on Thursday, the night of the crime, while crossing to New Jersey on the Cortlandt Street ferry, he was overcome by an awful stench resembling decaying flesh coming from the ladies' cabin. This caused many to think the body would be found in New Jersey.[9] Hilton informed the police, but again they rejected the lead. Their focus was still on the churchyard and the desecrated vault.

On November 8, the day after the grave robbery, the police tracked down the source of the shovel and lantern used in the crime. They were purchased at Seymour's hardware store, at Chatham and Divisions streets, where the salesman was questioned and gave a description of the buyer. The police also interviewed a man who saw six men carrying a box near the churchyard at 2:15 a.m. After he described the men as well dressed and jovial, the police quickly dismissed the story.

At this early point in the investigation, the authorities were trying to determine how the thieves were able to learn of the exact location of the vault opening. As such, some suspicion was still on the sexton and his assistant. Interestingly, Hilton and William Libbey were never suspected, even though they, too, knew the location of the vault.

The police made a significant discovery on Friday. They determined that the thieves could easily have entered and exited by crossing the fence at the extreme western end of the churchyard. At that location there were two, low, cross-braces that could serve as steps for climbing up the fence. There was also a forked tree conveniently close to the fence. From there the robbers could have reached the balcony of a nearby boardinghouse. It was deduced that the thieves used the braces and tree to get over the fence.[10] Therefore, no key was needed, thus taking some heat off the sexton and his assistant.

Late Friday afternoon, John H. McCullagh of the seventeenth precinct discovered something equally significant. While he was examining the churchyard, he discovered two large stains resembling tobacco spit on the pavement beneath the church portico. Taking a closer look, he was struck and repelled by a foul and nauseous odor, the likes of which he had never smelled before. It was too dark to search for more, and as he was sick to his stomach, McCullagh returned to police headquarters and reported his findings.

The next morning, McCullagh returned with Commissioner Nichols and the coroner. They examined the spots and found some others leading away from the church. They were satisfied that the blotches were caused by liquid dripping from Stewart's body. A large bloodhound—or a small Scottish terrier, depending on which newspaper was more credible—was brought to the churchyard to sniff out the trail of foul blotches.[11] This was done more for show than anything else, for the path taken by the thieves was clear from the ground evidence. The trail went past the church toward the western end of the churchyard, leading to the belief that the thieves stepped on the granite walk as they carried the body, thus the absence of footprints on the grass.

Mud was found on the fence braces, and more of the foul, greasy smudges were discovered on the spikes atop the fence. The police reasoned that the thieves lifted the body over the fence using the forked tree, the fence cross-braces, and the balcony of the nearby residence. It was with some relief that they had come to some conclusion other than the fact that Stewart's body had been stolen so mysteriously.

The boardinghouse whose balcony probably facilitated the robbery was at 129 East Tenth Street. It was operated by a woman named Newton and was soon to become an attraction. The police spoke to one of the residents, who recalled hearing a loud thump during the night and someone say, "Come. It's about time for us to be out of here," or similar words. He attached no significance to it, however, for it was common for young couples to sit on the balcony "billing and cooing" late into the night.

The police found another trail of drippings leading from the courtyard gate of the boardinghouse to the outside curb. It was here that the body must have been loaded into a box, put aboard a waiting wagon, and hauled away to a predetermined hiding place.

The foul-smelling droplets were subjected to chemical analysis by students at the Columbia School of Mines and were determined to be decomposed animal matter.[12] This conclusion was no surprise to anyone. The telltale drops most certainly marked the path of the grave robbers as they hurriedly spirited Stewart's rotting corpse out of St. Mark's churchyard on that cold and gloomy November night.

The *Herald* seized upon a "clew" that was all but ignored by the *Times*, and while it had a short-lived significance, it seemed, for the moment, the best thing going. A reporter from the *Herald* recalled that several months past, his newspaper published a detailed article about a new discovery, called Allekton, a colorless liquid that promised to preserve the dead, even badly decomposed bodies. It was created by a Dr. Rogers and was sold by an undertaking firm called Middleton and Warner, located at 28 Bond Street.

On October 7, the day of the first attempt to rob Stewart's tomb, C. N. Middleton remembered that a strange man came and inquired about Allekton. He wanted to buy some "for a friend." The stranger also tried to buy a "patent needle" used for injecting Allekton into a body. Middleton boasted that a quart of this concoction could deodorize an entire body simply by sprinkling the liquid on it.

Middleton was suspicious, and since he only sold the new body preserver and the needle to professional undertakers, he engaged the stranger in conversation. He could get nothing from the man but furtive glances and a weak insistence that a friend merely asked that he buy some Allekton. Middleton refused, and the man left without the new concoction. He never returned.

After the Stewart incident, Middleton contacted the police, Hilton, and Libbey, believing the stranger seeking Allekton was one of those involved in the grave robbery. Middleton was taken to a police station, where he was asked to review photographs and sketches in a "rogue's gallery." When he came to number 1,267, he recognized the face of his would-be customer, who he said was "by no means a bad-looking man." This face was also identified by the hardware sales clerk as belonging to the man who bought the lantern found at the crime scene. Number 1,267 and the face that went with it belonged to Thomas McCarty, age twenty-two, who had a minor criminal record for "watch snatching."

A *Herald* reporter present when Middleton fingered McCarty, set out to find suspect number 1,267, and apparently got to him ahead of the police. McCarty was found standing on Greenwich Street, gazing innocently into the light of a gas lamp. He identified himself and spoke freely to the reporter, even admitting he was once arrested for stealing a watch but was otherwise squeaky-clean. After a few moments of rambling conversation, the reporter concluded the "alleged ghoul" was just that. It was clear to the journalist that "in some other quarter, the invaders of Stewart's tomb must be found." McCarty was an innocent dreamer, an "ordinary corner lounger," not the stuff of cemetery ghouls.[13]

Then on November 11, 1878, the *Evening Post* learned that Middleton and Warner received a letter the day before from a man who called himself "Me Who Caled." Like many other pieces of correspondence dealing with the great mystery, this one was poorly composed, and it probably came from the man who attempted to buy the Allekton:

Midleton & Wurner:

jents I caled at your offic for your alukto non oct seven but i did not stele Mr. Stewout's boddy i got it or wanted it for a feller who red of it in the post and herald and jept asking me to get him sum. When he red in the boston papers about your taking up the body there and preserving it he was crasy on the subject, and i caled for him don't be to fresh and give away your guts, & try to get me in a hole, look out for yourselves.[14]

Interestingly, the misspelling of many of the words looks intentional, especially in light of the fact that certain words like "preserving" and "subject" were spelled correctly. It seems unlikely that a semiliterate person wrote this letter; more likely it was cleverly conceived and written by someone with less than innocent intentions. Still the curious letter shed no light on the identity of Middleton's visitor.

All the fuss over Allekton and its speculative role in the mystery caused reporters to visit the Bond Street store. While he vehemently denied using the occasion for free advertisement, Middleton couldn't resist bragging about the new product, stating, "If the man who applied here for our preparation on the seventh of October succeeded in obtaining any, he would have been able to within an hour, if one of the snatchers, to have rendered the body of Mr. Stewart totally inoffensive to the nostrils."[15]

The *Herald* suddenly turned its attention away from Allekton and toward Washington DC, where detectives offered both a theory and a suspect. The latter was Dr. George A. Christian, soon to be known to the world as the "Washington Resurrectionist." Christian, who was not really a doctor, was a convicted and infamous body snatcher whose reputation in that line of work was acquired prior to the Stewart outrage.

Because Washington detectives enjoyed a fine reputation as crime solvers and were especially good at arresting grave robbers, their ideas were worthy of respect. They theorized that the Stewart break-in was planned well in advance. The thieves were professionals and were present at Stewart's funeral. As such, they knew the exact location of the vault and were not fooled by Hilton's attempt to disguise it. They understood the size and interior of the vault, and probably made a sketch of it for future use. They studied the area many times at night and had, after careful planning, decided exactly when and how to strike.

According to the detectives from Washington, only one man in America was shrewd and daring enough to pull off this grave robbery: George A. Christian. Find Christian and you find the man in charge of the team of grave robbers that struck Stewart's vault.[16] Of this, they were certain.

The *Herald* was enthralled with finding Christian, as his likeness was quite similar to that of the man (first thought to be McCarty) who was described by Middleton and the hardware store sales clerk. Another dispatch was sent from the nation's capital, where the police had a description and a photograph of Christian taken on November 11, 1874, when he was arrested for stealing two bodies that were crated for shipping to Ohio. At that time, Christian was described by the *Herald* as a hospital steward from England, twenty-three years old; five feet, seven inches tall; weighing 120 pounds, with a sallow complexion, dark eyes, "dark flowing hair, high cheek bones and prominent nose."[17] He had the annoying habit of rolling his large eyes when he spoke while twisting and re-shaping his mouth. It gave him an unforgettable, wicked demeanor.

Christian was first arrested for grave robbery in December 1873 and was sentenced to one year in jail and a $1,000 fine. He was released by order of President Ulysses S. Grant on September 15, 1874, at the urging of his (Christian's) friends.[18] He was arrested again on November 10, 1874, along with two others known as Maud and Percy Brown, husband and wife. They were charged with stealing two bodies they planned to sell to an Ohio medical school. When arrested, Mrs. Brown was washing clothes taken from the corpses.

Christian was escorted to the police station and searched. Police discovered a notebook containing information about bodies sold to medical schools and the prices obtained for each. He posted bail, skipped out, and was not seen again until May 7, 1876, when he was arrested on board a train between Baltimore and Washington. Once again he escaped and disappeared. When news of the Stewart break-in reached Washington, the police were confident that the deft hand and thoughtful planning of the notorious Christian were at the heart of the crime.[19]

The warden of the District of Columbia jail thought so, too. He read the *Herald*'s description of the man who purchased the lantern and attempted to buy the body preservative, and he said confidently, "The description is as perfect as a picture of Christian."[20] The notorious abductor of the dead was back and up to his old tricks.

New York police, however, didn't seem interested in the theory of their fellow officers from Washington. Perhaps it was because they were too busy deflecting a barrage of other theories. By the second day of their investigation, the police were already inundated with tips, leads, and "clews" from the public.

Many people reported seeing wagons of various types in the vicinity of the cemetery on the night of the grave robbery. A "well-dressed" man spoke to Superintendent George W. Walling and offered an unusual theory: Stewart was stolen so that his head could be used by a "phrenologist." The gentleman was certain the body was already on its way abroad and insisted that police cable various foreign ports so the cargoes of ocean steamers could be searched. Walling would have none of it. This made the man very angry, and he stomped out of the police station in "high dudgeon," saying this was the first and last time he would ever offer help.[21]

A frustrated and tired Walling could only shake his head, for he must have known that before long, innumerable cranks would put forth equally absurd theories with equal or greater exuberance. The police would have to listen to them all and sort through the nonsense for reliable clues. It would be impossible to hold the public back from the investigation. It was just too good of a story and had the makings of a great mystery, just the kind of thing needed to relieve the collective boredom that habitually plagued the poor and the unemployed.

Rumors were flying around like passenger pigeons. Among them, someone suggested Stewart's body was stolen by some of his own relatives who suspected he had been poisoned to death. These suspects, presumably in-laws, wanted to have his remains examined for traces of poison[22] and decided against using established legal procedures for an exhumation. This rumor vanished soon after it appeared.

A private investigator of dubious reputation brought his own story into the act. Bernard Russick called at the seventeenth precinct and laid out his ideas. He was confident that Stewart's body was on its way to Havana, Cuba, concealed in a barrel of spirits. He was "possessed of information" and had "obtained evidence" to support his theory but would not reveal it. Instead, he booked passage on a steamer for Havana to intercept the remains. The police were glad to see him go.

Attention was also directed at New Jersey and a "mysterious box" on a milk wagon that was hauled on a street ferry to Hoboken and then to Newark. New York detectives, along with a Pinkerton agent, converged on Newark, checking the morgues and mortuaries, looking for a missing corpse. They came across the suspicious wagon and found that, while smelly, it contained only rotting fish bones.

A Newark newspaper expressed no surprise over this suspicion, as "Newarkers have become accustomed to having this city brought up in connection with all the sensational events throughout the country."[23] Why should the Stewart mystery not be laid at the feet of the people of Newark? After all, the Pinkerton detectives were in town looking for clues. The Newark police, however, ridiculed the notion that Stewart's body was taken to their city, and the Pinkertons denied any connection with the investigation. It was another dead end.[24]

Of greater concern was a letter sent to the *Herald* from "A Company." The message was terse and intriguing: "If the executors of the late A. T. Stewart will donate $500,000 for some needed public charity in the city of New York the whereabouts of his remains will be immediately divulged and not one penny will be asked for the expence [sic] we have incurred." The editorial staff of the *Herald* admitted the letter might have been a joke, but nevertheless called it the "coolest thing of the season."[25]

The Company letter was greeted with thoughtful curiosity because Stewart was not known as a charitable man. When a friend suggested he donate his palatial home to the city for the mayor's mansion, Stewart snapped back, saying he did not "slave in business to decorate the municipality."[26] His will bequeathed nothing to the city or its charities—not a single example of generosity that would create for him a sense of immortality that comes from giving.

A Company: were these the grave robbers? If so, were they trying to make a political statement or take revenge—or both? These thoughts had support because of the level of anti-Stewart hostility in the streets of New York. Many people remembered him as a cold, Scrooge-like man ruled by money. A reporter recalled walking along Broadway on the morning following the vault break-in and hearing many people mutter "served him right." Yet the crime was so horrible that the negative chorus was tempered by those who thundered about "what an outrage" it was.[27]

While the climate was ripe for revenge of some sort and, on the face of it, A Company appeared to be making a political statement, there was more. An anonymous person or persons placed this small, cryptic ad in the *Herald*:

NICHOLS & HILTON.—CALL OFF BLOODHOUNDS and discipline the Police. P. X. Y-8—$100,000.00.

Was this some kind of a ransom note? Was it a signal of some kind? Apparently no one thought it was either one. Hilton expressed amusement, and the police humorously suggested it was done by the *Herald* staff itself to fill up space in the personals section.

The *New York Herald* had a reputation for dabbling in scandal and working personal ads to the limit. Everyone had access to a little sounding board in the *Herald*. The newspaper was begun on May 11, 1835, published by the cantankerous, cynical, and hard-driving James Gordon Bennett, who seemed to possess but one goal: to produce the most popular newspaper in the world. With his life's savings of $500, Bennett rented a cramped, dingy basement at 20 Wall Street and, all by himself, started his newspaper and set out to "get the news."

Bennett's plan was to publish a newspaper that contained a mixture of hard news and sensationalism and sell it for a penny a copy. The *Morning Herald* was an instant success, and by 1840 it was the circulation leader in New York, surpassing the *New York Sun*, the city's first "penny paper." By 1860 the *Herald* boasted the largest circulation of any newspaper in the world.

The apolitical Bennett was not afraid to get down and dirty, and he attacked political corruption and hypocrisy with special glee, all the while promoting New York, its commercial interests, its art, and its people. He had a talent for finding a story that would engross his readers. When he came upon scandal or crime, he exploited the story to the hilt, despite merciless criticism from detractors, including churches and rival newspapermen.[28]

The *Herald* was popular because it was cheap, allowing low- and middle-class people to buy and read it. Upper-crust folk might have sneered at Bennett and his penny paper, sticking to their six-penny *Wall Street Journal*, but they undoubtedly read the exciting *Herald*, especially the new-money snobs like A. T. Stewart. As time went on, Bennett raised the price of his newspaper so that it was no longer a penny paper.

Bennett died in 1867, and his son James Gordon Bennett Jr. assumed control of the *Herald*, adopting his father's successful formula. The younger Bennett had his father's talent, including the rough edges that frequently collided with others. What he lacked was his father's drive to be the first with the best. His forte was making news and creating sensations, like the time he published an editorial titled "To Hell with the Pope."[29] In this instance his bad taste in journalism was attributed to his fondness for the good taste of champagne.

Bennett Jr. loved the newspaper business and found the Stewart case to his liking. His newspaper immediately became a magnet for those who wanted to place ads and submit letters with clues. Like his thick-skinned father, Bennett knew what sold newspapers, and he cared not that many of the letters and personal ads were outrageous, phony, and awkwardly humorous.

Under the younger Bennett, the success of the *Herald* went unabated throughout the 1870s. The depression following the Panic of 1873 barely diminished its readership, although Bennett did decrease the price per copy from four to three cents in 1876. Its circulation during the decade sometimes hit 150,000 per day when news events of great importance or public interest hit the streets.

The primary rival of the *Herald* was the *New York Tribune*, begun on April 10, 1841, by Horace Greeley, who became the best-known and best-liked newspaperman in America. In addition to his daily paper, Greeley published the *Weekly Tribune*, which became the best-circulated national newspaper of its time. Unlike the paper of his hated rival, James Gordon Bennett, Greeley's *Tribune* was unabashedly political, as he felt a newspaper should inform and instruct the public and be a strong moral influence. Throughout his long and colorful career, the wildly whiskered "Uncle Horace," as he was known, cranked out editorials that called for reform and progress.

To his critics, however, Greeley was known as a quirky, unsteady sort of fellow who never seemed to take a consistent stance on the political issues of the day. He was antislavery, antibooze, and antiseduction, to name a few of his many causes. While he was always busy stamping out undesirable influences, he was pragmatic enough to know that he had to cover crime and scandal to keep pace with his rivals. He did so freely, all the while hoping that readers would learn from the mistakes and misfortunes of others.[30]

Greeley died in 1872, and management of the *Tribune* fell to Whitelaw Reid, its managing editor for many years. Under Reid, the *Tribune*, like other New York dailies, threw itself into the investigation of the Stewart mystery with determination and zeal. Overall, its handling of the story was more circumspect and careful than the *Herald* or the *Times*.

By the late 1870s newspaper reporting had advanced to the point where journalism could be called a profession. Decades of investigating the bizarre and the unusual, along with political and business analysis, produced a corps of seasoned reporters whose dedication to a higher standard was noticeable. Many reporters were college graduates who took pride in crafting stories around their articles.[31] Readers of the Stewart mystery were beneficiaries of this improvement. While the investigation emphasized the ghoulish and the shocking, articles were nevertheless very factual in content, insofar as the facts could be ascertained.

This is not to suggest that editors and reporters were satisfied with a bland, obituary-like statement of facts. They eagerly attacked exciting events like the Stewart grave robbery and played them for all they were worth, but they did so with an eye for satisfying the public's need to understand what was happening in its city and neighborhoods. They were thoughtful, as well as shocking, and appealed to a growing level of sophistication. The rise in the quality of reporting went hand in hand with the ascendancy of education and literacy. A newly found clarity was emerging to meet the demand for more than sophomoric sensationalism.

The reporters and their newspapers became the primary carriers of ideas during the later stages of the nineteenth century. While books and magazines continued to be very popular and authors were often given the star treatment, it was the newspapers that embraced the idea of community service, called "the essence of turning away from the image of newspapers as reflections of strong publishers." While the publisher and editor were not yet ready to subdue their aggressive personalities and work in the background, public needs and interests were often at the forefront for the first time in the history of the American newspaper.[32]

For instance, when the awful subject of grave robbing appeared in print, a long, colorful, fact-by-fact explanation of the crime was often followed by an editorial that spoke for public morality. The evils of the crime were self-evident, so the editors stressed the need for a remedy, calling for repressive laws that proscribed greater punishment as a deterrent or modernized laws that allowed the use of cadavers in medical schools.

Rector Dr. J. H. Rylance had New York newspapers in mind when he delivered a powerful sermon at St. Mark's church on the Sunday following the grave robbery. Rylance attacked depravity in general and those who desecrated the Stewart vault in particular. With passion and eloquence, he lambasted American society and its insidiously dangerous gravitation toward increased criminal behavior. Modern man, he insisted, had become profoundly immoral despite many years of material progress. He warned against a coming "tidal wave" of crime committed by debased and depraved men who have no respect for life and property. Such men, often produced by poverty and despair, threaten to destroy all that is good. It was the ancient good-versus-evil theme revived with great vigor.

Rylance had sharp criticism for men of wealth, saying, "our millionaires die; but no one disturbs their last moments by reminding them of the hard conditions amid which thousands of their fellow creatures are doomed to live, and which a little of their superfluous wealth might do something to mitigate." People who live lives of constant sorrow and overpowering poverty, "never darken our church doors."[33] It's not that the poor were irreligious. Rather their lives had been reduced to a desperate, animal-like struggle for food and shelter, denying them the time for anything spiritual or intellectual. In a sermon that sternly cast blame for crime and poverty toward men like A. T. Stewart, the reverend reminded his audience that we do, indeed, reap what we sow.

Next, Rylance singled out the city's newspapers for special criticism. Newspapers, in their haste to get a good story—he believed—added to the problem by encouraging an "imitative instinct" in impressionable folk. Books and newspapers, he said, "augmented the liability of the weak or viciously disposed," causing them to do what they would not ordinarily do.

Rylance even took a crack at Hilton, saying he had no business interfering in cemetery matters after someone had tampered with the slab on the Stewart vault prior to the break-in. Had this been reported, the awful outrage that followed might have been prevented. Given the horrible nature of the crime, Rylance had an ideal forum for lashing out against sin and error, and he made the most of it, even blaming himself.

Other parts of the country seemed to wear a sour expression, too, as if tuned into the mood of Rylance's sermon. The editor of the *Chicago Tribune* warned that dire consequences would follow should the thieves go unpunished. Society lays out rules of conduct for treating the dead, holding them and their resting places "with reverence." A cemetery, like a church, is a holy place, one that even crude men are reluctant to blaspheme. Yet some men crossed that line and committed the ultimate act of disrespect. To the *Tribune*, this was unpardonable, and the violators surrendered all right to receive respect from others.

The *Tribune* called upon Hilton, Mrs. Stewart, and the New York Police Department to use all their resources and energy toward solving the crime. New York was called the "least protected" city in America. While the *Chicago Tribune* acknowledged the skill and daring of the thieves, it asserted that their success was primarily the result of police incompetence. The police were cited for encouraging the criminal element of the city by allowing crime to get out of control. As long as the thieves were free, no cemetery and no grave were safe. As long as some men were willing to cross over into the outrageous and do the unthinkable, every man risked walking complacently into the hellish abyss of immorality.

In urban areas, the *Tribune* saw grave signs of a general moral decay that was caused by a diminished respect for decency and honor. It hinted that political radicalism was at the heart of this dangerous trend and that the "principles of Communism" were at work, threatening social order. If the authorities fail, then communities should resort to vigilantism to weed out the evil element. The prospects for further grave plundering were great, stressed the *Tribune*, and would remain so until the crime in New York was solved. The editorial was a long, tiresome lament, written for a vulnerable, hand-wringing world that was wrapped in the garb of mourning and anxiously waiting for deliverance from its fears.[34]

Things looked better on Monday morning, November 11, 1878, when the *New York Times* said Stewart's body had most likely been recovered and was being held in a safe location. Calling it a "rumor," the *Times* nevertheless thought it significant, drawing conclusions from an interview with Hilton. The day before, the judge was playing coy, smiling and hinting that he was in possession of the body.

A reporter was sent to his house on Monday and was pleasantly greeted. Their conversation went like this: "It is reported at the Central Office, Judge, that you have Mr. Stewart's body."

Hilton replied laughingly, "I deny that, but we are looking for it."

The reporter tried another approach, asking, "It is not alleged that you have the body in your actual possession, but that you have found it, know where it is, have it well covered, and are merely guarding it and watching for the robbers to come to it?"

After a moment's pause, Hilton said, in a wry, artful voice, "I have no reply to make to that. I am under injunctions of secrecy, and cannot tell you anything more with propriety. I would cheerfully, if I could. You must, therefore, pardon my refusal to say any more."[35]

With that the *New York Times* concluded the investigation was almost under wraps, for Hilton had provided a coded answer, as accurate and revealing as could be expected from a representative of a dead multimillionaire. Stewart's body was located and would be picked up in due time, so everyone could relax. Before long his remains would be resting again, in an undisclosed location or, better yet, in the new crypt in Garden City.

It was not to be, however. Despite the optimism of the *Times* and its reliance on Hilton's hints and proclamations, hard, frustrating work lay ahead.

A reporter for the *Evening Post* must have had a sense of frustration when he called at the Stewart residence on that same Monday, asking about Mrs. Stewart's well-being. He was met by a servant who sent for a Mr. Smith, probably a relative, who said only, "She is more comfortable than she has been."

"I presume she is more cheerful in view of the prospective speedy recovery of her husband's body?" asked the reporter.

"Well, yes, she is."

"I believe you have discovered the exact place where the body now is?"

"I believe they have, but really I can't say anything about it."

"Can you tell me whether the body was found in this city or not?" quizzed the reporter.

The man replied, "You really must excuse me. I can't say anything about it. In fact, I don't know."[36] That was the end of the interview. Smith all but admitted that the body had not been found, and the *Post* reporter probably left feeling as if no solution was in sight. Smith couldn't be faulted if he was confused by conflicting signals, even if the *Times* reporter was not.

An old detective was interviewed by the *New York Weekly Tribune* and offered his outlook. He believed the body was miles away from the city, safely hidden. The robbers had been successful up to this point and would simply bide their time. Unless one of them broke ranks and ran for the police, perhaps hoping for the reward and/or immunity, their conspiracy would remain intact. After the police had exhausted all avenues of investigation and Hilton and Mrs. Stewart despaired of finding the body, the robbers would make their move. The veteran police officer, whose name was not included in the article, was certain the police would be contacted through a third party who would demand money and give instructions for the exchange and delivery of the body.

CHAPTER 6

In Search of the Ghouls

> Several persons of hitherto unquestioned respectability, who would never be suspected of complicity in such a crime, are among the most guilty participants in the hellish plot.
>
> *New York Times*, November 15, 1878

During the week following the theft of Stewart's body, the New York City Police Department devoted itself to finding the "participants in the hellish plot." Detectives worked day and night, traveling about the city and its surrounding area, checking leads, knocking on doors, and questioning people, throwing themselves into the awful mystery with an exceptional, although at times clumsy and ineffective, dedication. Everything else, it seems, was put on the back burner as searchers—both official and unofficial—grasped wildly at even the most ridiculous leads. By offering a reward, Hilton launched a great treasure hunt, and a legion of inspired treasure seekers took the bait, all believing that a handsome payment was in the offing.

A cagey reporter from the *Baltimore Gazette* said that Stewart—who employed thousands while he lived—was still providing work for the multitudes. The reporter pointed out that although he was dead, Stewart was keeping "thousands of honest, hard-working persons" very busy searching for his remains.[1]

The police saw the situation as anything but mirthful. From the outset they treated the case as if it were the kidnapping of a live person. The investigation took on the kind of urgency one would expect from the abduction of a celebrity. Under the crack of Hilton's whip and the demands of an anxious public, the police scurried about the city as if they had to locate a bound and gagged victim before his kidnappers killed him. It was as if a living A. T. Stewart was waiting for rescue and time was running out. Although they constantly referred to Stewart's "remains" or "body," at no time did the police act as if they were hunting for a mere bag of bones. Never in the history of New York City had anyone seen a greater police effort devoted to the solving of a single crime.

Reporters were equally busy, tracking down stories and interviewing people, all hoping for a "sensation" to write about and some share of the glory. Anyone driving a wagon with a rectangular box in it was fair game. "Suspicious wagons driven by mysterious men for unknown purposes" on the night of the crime were reported by people all over New York, including undertaker's wagons that roamed the streets, day and night, carrying the dead. Hardware men stepped forth with stories about shovels and lanterns they sold in recent weeks.[2] Vigilant noses sniffed out suspicious places, hoping to detect the scent of death and decay.

The police staked out all the ferries, and the woods and hiding places on Staten Island were thoroughly searched. "Mysterious" men and women who went in and out of police headquarters on Mulberry Street were pursued with wonderment.

The press would swoop down on a cemetery at the slightest hint of suspicious activity. A reporter from the *Times* was stationed at St. Mark's churchyard, where the morbidly curious gathered every day to stare vacantly at the desecrated ground. The city's appetite for the sensational and the macabre was peaking, and "glory be" to the reporter who locked in on the right clues and delivered the story that cracked the case.

Jacob A. Riis, a young reporter for the *New York Tribune*, credited the "Stewart ghouls" for giving him the chance to advance his career as a journalist. Riis was a politically charged immigrant, a reformer who understood and sympathized with the ghetto dwellers. He was active in popular and unpopular causes, such as preventing water pollution and alleviating the suffering of the poor crowded in the tenements. He was a good writer, and his columns about crime were crafted into small, human-interest stories. He said, "the true journalist was an investigator who was never satisfied until he found the cause of the disaster."[3]

The Stewart mystery put his theory to the test. In later years, when Riis was a national figure, he called the Stewart case one of the great sensations of his time. He summoned all his energy and talent and plunged into the dark mystery with enthusiasm. Riis wrote in his book, *The Making of an American*, "Of all the mysteries that ever vexed a reporter's soul, that (the Stewart case) was the most agonizing."[4]

Other journalists shared his opinion, as did people who bought and read newspapers. A front-page article in the *New York Evening Express* captured the November mood of the city: "That the body of the merchant-millionaire should have been carried away from a teeming centre in this populous city set every soul in it agog."[5] The same article urged Hilton and the police to come up with answers and be quick about it. Citing the rash of grave robberies in 1870s, the *Evening Express* called the Stewart case an example of "cryptomania" and suggested that the culprits came from the "West," meaning Ohio and Illinois, looking for a new field of labor.[6]

The autumn of 1878 was a busy season for grave robbers in Ohio. Just as the peaceful, golden hues of fall were settling in on the trees, disruptive headlines shouted: "Body-Snatching in Ohio." Another chapter of horrors had begun.

An article in the *New York Times* on September 18, 1878, told the story of the theft of the body of a prominent Cleveland businessman, Edwin French. He took sick with typhoid fever at the home of his brother-in-law in the village of Willoughby, some twenty miles to the east of Cleveland. He died and was buried in the Willoughby cemetery after a splendid funeral attended by family and friends, many of whom came from Cleveland.

His son, Julius E. French, hired a young man to guard the grave because he believed that someone might attempt to take the body. Young French was knowledgeable and cautious. Nevertheless on the first night of what was expected to be his father's eternal sleep, grave robbers (believed to be two in number) managed to sneak into the cemetery, avoid the guard, open the grave, drag the body out by the neck, and cart it away in a buggy. This happened at about 1 a.m. Despite his vigilance, the guard found an old coat left by the fast-working robbers beside the empty grave, then discovered the body was gone.

When news of this latest Ohio resurrection was circulated, the townspeople were up in arms. In an angry group, they descended upon the hardware store, buying knives and guns for the hunt. "Squads of men started in every direction from the village" as a mob mentality took control of Willoughby's citizens. Wagon tracks from the cemetery pointed toward Cleveland, and a band of vigilantes hurried in that direction.

In Cleveland, Julius French received a dispatch stating, "Your father's body has been stolen; put Police on the watch for it immediately." French alerted the police, and detectives were hastily dispatched to stake out the Cleveland medical colleges. The police came upon a buggy at a stable on Rockwell Street that attracted their attention, as it was coated with fresh mud. It was examined and "gray hairs were found on the footboard." The proprietor of the stable was questioned, and he identified two young men who rented the rig, returning it at 3 a.m., along with an exhausted horse.

Soon two men were in custody. One of them was a "professional body-snatcher" named Eugene Joiner who, with a little encouragement, made a full confession to the crime. He implicated another young man, Dr. Erwin C. Carlisle, who lived in the suburbs of Cleveland. Carlisle caved in easily, too, and told the police the body could be found at the Homeopathic Hospital College. The police were reluctant to believe a grave robber—even a doctor—and search warrants were obtained for all the local medical colleges.

Two detectives hurried to the Homeopathic Hospital College on Prospect Street. They went to the dissection room, searched it, and when they were about to leave, noticed the sawdust on the floor beside the dissecting table looked disturbed. Prying up the boards, they found the body of the late Edwin French "in a box ready to be lowered into the pickling vaults." It had been injected with arsenic. Ironically, French had been a "friend of the Homeopathic Hospital" and donated $100 toward the erection of a new building, only to be treated so rudely in death.

Arrest warrants were sworn out against several doctors, college faculty, and other personnel. The body was reburied amid speculation that "lively litigation" would be brought against all those implicated in the splashy event. The French article was brought to a close with a warning: the college would likely be subjected to destructive mob violence as the anger of the people had yet to subside.[7]

Just a few days later, another Ohio grave robbery made news, and once again, the Homeopathic Hospital College was the center of attention.

The bodies of two old ladies were discovered there. "The bodies had been crushed into the smallest possible compass, and packed away in barrels like so much pork for winter use." Gold from their teeth had been removed.

One of the corpses was identified as that of Mrs. Angeline Higby of Garretsville, Ohio. Julius French, who was apparently on hand with the grisly discovery was made, telegraphed Higby's family with the horrific news. A son-in-law immediately summoned help and drove to the cemetery where the burial had recently taken place. The grave was opened after hard digging, revealing an empty coffin. Arrests were made, and the bodies, which bore the evidence of a terrible violation, were reburied.

If that were not bad enough, a third body was found at the college, that of a nine-year-old boy "who had been remarkable for his proficiency in music." The college authorities begged to be allowed to rebury the body of the budding musician themselves, and strangely, the request was granted.[8]

When grave robbers struck, they often had no idea who it was they were bringing back from the dead. It was as if death was the ultimate leveler: a stiff was a stiff. They were in the market for bodies, old or young, rich or poor; they were in it for the money and had little or no respect for the reputations and personalities connected to their plunder. For those who gathered the news, however, the strange mix of talents, ages, and personalities that emerged from this short series of Ohio resurrections seemed to raise the stories to a level of titillation that went beyond the ordinarily macabre. Old ladies with gold in their teeth, a child prodigy, and a prominent businessman—all were looked upon as helpless victims of body snatchers. In life they had no connection, no ties, and likely left little or no record of their lives. Yet as the result of some mean, posthumous intervention peculiar to their time, they were brought up and out together, with bits of their lives laid on slabs of newsprint for all to see.

Did Henry Hilton read about these and other sad affairs? Was he feeling overwhelmed by the ghoulish business? He had about forty of his own private detectives in the field searching for Stewart's body, with the police working on the case as well. Glum or jolly, he was seen almost daily going in and out of police headquarters, huddling with officials and plotting strategy. When he wasn't with the police, reporters usually found Hilton in his office at the corner of Broadway and Chambers. His son-in-law,

Assistant District Attorney Horace Russell, was an integral part of the team.

Hilton's role had assumed large proportions; and he was sought out by the press as much as any police captain or inspector. At night Hilton conferred with officials in his home, the meetings extending into the early morning hours. More likely than not, when he emerged a reporter or two were there to ask questions. Henry Hilton was running things again, a role he relished.

The press, including the *New York Times*, which was usually sympathetic to Hilton, was kept at bay as much as was possible, causing reporters to speculate and draw conclusions from hints, innuendos, and body language. Articles were often written based on what was not said rather than what was said. It was frequently assumed that those in a position to talk authoritatively were holding something back, leaving reporters to interpret assorted winks and nods. As a result the press was often frustrated and angry.

The police, on the other hand, were often upset and impatient with the press, especially those reporters who beat on their doors in the middle of the night. Superintendent George W. Walling, for one, complained about the persistence of the press, believing the investigation would be better off with more secrecy. While he was usually courteous, Walling objected to journalists who wrote elaborate stories without foundation, and he criticized those in his department who leaked information to the overeager reporters.

"Wash" Walling joined the New York Police Department at age twenty-four in 1847. He was a gutsy, well-built young man from colonial New Jersey stock. He learned the ropes of police politics quickly and wasted no time in becoming one of the city's top cops, having played a role in the Dead Rabbits Gang riot of 1857 and faced the bricks and bottles of the mobs during the terrible Civil War draft riots of 1863. In one instance, Walling single-handedly turned back a portion of a mob set on looting a gun shop, killing one man and scaring the rest away.[9] Still, for all his heroics, Walling, like other courageous cops, was often subjected to severe criticism by the public and press.

While some members of the press complimented the efforts of the police, others were particularly scathing and unmerciful in their attacks. The *Evening Telegram*, another New York daily, snidely said the police were good at finding crimes but not criminals and were well known for "clubbing innocent men and women almost to death."[10] The *Evening Telegram* poured on the sarcasm as each day passed without a solution to the Stewart crime.

The *Herald* was also quick to take the police to task for the perceived slowness of their efforts. Everyone wanted answers and none were in the near future—nothing but crumbs of information and "glittering generalities."[11] The guessing game led reporters to believe that the body had most likely been found and that it was concealed in some safe place until it could be secretly deposited in the crypt at Garden City.

Thus, it became the reporters' goal to confirm their suspicions—or to refute them. To do so reporters dogged anyone who might have anything to do with the mystery. One of Hilton's agents, said to be a shrewd man, left town quietly, attracting the attention of the *Times*, which thought it was odd for him to be absent from New York at that particular time of the year. Such an occurrence had to be significant. Was he going somewhere to retrieve the body? Was there a deal in the works with the thieves? Was an arrest imminent?

While everyone of importance (and some of no importance) was under surveillance, it was Hilton himself who became the primary focus of the press. However, he was not always a fount of information, despite his reputation for bluntness and candor. Reporters were sent to his house only to be politely turned away. When he did speak he chose his words carefully, revealing only what he wanted to be made public. He spoke like a confident man, revealing facts when he so desired or artfully deflecting questions when it suited him.

Throughout that November, Hilton behaved like a man in charge—a man who liked being in the spotlight. While much was done in secret, it appears as if he was consulted and briefed on every aspect of the case. The police depended on him for decisions, and for all practical purposes, Henry Hilton, the former judge, was in charge of the investigation. Within a few days following the crime, some in the press were certain that if and when the body turned up, Henry Hilton, not the police, would be the first to know.

Superintendent Walling was in close contact with Hilton during the early stages of the investigation. Since he was a well-respected veteran of the police force, Walling was sought by the *Herald* for an interview. It is apparent from what transpired that both the reporter and the superintendent were frustrated with the lack of progress. When asked if the thieves had been located, Walling angrily replied, "That is another absurd story." He then suggested that anyone who made such a statement should be "kicked over the East River and never allowed to come back." He did, however, express confidence that the body would be recovered.

As for the thieves, Walling said, "That is another matter." Raising his voice, he said, "Suppose you had the thieves right before you—how could you prove that they went into that graveyard and took the body? Nobody saw them and no jury would convict them without some evidence of their guilt."[12] This was a crime like no other in the history of New York—a city whose future greatness seemed to depend on upstaging everything in its past.

Walling's outburst mirrored the frustration of the entire police department. They were under great pressure and were worried, knowing the public would watch this investigation as none other in the past. Because of the burden of public scrutiny, they resorted to desperate measures, such as recruiting thieves to join the spirited pursuit. For this they were mocked by the *Herald*, which said that "every thief in the city who is under the thumb of the detective force has been pressed into service."[13] The police were apparently willing to accept mockery, if in doing so they enhanced their chances at putting the frustrating mystery behind them.

It was, however, futile. The police and other governing authorities were up against an invisible force whose power exceeded their collective abilities. New York was unstable and unmanageable because of its rapid growth, its great ethnic diversity, an influx of new immigrants, and its dense population—much of it poor. The pace of rising instability was far faster than the ability of those in charge to keep up and manage, no matter how hard they worked.

Crime was out of control in New York, and it wasn't fair to blame law enforcement, but that didn't matter to some in the media. The *Evening Telegram*, for example, poured on the derision, calling the police "dogberries." These "dicks" were a collection of poorly educated incompetents who had no business posing as America's "finest police force." According to the *Telegram*, it was no wonder the thieves were able to pull off the daring crime. They understood the competence level of New York law enforcement and had little to fear from it.[14]

Meanwhile, communications from various sources made their way to Hilton and the police. Each one offered some form of help, usually in exchange for cash. By November 11, four days after the break-in, Captain

McCullagh had received 150 clues from a variety of sources.[15] Hungry and angry, New Yorkers were aroused, as many weary arms and urgent ideas thrust themselves up and out from the chaotic sea of poverty, hoping for rescue or at least the chance to be heard. The world was witnessing a great struggle for the reward, with thousands of people grasping for a tiny, belated share of a millionaire's estate. If this demonstrated anything at all, it was the degree of desperation that hovered over New York during a time of awful economic uncertainty.

A titillating lead surfaced in Tuckahoe, Westchester County, New York, where stone for the Stewart mansion was quarried. Construction of Stewart's imposing Fifth Avenue house started before the Civil War. After the war commenced the cost of materials and labor soared, causing the contractors, including the builder, Alexander Maxwell of Harlem, to go broke. The author of this theory said Stewart had been unfair to the building contractor by refusing to release him from the contract. All this caused the contractor to despair and die before the house was finished. This perceived unfairness gave the contractor's family cause to plot and carry out the theft of Stewart's body. This was never more than a theory,

The Stewart mansion at the northwest corner of 34th Street and 5th Avenue. Image courtesy of Garden City Archives.

Interior of the Stewart mansion. Image courtesy of Garden City Archives.

and the contractor's family was never under official scrutiny. Still, the story of Stewart's unfairness circulated among New Yorkers for many years prior to the crime, only to resurface when his body was stolen.[16]

The story, like many others about Stewart, contained elements of truth and folklore. Stewart did, in fact, have a dispute with his contractors that led to a lawsuit and a judgment. With regard to Maxwell, one version of the event holds that Stewart did not enforce the judgment and thereby spared the building contractor from financial ruin. Another more fanciful version has an angry Maxwell storming into Stewart's office, laying on verbal abuse until he was ordered out. The poor fellow, it was said, was so worked up that he died from a stroke before he could get outside.

Believers of this story claimed that the death of the building contractor, along with the accidental death of a worker, put a hex on Stewart's new house. Because of this and Stewart's notorious tendency toward superstition, he delayed moving into the mansion until 1872, although it was ready for occupancy by 1870. Of course, there were those who recalled that not long after moving into the house, Stewart took ill, never fully recovered, and later died in his marble mausoleum.[17]

While the police were not unduly concerned with this or similar explanations, they were looking for a former Stewart employee who had been discharged by Stewart sixteen years earlier for embezzlement. He had been apprehended and charged with theft. He begged Stewart for forgiveness and promised to, and did, repay some $14,000. Forgiveness was not forthcoming, however, and he was prosecuted to the fullest. Feeling betrayed by his former boss, the convicted embezzler swore vengeance and, after his release from prison, sank deeper into criminal activity. The police thought he might have, at long last, struck back at Stewart. Finding him became a priority.

Out of the morass of nonsense, there came an occasional practical suggestion. Someone surmised that the thieves had buried the body, giving it an assumed name. To accomplish this, the thieves would need the complicity of an unscrupulous doctor to sign a fake death certificate, along with a crooked undertaker to handle the burial arrangements. It was a logical theory, as it would have been a good way to hide Stewart's remains pending ransom demands. However, records of recent suspicious burials were checked without results.[18]

The police had their hands full with site inspections, the search for suspects, and sifting through reports. Any dead body in transit was suspected of being that of A. T. Stewart and had to be checked out. The police were so thoroughly saturated with letters and notes regarding the whereabouts of Stewart's body that had the real thieves wanted to communicate their intentions and demands, their correspondence would likely be lost in a sea of paper. The ability to identify a genuine lead became a problem.

The police were, however, able to determine that the thieves could have exited the cemetery by climbing over the iron gate at the Eleventh Street entrance. While this didn't eliminate the "boardinghouse corner" theory, it made the mystery a bit more complex, and the police were still at a loss to explain where the thieves went after leaving the churchyard. They felt certain, however, that the wagon used to carry Stewart's body away was of the "pattern used by vendors of condensed milk," and was drawn by a roan horse.[19] This was another tantalizing but unsupported conclusion.

A Company was heard from again. This esoteric group, which displayed a sophistication lacking in other entreaties, published another letter in the *Herald*, once again urging Mrs. Stewart to donate $500,000 to some "needed public charity." While the tone of the message lacked emotionalism, the people behind it plainly called for immediate action, saying they were "unable to conceal the body longer than Wednesday night." By noon Wednesday they must have proof of the donation or they would have no choice but to destroy the body "in order to avoid detection."[20] They were ignored while the police focused on less complicated matters. Officials were not prepared to believe that a radical group would use grave robbery to make a political statement.

Through the practical assistance of Sexton Hamill at St. Mark's, the police discovered how the thieves could have located the cover of the underground vault. Hamill pointed out that all the vaults were situated in rows and all were beneath two and one-half to three feet of dirt. Ringing the vault cover was a raised border of granite. To locate the stone, the thieves used a "resurrectionist's sounding rod," which they apparently did not have on their first visit. Once the raised border was "sounded," they needed only to dig down, take out the dirt within the raised border, remove the slab, and enter the tomb.[21]

Moving the name tablet did not deceive them either, since they had been there before and knew the location of the vault in relation to the others on either side. They could judge the location of Stewart's vault by the other grave markers, even if its exterior marker was moved. Moving the marker would only fool those who had never been to the cemetery before. While the marker could be moved, "they knew we could not have carried the vault off," said Hamill, with a sweeping sense of vindication.[22] It was simple logic, he declared. It proved timely as well, for it established his innocence, and the police and Hilton bothered Hamill no more.

With Hamill and Assistant Sexton Parker in the clear, the police had no suspects—at least none they were talking about. Their focus was now on the silver nameplate and the swatch of velvet that had been cut from the casket lining. It was believed that in the event they or Hilton's people were unsuccessful, the thieves would eventually send some communication along the lines of "bring money and a wagon," making it known they had verifiable evidence to prove the identity of Stewart's body.[23]

On November 13, the *Times* again expressed confidence that Stewart's body would be recovered soon and the mystery laid to rest. Hilton and the police were enthusiastic and did nothing to hide their good feelings. Hilton expressed full confidence in the police, saying, "Both the police and the private detectives are following up every point that seems worthy of investigation." By now his daily pronouncements were regular fare in the press.

Quite expectedly, the usual oddities surfaced in the newspapers as well. A sleazy private detective named Bernard Koenig was prancing around the precinct, demanding to be heard. Koenig's office consisted of a desk in the corner of a tailor's shop, where he supplemented his detective's income by notarizing documents. His credentials consisted of a badge borrowed from a sanitation inspector that allowed him to enter private homes. He was just one of a legion of so-called private detectives operating in New York. Overwhelmingly incompetent and dishonest, these desperate hustlers worked the streets in predator-like fashion, following, lurking, and spying while earning a few bucks in blackmail.

Koenig claimed he was in the employ of Hilton, but was not in it for the money. Principle, not cash, motivated him. He broke through the surrounding din by declaring that he knew where Stewart's body was hidden. He used a reporter for the *Times* to chastise the police, thus, building himself up at their expense. Koenig insisted he was not after newspaper publicity and was willing to divulge the location of the body. However, if Hilton failed to pay, he would stop his investigation and the entire city would be slighted.[24]

Keonig was typical of the many hungry charlatans who hoped to profit from the mystery. Hilton had cast his bread upon the waters, and a desperate swarm went after the tempting morsels. Among this class were self-styled spiritualists, clairvoyants, and assorted dreamers, all who had "critical information" (for sale, of course) and none of whom were taken seriously. These people were especially troublesome to Hilton, a hardheaded businessman who was loath to admit the existence of such a widespread belief in the supernatural that drifted beyond the borders of conventional religion.

Hilton was, in turn, both amused and angered at the tenor of the information that surfaced. He must have been especially galled at the person who wrote to the *New York Herald* blaming Stewart himself for the outrage. This writer claimed righteous vengeance had been visited on Stewart, for in the early 1860s he "desecrated the bones of those who were buried in the old Amity Street Baptist Church-yard."

Hilton lashed back, calling the letter a vicious, slanderous falsehood, for Stewart bought the land long after it ceased to be used as a church and a cemetery, well after the bones were removed. To be sure a few stray bones were discovered when workers excavated a foundation, but these were "gathered faithfully" at Stewart's instructions and "sent to the Morgue."[25]

Others remembered it differently. One man who lived in the area long enough to "know the history of nearly every man, woman and child in the district," placed blame squarely on Stewart. George P. Fox, a "venerable gentleman," recalled with clarity the time that Stewart bought the old church property. People who had relatives buried there were shocked and indignant when they learned that Stewart was set on excavating the sacred dirt to build a stable for his horses. A fence was built around the site, but it didn't stop people from seeing carts of bones and skulls. Word spread, a crowd gathered, and a riot was imminent. Then the police dispersed the angry crowd, the work went on, and a rich man had his horse barn. For those who had family buried in the churchyard, this was blatant desecration, and they never forgave Stewart.[26]

A beleaguered Henry Hilton wanted to focus attention away from old controversies and toward the discovery of Stewart's corpse. To that end he spoke to a reporter for the *New York Sun*, saying he was sparing no expense in the monumental search for the truth and a decent end to this terrible indecency. Choosing his words carefully, he said, "I do not wish to conceal from the public the fact that I have the best detective talent in the country covering every possible point."

Despite the shabby reputation of the police among the public and press, Hilton expressed every confidence in them, explaining that his decision to use a large number of private detectives was not a negative reflection on the New York City Police Department. In fact, he had the approval and full cooperation of the police to engage private detectives. His brief interview gave notice that his entire force of hired detectives and the police would be united in a mighty team, dedicated toward a single goal.[27]

Still there were the unstoppable, irritating diversions. A Company also brought up the desecration of the old Amity Street Church burial ground in its third and final installment to the *Herald*, appearing on November 13, 1878. Reminding everyone that the Wednesday deadline had come and gone, the writer said that at 1 p.m. that day, the body had been "divided into small particles," and was "wrapped separately in comparatively small bundles, handsomely put up." The writer went on to claim that these were sent to "different towns in different countries" where they would never been found.

A man from Savannah, Georgia, claimed he received one of the small bundles. He sent a letter to the *Herald* after receiving a "few bones of the late A. T. Stewart," along with a letter signed by A Company. He said he was asked to keep silent about his identity until A Company furnished him with "additional information that I should make known publicly at that time." He promised the *Herald* that he would keep silent, but if he did not receive the promised information, he would forward the bones. The man signed his name "Resurrection." The *Herald* called him "A Georgia Joker."[28]

A Company's motive, one letter writer suggested, was far from funny. They wanted to avenge the desecration of the Amity Street churchyard, "the sacred burying ground" that was forced to "give way to the stables of A. T. Stewart." He (or she) went on to explain that the body was stolen in October by a team of nine men who carted it off to an apartment where it was deodorized and hidden. Since Mrs. Stewart had not responded to the demand for the charitable contribution, the body was destroyed. The writer closed by exonerating Hamill, implicating "some influential, well-to-do citizens," and saying all further searching would be futile.[29]

Stories such as these were undoubtedly worrisome to Mrs. Stewart, but she was seldom mentioned in the press. In a violent era where sensationalism and vicious personal attacks were commonplace and few, if any, were insulated from exposure, everyone seemed to respect her privacy. She was left alone. Hilton, of course, saw to it that she was shielded and would have caused quite a stir if someone penetrated her zone of safety.

However, Mrs. Stewart most likely followed the investigation closely, praying for the return of her husband's body. If she read the front page of the *New York Times* on Friday, November 15, 1878, her sagging spirits must have taken flight, for the *Times* announced to the great surprise of all: "A. T. Stewart's Body Found."

It was the most strident and forceful headline printed during the early stages of the investigation. In positive terms the *Times* explained that the guilty parties were all known and the evidence against them was irrefutable. While no arrests had been made, all parties were beyond escape and would receive punishment. Hilton said so, declared the sensational headline. Other New York newspapers fell in line, including the *Evening News*. That newspaper reported the body was most certainly found at or near Shamony, Burlington County, New Jersey, about forty miles southeast of Camden.[30]

The *Evening News* did not provide details, but the *Times* did. Citing the "highest authorities," the *Times* said the body had been found and each of the guilty parties were (almost) in the clutches of the law. Furthermore, and perhaps as shocking as the crime itself, the names and positions of the criminals "will raise the hair on the heads of the people of New York." Several were important men, and one of them was a "prominent attorney." Except for the "principal," all were in New York and under strict surveillance, and when the order was given, the police would haul them in.

First the police had to get Hilton's consent to arrest the conspirators. Two days before, the police had wanted to arrest the "principal" and sent a telegram to Hilton asking for his permission. Hilton replied in the negative. He wasn't quite ready. It was, as he said, necessary that a "full and severe example" be made so that a similarly heinous crime would not be committed later. Finding the body was no more important to Hilton than exacting punishment on the thieves, which he would do for the good of society.

Clearly wishing the awful mess would disappear, the *Times* rejoiced. "The probabilities are that a complete swoop will be made to-day, and the entire gang lodged in jail at the same time."[31] Reporting on the ghastly crime was exciting, but it had become a tiresome job, and the staff of the *Times* seemed to long for mundane stuff like cutthroat business practices, corrupt politics, society parties, and the unpretentious obituaries of plain people.

The *Times* was founded by Henry Raymond in 1851, making it the fourth penny paper to appear, following the *Sun*, *Herald*, and *Tribune*. Raymond, who learned the newspaper business from Horace Greeley, wanted to publish a newspaper that steered a middle course between Greeley's *Tribune* and James Gordon Bennett's *Herald*, the twin pillars of New York journalism. Raymond's penny paper would avoid the excessive sensationalism of the *Herald* and the uneven political crusading of the *Tribune*, focusing on the impartial reporting of news. The public liked this concept, and the *Times* was a success.

Raymond died in 1869, and by the 1870s his newspaper had lost much of its pragmatic attitude, along with its dispassionate editorials and articles.[32] It entered a long period of decline. The changed *Times* eagerly lapped up even the most ridiculous stories concerning the Stewart investigation as if it was trying to "out-Herald" the *Herald*.

On November 15, 1878, a *Times* reporter located Hilton and asked for his opinion of the latest developments. The reporter found him especially amiable but shifty and reticent nonetheless. When asked to confirm that the body had been found and arrests were imminent, Hilton hesitated and said, "I will not confirm it."

"Will you deny it?" persisted the reporter.

"I will not," was Hilton's firm and immediate reply.

The reporter attempted to probe deeper by asking whether the search was nearly at an end. The smiling Hilton simply said, "Have patience, and you will get a story to fill three or four columns. I am very hopeful. We are much further advanced than yesterday. I will say that."

Undoubtedly, many people who read the interview were disappointed and probably quite skeptical. Hilton cast no hints as to the identification of the "prominent" people involved in the crime. The story conveyed an unmistakable ambiguity, and Hilton's responses contradicted the information previously dispensed to the *Times* by the "highest [but unnamed] authorities."[33]

When interviewed by the *Herald*, Hilton put on another face, expressing greatly enlarged fears about the ghouls who stole Stewart's body. He was anxious to cooperate with the press, he said, as this crime transcended New York and was the "great question" that "affects society at large." The reporter didn't ask Hilton to explain, choosing instead to eagerly listen while Hilton spoke freely.

"If they are to succeed in stealing the dead there is no telling how soon they may turn their attention to carrying off the living. Why, I understand it has been proposed to steal me—to carry me off, in hope of getting a large reward. Just think of it!" he said with more than his usual bombast.[34] In the two interviews Hilton refused to reveal any information regarding those whom he suspected of complicity in the great crime.

Beyond cliffhanger headlines, interviews, finger pointing, adamant denials, and Hilton's views, the newspapers offered something that resembled substance. News leaked out that a boardinghouse at 44 Stuyvesant Street was under surveillance, where three suspicious men had been staying at the time of the break-in. This boardinghouse was operated by a German named Frederick Wickman. It was directly across the street from St. Mark's churchyard and close to Mrs. Newton's now famous boardinghouse.

The three suspicious characters stayed up late at night at the Wickman house. Other residents thought the three men were often in consultation in their upstairs room that faced the churchyard.[35] Strange, loud, pounding noises came from the apartment, and neighbors were concerned, but nothing came of it.

Then early in the morning following the infamous crime, witnesses saw the men loading several trunks into a hack (a horse-drawn taxi). There is some confusion in the newspaper record as to whether the hack was parked in front of the Newton house or the Wickman house. Witnesses said that a woman, presumably a landlady, angrily interrupted their work and demanded they pay up back rent. The men seemed a bit disconcerted over her presence. One of them gave her a $10 bank note and said, "Never mind the change, keep it all."[36] The men drove away with the trunks and disappeared. The police believed the body of A. T. Stewart was in one of the trunks.

CHAPTER 7

Hackman Kelly

> A hackman named Kelly ... has not been seen by his employer since Thursday (the day of the crime) and it is suspected that he might have some connection with the grave robbers.
>
> *New York Post*, November 15, 1878

The New York police said they had located and questioned the man who drove the getaway hack, but refused to name him. Members of the press, however, discovered that a hack man named Michael Kelly (also Kelley) was most likely the man referred to. It was said that right after the theft, Kelly, a man of modest means, was "flush with money" and talked about leaving town. Suddenly "Hackman" Kelly, known in his line of work as the "Night Owl,"[1] became the focus of newspaper reporters and the police. Could he be the man who drove the getaway vehicle on the night of the terrible crime?

The *Herald*, the *Times*, the *Sun*, and the *Evening Telegram* all eagerly expanded on the hack man story. While their stories are in conflict over minor details, they share some essential points that can be used to describe Kelly and his tenuous role in the great Stewart mystery.

Kelly was said to be a simple man of simple tastes, "slow going" with "methodical habits." He was a clean-shaven man; twenty-five to twenty-seven years old; five feet, eight inches tall; and well built with sloping shoulders, blue eyes, and thin lips. He walked around with his pants tucked into his boots. He also kept to his work and was apparently on good terms with his fellow hack men. When he wasn't driving, he spent his time in saloons or at the stable that also served as his residence. Like other poor men with limited potential and an angry outlook, he had his big dreams.

Occasionally he went on a "spree," and when he was "in his cups," he was often heard to say he wanted to "take a swag," a slang expression that meant hauling a burglar and his plunder. While he was a rough dresser, it was said that he liked to wear a soft, black hat—a feature that fit nicely with his new role as a villain. Michael Kelly had a brother, Edward, who also drove hacks.

It seems that Michael Kelly had a reputation for hanging out with unsavory, "sporting" characters, and while his employer, John Graham, trusted and vouched for him, things changed after Stewart's tomb was defiled. "Night Owl" Kelly, also known on the streets as "Bull," drove an "unusually capacious" hack for Graham's stable, which was located at 25 1/2 Sheriff Street in the city. When he was not conveying a fare, he parked his horse and carriage in front of St. Paul's church at Broadway and Vesey or at the Astor House.

On the evening of November 6, the night before the Stewart incident, Kelly was overheard to say that he wished he could pick up a drunk who could easily be robbed. At about midnight, he picked up some passengers near Chatham Square, and when next seen, Kelly was moving rapidly up Broadway with three or four passengers. Later, he reported back to Graham's stable between three or four in the morning and turned in only $2 or $3 in fares. However, he supposedly told a stable hand that he landed a "big stake" and proudly displayed a wad of bills.

The next day, after Stewart's empty coffin was discovered, Kelly was scheduled to drive for a funeral procession that would occupy most of the day. Later at the stable, a stranger came to visit—a man the *Times* called a boy and the *Herald* called Bill. The stranger had a message for Kelly, and after reading it, Kelly left in great haste. He returned late that afternoon and gave his employer $5 in fares, explaining that he had completed funeral duty and the corpse arrived late.

That night Kelly was said to be asleep at the stable when he was awakened by a stranger, presumably the same man who appeared earlier. Graham recalled that the stranger tried to shield his eyes as if he did not want to be identified. After a brief discussion, Kelly excitedly asked his boss for fifty cents, saying only that he had to visit his sister, who was very ill. He left with the stranger and later sent a message back to Graham saying that he would be gone for a few days. He was last seen at Chatham Square, with $300 to $600 dollars, spending freely among his fellow hack men, making it known that he was bound for some place far from New York.

"Night Owl" Kelly disappeared as if consumed by the darkness, and those who drank with him had conflicting ideas as to his whereabouts. Some said he went to New Orleans, others mentioned San Francisco or the Black Hills of Dakota Territory, and still others, the majority, said Washington DC. The *Herald* preferred the latter destination and once again tried to tie George A. Christian to the crime. However, Graham was unable to confirm that the stranger, known only as Bill, was the same man who purchased the lantern and attempted to buy the body preserver from Middleton. He also doubted that his missing employee was in cahoots with the grave robbers.[2]

Still the press and police had Kelly under suspicion. His spending spree and disappearance, along with his reputation for hanging out with shady characters, worked against him. It was believed that Kelly's coach was used in the crime, as it would be necessary, the morning after to carry the body away in a closed conveyance. The police seized Kelly's coach for examination while the missing hack man remained a suspect at large.[3] It was discovered that the carriage had been overhauled and repaired within a few days of the robbery, although someone detected a small, dark spot on the door handle that gave off a foul stench,[4] strengthening the belief that "Hackman" Kelly was the driver of the getaway vehicle.

Kelly's former employer, John Graham, was located by a reporter for the *Tribune*, but could offer no explanation as to the hack man's whereabouts. Graham had changed his tune somewhat, however, and said he believed Kelly was involved in the Stewart affair from the outset, but was told to keep his mouth shut around reporters.[5] Graham said he had important information concerning Kelly's alleged involvement, but refused to provide any details. The authorities thought Kelly went to Canada and were searching for him there.

Reports of suspicious activity kept coming in, and once again the Wickman boardinghouse at 44 Stuyvesant Street was in the news. Former senator Thomas J. Creamer lived at 46 Stuyvesant Street. Living with Creamer at the time was an "old lady" of the "highest respectability" who had something to contribute. She recalled that early in the morning following the theft, while Creamer was away, two young men emerged from 44 Stuyvesant Street carrying a black leather trunk that they loaded carefully into a carriage before driving away.

This report caused the police to surmise that sometime after Stewart's body was removed from the churchyard, it was placed in a black leather trunk by a small group of men who boarded at the Stuyvesant Street location. It was carried away from the graveyard in an open wagon and later, early the next morning, transferred to a closed coach driven by Michael Kelly, and transported to a hiding place, possibly in New Jersey.

Upon investigation, however, the police were left with a weakened theory. They inspected the room rented by the suspicious strangers, and while it reeked of a strange odor, it was not the stench of a dead body. They now thought the young fellows who removed a trunk from the apartment were indeed involved in some illegal transaction but had nothing to do with Stewart's missing body.[6] There were, however, many other avenues to explore, including the whereabouts of "Hackman" Kelly, who was still under some suspicion. He was either a party to the conspiracy or an accessory who could furnish valuable information.

Strange people continued to show up at police headquarters. Among them a "lunatic" presented himself carrying a "citrate of magnesia bottle filled with some milky fluid smelling slightly of carbolic acid." When shaken, tiny particles like snowflakes floated in the liquid and slowly settled to the bottom. The man, who called himself H. Zelinski, told the police that the bottle contained the powdered remains of A. T. Stewart. Captain Kealy, chief of detectives, listened patiently and thanked the man for his concern. Apparently satisfied, Zelinski left without asking for a reward. He also left the bottle at the station, another souvenir.

Others who inquired in person or by letter were not shy in demanding money. Hilton conceded that he had received thousands of letters since the revelation of the crime. While a few appeared to be good-faith attempts to help, most were regarded as mere curiosities. The majority of the helpful correspondents were prepared to produce the body in exchange for sums ranging from a low of $5,000 to a high of $1 million.

One eager contributor informed Hilton that the Stewart remains were "beyond the possibility of discovery, and they are and will be kept in as perfect state of preservation as possible." Although he professed to be unconnected with the crime or the criminals, he was nonetheless prepared to facilitate the recovery of the body upon the offering of an "unconditional and suitable reward" through the columns of the *Herald*.

Another man was more direct. "Sir: If you make the reward fifty thousand dollars and no questions asked, the body of Mr. Stewart will be returned." Again Hilton was advised to signify his acceptance in the *Herald*.

Someone with fine penmanship, presumed to be a woman, wrote directly to Mrs. Stewart, calling her offer of reward unsatisfactory. She (or he) demanded $100,000 and a reply in the *Herald*, signing off with, "Until then, you will not hear from U. S." Another letter to Mrs. Stewart promised to reveal the location of the body but only if she would provide funds to finish the new Catholic church on Fifth Avenue between Fifty-first and Fifty-second streets.

Another correspondent accused the Jesuits. He confessed his "information may seem peculiar, perhaps ridiculous," but he nevertheless invited the police to continue searching graveyards and churches. Signing himself "A Correspondent in Danger," the man insisted he had reasons for his suspicions, yet failed to reveal them.

Most letter writers preferred some form of tantalizing anonymity. One such person wrote a short note telling the searchers to check out an undertaker's shop on Melrose. The note was written on a scrap of paper that was cut to resemble the shape of the piece of velvet cut from Stewart's casket.[7]

Yet another man advised Hilton and the police to look once again in the Stewart family vault, for he was certain that the body was still there. "If you will examine the coffin containing his father-in-law's remains, you will find there what you seek. Signed: A Friend."[8] Friends such as this man, Hilton did not need. He wasn't up to opening another coffin. Besides, Stewart's father-in-law was not interred in the St. Mark's vault.

A rather tentative and poorly penned letter came from "ONE OF THE ROBBERS." It read, "Dear Sir: If you will promise me not to lock me up, and give me $10,000.00, I will tell you where the body and the robbers of the late At. T. Stewart is." Another inept speller wrote, "THAT BODY HAS BEEN BERRED 1 YERE." One can be certain these letters were granted all the attention they deserved. The little people were speaking. The outrageous crime had aroused the masses.

Some letter writers purported to know the identity and location of the robbers, even to the point of quoting them. Often there were evenhanded letters apparently written by persons who genuinely wanted to help. Other letters were crudely and angrily written, calculated to insult rather than persuade, as personal bias was bound to surface. On November 11 a man wrote advising Hilton to "privately offer the Roman Catholic Bishop from $1000.00 to $5000.00 for the return of A. T. Stewart's body, and I think it will be returned without the thieves being rewarded for their labors."

Innumerable missives came from clairvoyants or from those who consulted supposedly supernormal people. In that vein there was the lady who contended that a medium told her that Stewart's body was "broken in two and carried away in two sacks, first to Tompkins-square and then to Ninety-second street, East River." Then there was the man who went to a séance and found himself in the company of the ghosts of A. T. Stewart, Cornelius Vanderbilt, and Jim Fisk. Stewart's ghost told the man to inform Mrs. Stewart to visit the medium and "he would tell her where the body lay and who were the thieves."

Stories, theories, explanations, visions, plots, and subplots were written in pen, pencil, and cutout letters pasted on paper—all emanated from an aroused and anxious public. Everyone wanted his or her share of the fame and money. A multitude of mostly anonymous voices, sounding their desperate, heartfelt opinions, turned New York into a crazy, hot-and-cold circus of the mind. Somewhere in this maze of data there were undoubtedly a few good clues and probably a letter or two from the actual thieves, but how was anyone to sift them out and identify them?

Spies were everywhere, especially in taverns and other low places where rough men hung out. Bits of secret conversations were picked up, noted, and quoted in letters to Hilton, the police, and the press. Without trying at all, it seemed as if Hilton had announced a contest: who among you can come up with the most bizarre solution to this crime?

An anonymous contributor pointed the finger of guilt at a former Stewart employee who, for the past ten years, had engaged in criminal activity. Theft and disposition of stolen property were his specialties. Supposedly this man was overheard in a gambling house discussing a plan to rob the Stewart vault for a "big reward." He was later heard saying, "It is all right. The body is safe enough." Unfortunately the letter writer refused to say more, apparently content with tossing out some tantalizing clues and standing on the sidelines to see what might develop. He did not "wish to mix in the matter publicly."

There were letters steeped in history. A "wall street banker" brought the Civil War into the mystery. He envisioned some kind of Southern conspiracy in retribution for Union soldiers rifling Confederate graves at Vicksburg, Mississippi, in search of valuables. Another man suggested the police should engage in a deception; they should announce that the body was found, pay the reward, and "await events." The robbers, he said, would surface if they thought their plans were thwarted. Among other suggestions, people called for a search of police headquarters, the city sewers, a niche in the Stewart vault, or one of the other coffins in the vault. An unending parade of ideas descended on those whose duty it was to solve this baffling crime.[9] New York had become a living theater of the absurd.

Two letters—one badly written, the other more skillfully stated—purported to come from the thieves themselves. The first one castigated Hilton and his puny reward. These men unabashedly declared, "We aint beggerers," and rudely rejected the $25,000 reward. They demanded "100000 or a half a million" for the "Rotton old carkase," as they didn't work cheap. As Stewart was "one of the meenest white men that ever god let live," they preferred to let him rot in some anonymous place rather than give him up for a pittance. It was signed: "GRAVE YARDS."

The second letter was literate and far more revealing, embodying the desperate politics of the times while reflecting the rich/poor dichotomy that was peculiar to the last half of the nineteenth century. The authors of this letter made it clear that if there was no way to contest and defeat the rich while they lived, perhaps it could be done by desecrating their graves and stealing their bodies. Maybe there was some economic value and political advantage in the lifeless tissue of millionaires.

The six men behind this letter expressed regret for having committed such a heinous crime. They pleaded poverty, however, saying they were simply trying to make money to feed their hungry families. The six men laid out a spooky plan for the payment of the reward ($5,000 per man) and the return of the body. They wanted all this to come off cleanly, as they desired to inflict no harm on society. They were not "bad men." To prove they were genuine, they offered to produce "a portion of Mr. Stewart's coat, pants, vest, necktie, collar, shirt and hair." In the event that their offer inspired no interest, they would revert to their other plan, which was to sell the body to "the proprietor of a museum" who wanted to make a cast from the remains.[10]

This appeal might have plucked some heartstrings had the author not mentioned that their group consisted of a lawyer, a physician, a banker, and three detectives (no journalists). Such a gathering of professionals in this particular conspiracy must have caused any number of readers to detect the obvious satirical content of the letter. It wasn't an appeal for social justice; it was, rather, an attempt to inject satire into the sadistic incident.

Inspector George W. Dilks received a letter constructed of "words cut out of a newspaper and pasted on brown paper." The note, directed to the chief of police, said only, "In 8 hour I will be in Canada with A. T. Stewart's body. A woman has the remains." There were no instructions or demands, leaving Hilton and the police to concede that it was as worthless as all the others that came in on a daily basis.[11]

Some letters were couched in language that taunted Hilton and the police, emphasizing their lack of success. One such letter came from someone who called himself "Xerxes:"

> November 14, 1878.
> Dear Sir:
>
> One week last night Mr. Stewart's body was taken. Your detectives have been within a block of it within 48 hours, and they may hunt until doomsday, they cannot find it, but for $200,000 and no questions asked, it would be delivered. A personal in the *Herald* saying you will pay this amount, with guaranty, will be answered.
>
> Yours,
> Xerxes.[12]

This letter could well have come from the actual thieves, trying to draw first blood. If so, it was a message to Hilton that his puny $25,000 reward and insistence that he would pay no ransom were unappreciated, to say the least.

With all the various ideas floating about, credible and otherwise, many of them reflecting personal prejudice, it should surprise no one that someone blamed the Jews. Among his mail, Hilton received the following letter:

> DEAR SIR:
>
> My opinion is that the Jews have something to do with the affair. It would do no harm to search the large safes in and around Broadstreet. In one particular office the smell is far from pleasant.
>
> Excuse Pencil.
> November 15th, 1878[13]

The letter probably pleased Hilton, who was overtly and notoriously anti-Semitic. Indeed, he had a well-publicized and long-standing feud with the Jews of New York.

The feud started in the summer of 1877, when Hilton announced that Jews would no longer be admitted as guests at Stewart's Grand Union Hotel in Saratoga Springs, New York. Hilton was managing the hotel as part of the Stewart estate. The hotel wasn't making money, and Hilton blamed the Jews, claiming their presence was keeping others away. This enraged many Jews, especially the wealthy Joseph Seligman, who had been a guest at the resort hotel for the previous ten years. The *New York Times* and other newspapers took Hilton to task, but he stood his ground, feeling secure in his Aryan sense of superiority and causing lasting enmity between himself and Jews.[14]

It mattered not to Hilton that it was the poor economy of the 1870s that caused a downturn in the hotel business. He was apparently content to use the opportunity to exploit his bias against Jews and his personal dislike for Seligman. To his credit, he ignored the accusatory letter published in the *Times* and chose not to use it to air his anti-Semitism. Besides, he was behaving as if the case was all but under wraps, and he wasn't blaming the Jews for stealing Stewart's body.

Actually, by as early as November 13, many thought the denouement was at hand. It started with the "disappearance" of Superintendent George W. Walling of the New York City Police Department's central office. Walling was seen in New Jersey, with a dog and a gun, heading in the direction of "one of the most desolate" areas in the state. He was in the company of Charles B. Waite, a wealthy hotelman who owned thousands of acres of wild hunting land. Since Walling was known to have been working diligently on the Stewart case, people assumed he was in the country looking for the body.[15]

The rumor was picked up and spread from mouth to mouth. Soon the area between Philadelphia and New York City was ablaze with speculation and excitement. Throughout the towns and villages in the area, the talk was of the discovery of Stewart's body in a remote part of New Jersey.

In Philadelphia, near panic erupted among the various newspaper offices as anxious newsmen scrambled to secure transportation to Waite's hunting preserve. They even tried to book a special train. The hunt for Stewart's body was creating celebrities du jour, and "Wash" Walling was one of them.

It was later revealed that the source of the rumor was the arrival of a "sailing vessel" at Port Monmouth, New Jersey. Aboard were ten men from New York, armed with guns, ostensibly out hunting. The vessel deposited a "mysterious box" in a cove near the port. Reporters pieced together all these facts and suspected that, at the very least, the astute Walling was on to something. The rumor faded, however, and nothing came of the story except that Walling was probably engaging in some rest and relaxation, and his targets were quail, pheasants, rabbits, and ducks, not a group of dastardly grave robbers. Exciting for him perhaps, but a major disappointment to the newspapermen and the locals who expected to be a part of some great discovery.[16]

Nevertheless, the police hinted strongly that big news was in the wings. It was revealed in the *Times* that by November 15, the police had all the facts in order to their satisfaction. They knew the exact time the grave robbers entered the tomb (3:17 a.m.) and that they left the cemetery within an hour. Since it had rained that evening until about 3 a.m. and the copy of the *Herald* found at the crime scene was dry, it was deduced that the thieves entered the churchyard soon after it stopped raining. It was believed that a man named Mahoney "did the principal work." He was under surveillance and could be "arrested at any moment."

The corpse was "doubled up inside the vault and thrust into a canvass bag," then loaded aboard a wagon and taken directly to Weehawken, New Jersey, where it was turned over to a man named Murphy who ran a saloon. Murphy was an unsavory character who had recently been caught with two dead bodies on his premises. According to the police, Stewart's body was kept there for a time and then moved to another secret place.[17]

Beyond this, the police would say no more, but people were led to believe that revelations and arrests would be forthcoming. Soon the public would see the faces of the men who committed the ghastly and infamous crime. The ghouls would soon make their appearance. All of New York waited, like an enthralled audience, for the next act to begin.

CHAPTER 8

Closing In on the Ghouls

> Late last night, the *Times* reporter learned that a grand movement was taking place to capture the robbers of Mr. Stewart's grave.
> *New York Times,* November 17, 1878

On the evening of November 16, 1878, New York was rippling with more than the usual excitement. People were enthralled with the Stewart mystery; it was considered the greatest sensation since the disappearance of Mayor Abraham Oakey Hall of Tweed ring fame.

The Stewart excitement was front-page news all over America, and the country was agog over stories of grave robberies. The *New York Herald* reminded its readers that "not so very long ago ... the grave of Henry Clay was tampered with."[1] In Springfield, Illinois, nervous officials at the Oak Ridge Cemetery again hurriedly moved Abraham Lincoln's body to a new grave in the labyrinthine outside the Memorial Hall, fearing that it was not safe from plotting ghouls.[2]

The *Chicago Tribune* recalled both the desecration of Lincoln's tomb and the disappearance of Stewart's body while covering a low-profile grave robbery that occurred in November 1878. The *Tribune* lectured its readers about the prevalence of this crime and then expended two columns explaining the ghoulish deeds of two losers: Sam Johnson and Frank Brown. Shortly after stealing a body, they were arrested and willingly revealed the details of their crime to police and reporters.

Brown, a young man who studied medicine at Rush Medical College, had arranged to steal and sell a body for $25 to a professor at the Chicago Homeopathic College. He recruited Johnson to join him and rob a grave, promising there was "big money in it." Johnson showed some false bravado, bragging that he had experience in stealing stiffs in Cincinnati, St. Louis, and other places.

Actually, Johnson was a middle-aged black man from Elgin, Illinois, who worked as a hostler. He was a poor man with a family and not enough money to feed it. He later insisted he was loath to engage in such foul activity but did so out of poverty. Brown guaranteed that, should they be successful, Johnson would be well paid for his night's work.

Johnson was sent ahead to the targeted cemetery in Elgin to find a suitable subject, and he selected the grave of a recent suicide. He and Brown returned to the cemetery that evening and went to work. Johnson did the digging, and when it came time to remove the corpse, Brown weakened, so his nervous assistant, now determined to see it through, uncovered the coffin and wrapped the body in two sacks. They carried the rotting corpse to the wagon, covered it with a robe, and strapped it down to the bed. During the course of this gruesome exercise, Johnson perspired heavily and felt sick and nauseous because of the horrible stench. Sweat poured from his forehead, and he "trembled like a leaf." Clearly, he was out of his element.

Yet they were alone and succeeded in hauling the body to their Chicago destination, traveling forty miles over muddy roads in six hours. Later Johnson was arrested at the stable as he turned in the horse and wagon. Brown was also taken into custody, and they both spoke freely of their crime, but each man implicated the other, trying to deflect blame. It was then that they learned they had robbed the wrong grave. Instead of the fresh grave of the suicide, they dug up a woman's body, that of Mina R. Schraeder of Hanover in Cook County.

The city marshal, upon hearing the two unfortunates relate the details of their ghastly night's work, said to Brown, "You must have made a mistake, you got a woman."

"Good God," exclaimed Brown. "Is that so?"

It was so. Johnson tried to make the best of a badly bungled body snatching by saying he was certain they had the right grave, but it was dark, and neither man got a look at the badly decomposed corpse. It was delivered to a janitor at the medical college, and he didn't bother to take a look at it either.

It gets even stranger. The woman whose body was purloined by mistake had died of pneumonia on September 20, 1878, and during her illness, she was cared for by Dr. S. P. Brown, father of the young grave robber. Brown's name was on the death certificate.

Poor Sam Johnson, when he spoke to reporters and the police, muttered repeatedly that he was a "simple, damn fool for going into the business." He said that the "Lord would paralyze his tongue if he was not telling the truth" and insisted that this was his first and last act as a grave robber. Yet he can be credited for adding a small bit to the growing literature of grave robbing, so that New York and A. T. Stewart didn't grab all the headlines.[3]

In New York, the police were everywhere, devoting the brunt of their resources to the Stewart case as if it were the only case of any importance, as if in one grand sweep, all the guilty would be found and arrested. Finding a single dead body had become a priority that superseded all other police business, and the forces of justice appeared ready to produce the desired results. Hilton and the police announced that "they had obtained sufficient evidence to insure the conviction of all the guilty parties beyond the possibility of a doubt."[4]

The famous Pinkerton Detective Agency sent a contingent of agents from Chicago into the investigation. The agency was staffed by skilled and dedicated detectives and had a reputation for getting results. During the Civil War, several Pinkerton agents infiltrated the South, gathering valuable military intelligence for the Union. After the war the agency opened a New York office headed by Robert Pinkerton, son of the company founder, Allan Pinkerton, America's original "private eye."

If the Pinkerton's were not enough, private detectives from various parts of the United States had descended upon New York and were hard at work, as were all the local "shadowers" who could be recruited. These men were grouped in squads and sent scouring the city for evidence and suspects.[5]

A force that large and determined had to produce something. From the outset, the authorities made bloated pronouncements and predictions aplenty. To fail now would be to risk massive public ridicule.

A dead body had to be found, but equally important, live bodies had to be produced, paraded before the public, and put behind bars.

So they were. From among the denizens of crime-ridden New York, the police and their private detective allies located and arrested two men in connection with the Stewart grave robbery. The first man arrested, Henry "Hank" Vreeland, said to be twenty-five years old and from Brooklyn, was taken into custody as a "suspicious person."[6] The second suspect was William Burke from New York.[7] Burke was about forty years old and, upon being consigned to jail, said he was a "speculator."[8] Both men were locked up in secluded places, and the police were very secretive, refusing even to say why the arrests were made. Once again the press was kept in the dark, and there was a concerted effort to keep reporters away from the suspects.

Both Vreeland and Burke had criminal records and were suspects in another recent spectacular crime, the Manhattan Bank burglary, which was upstaged by the Stewart outrage.[9] Burke, whose "hang dog" face was among those in the police headquarters' rogue's gallery, had served five years in state prison for a burglary committed in 1872. He was described as having a "natural sneaking, cur-like expression" and being one of the "meanest-looking of thieves." The *Times* concluded that he was so thoroughly distrustful in appearance, he wasn't even fit company for other thieves. He was, in other words, what people in those days called a "criminal by nature."

Vreeland, alias Whalen, Wilson, and Wheeler, was also a petty criminal—a pickpocket—who had served three years in state prison. He also served six months in jail for stealing a pair of shoes. He was a cooper when he worked and was once employed by Colgate and Company. The *Times* called him a "sneak thief." Vreeland was described as "manly-looking" but possessing a "hard, villainous face." On the plus side, there was a "redeeming dash of pluck" in his appearance.[10] It was reported that he was living with Burke's sister—identified only as Mrs. Wright—in a tenement, "under very intimate relations."[11]

The police concluded that these men were hired to do some of the dirty work, "as they were not possessed of brains enough to devise so good a plan themselves."[12] These men were considered to be too dumb to have successfully planned and pulled off the St. Mark's grave robbery. Still the arrests gave the police some much-needed momentum, despite the shabby nature of the suspects.

While the forces of the law were engaged in their grand sweep of the city, journalists from the city's newspapers descended on Hilton. Their mission: to determine, once and for all, whether Stewart's body had been found. The newspapers concluded that since arrests had been made, the body must have been recovered. Hilton was tight-lipped, however, saying only that he did not want to compromise the search in progress. For the next four days he would send mixed signals to the press.

The press then turned to the police. A reporter for the *Times* questioned Inspector Dilks, who was on duty at the central office on the night of November 16, 1878. The reporter told Dilks that word was out claiming Captain Kealy had gone to Weehawken, New Jersey, to "take possession of the body in the name of Judge Hilton." Dilks reacted with surprise and said only that he was expecting, at any time, a telegram announcing that Stewart's body had been found.

Having tossed out some juicy tidbits, Dilks found himself cornered by the determined reporter. When pressed, he admitted that detectives had pinned down the whereabouts of the body, and "their business last night was to find it." That explanation was not good enough. The reporter asked point-blank, "Will the telegram announcing the recovery of the body be given to the public to-night?"

Dilks unhesitatingly replied, "It will if it arrives in time."

The reporter left but soon returned, this time rousing Dilks from his sleep. The gutsy journalist put Dilks through another round of the same questions and received essentially the same answers. In concluding he said, "This is a very serious matter, Inspector Dilks, and we are going to print it." Dilks replied, "All right."[13]

Although Dilks later denied making any such statement, it was thus reported, and once again the people of New York were pumped up with the expectation that the body of the Merchant Prince would return to some safe, permanent resting place and resume its long, dreamless sleep without further interruption. People everywhere awaited news that would put an end to all the bizarre events that followed in the wake of the unnatural crime.

Rich or poor, people preferred stability. While most people at that time lived meandering, edgy lives of boundless uncertainty, there was something fixed and certain about death. As sure as death brings forth grief and a taste of dust, bodies were put in the ground to stay. A cemetery and the gravestones within are symbolic of spiritual immortality, one of the more unchanging features of our cultural attitude toward death.

To disturb the dead was to violate an ancient taboo and summon superstitious feelings that were better left alone. Any unnatural act toward the dead aroused and offended the human psyche, asking more of it than it could be expected to understand and tolerate. It was as if the titillating horrors handed down by Edgar Allan Poe had acquired unintended qualities and consequences. Reading about the macabre was one thing; it was entirely another to live it.

The Reverend T. DeWitt Talmage of Brooklyn was living the macabre every day as he deftly and courageously dodged the bullets of sin in a dangerous and hopelessly corrupt world. He was devoted to exposing and destroying as much evil as he could, and toward that end, Talmage embarked on a series of sermons called "Night Side of City Life." The crusading pastor used his pulpit and pen with great vigor to chart the growth of crime and the downward spiral of morality. He personally visited the saloons, bars, brothels, and other dens in the city in the official company of the police, of course, to get firsthand knowledge of the sinful activity.

The outrageous theft of Stewart's body gave Talmage another cause to add to his wilderness crusade against evil. While preaching against alcohol, thieves, assassins, and prostitutes was his specialty, the popular evangelical minister was especially troubled with this particular example of sin. He was seen at St. Mark's after the break-in, making his own inspection.

On the evening of November 8, 1878, while he addressed an audience at the Brooklyn Tabernacle, Talmage diverted from his text to express his personal horror over recent events. He admitted that news of this sort was not unusual and "humanity is sliced up on the dissecting tables of our medical colleges for the advancement of science." He angrily concluded that there can be no scientific rationale for the acts of those who stole Stewart's body. This man of religion received immediate applause when he condemned this sacrilege and demanded that "no money be paid to such blackmailers, who deserve bullet and quick trigger."[14]

The epic crime was the topic of another powerful, soul-stirring sermon that Talmage gave at the Brooklyn Tabernacle on the night of November 15, 1878. He called the crime a horrible deed that "shook all Christendom." He found it literally incomprehensible, saying this was a "burglary against the resurrection day," a belief, no doubt, shared by his enraptured listeners, for after a body is placed in its grave or tomb, "no hand but the hand of God has a right to lift the dead." Yet the unholy culprits who lifted Stewart's body from its tomb weren't playing God; they were acting under the influence of the devil.

Talmage called for universal condemnation of those responsible, knowing that all of America and much of the world was following the case and trusting in a favorable resolution.[15] For some people Talmage was courageous and inspirational; for others his torrid sermons, laced with colorful metaphors and self-deprecating remarks, were comic relief. Others just thought he was a hypocritical prude.

The Stewart story had been the talk of the town from the moment the news broke. By now, some people were sick of it. Others hoped for a solution but, at the same time, were irresistibly drawn to the story. They looked forward to the next newspaper report as if it were the next episode in an adventure series. Then there were those people whose appetite for the bizarre was limitless. Those people probably wanted Hilton to parade Stewart's corpse down Broadway, then put it on display. Only then would their morbid curiosity be satisfied.

This, of course, would never happen, but with arrests made, people were counting on the trials to be good theater. It began with the arraignment of Burke and Vreeland. While the focus of public curiosity was on them, their first court appearance was brief and secretive. At 2 p.m. on November 16, 1878, the suspects were ushered into court surrounded by police officers. They wore hats pulled down over their faces and overcoats with pulled-up collars.

Burke's mother and his wife, the latter a former circus rider, attended the proceedings. They sat quietly, tastefully dressed but pale and nervous, while Burke and Vreeland were charged with robbing Stewart's body from the family vault. It was clear from their demeanor that this was a difficult and embarrassing experience, but they bore up well and were steadfast in their support of Burke.

The women left without talking to the *Times* but spoke freely to a reporter from the *Herald*. The woman who identified herself as Burke's wife (or sister, no one seemed to know for sure) maintained he was innocent. "He's a speculator," she said, matter-of-factly, not a grave robber. When asked what kind of speculator she said quickly, "any kind of a speculator."[16] This kind of ambiguity, however, only tended to draw more suspicion to Burke and his companion. To a public thoroughly involved in the mystery of the moment, a speculator sounded like someone who would steal the body of a rich and famous man, risking arrest and eternal condemnation for the chance to make his pile. Were the arrestees—Burke and Vreeland—made of this stuff?

Burke's mother didn't think so. When asked about the arrests she told a reporter for the *Sun*, "It is so silly.... I had to laugh when I heard." Showing maternal drive and some guile, she lampooned the police, saying that if she had any knowledge of the whereabouts of Stewart's body, she would bypass the police, head straight for the reward (meaning Hilton), and let her son and his friend fend for themselves.[17]

It appears the police paid little attention to her brave front and her opinions. Their sights were on the two men in custody, and they must have felt some relief at bringing the pair before the court. Of course they still had to keep the suspects away from reporters. After brief formalities the prisoners were secretly whisked away, leaving the reporters unfulfilled and within a word or two of a good story.

The *Times*, acting on good authority, said Burke and Vreeland denied any connection with the Stewart grave robbery.[18] Besides, Vreeland had a good alibi. On the night of the grave robbery, he was dead drunk in Mrs. Wright's room and, therefore, unable to participate in such a complex crime.[19]

Despite all the fanfare and press coverage of the arrests and the intrigue caused by the arrest of an additional "mystery" suspect, neither the police nor the press were much impressed with the haul. The police could only claim that Burke and Vreeland were, at most, mere "tools" in the crime. There was no concealing the general belief that these men—if indeed they were guilty—were directed by others.

Who and where were the others? It was believed that Michael Kelly, the missing hack man, had been murdered to keep him from squealing. The two men identified only as Mahoney and Murphy were never brought in.[20] Nevertheless, the police kept their focus on a five- or six-man conspiracy. It was also reported that three other suspects who were targeted for arrest had bribed private detectives into allowing them to escape.[21]

Almost from the outset Hilton and the police had been promising tasty, "big name" revelations. What had been served up to the public was a mere appetizer. The main courses were yet to come, and the police expressed, with confidence, that more exciting arrests were expected in the near future.

The *Herald* maintained its belief that "Christian, the Washington resurrectionist," was connected with the crime because of his reputation as a grave robber par excellence. Like a haunting dream returning again and again, the *Herald* was not able to shake off the striking similarity between Christian and the man in picture 1,267 in the police rogue's gallery. This was the man that C. N. Middleton fingered as the customer who appeared in his store asking for the body preservative, Allekton. "He had a peculiar way of turning down his mouth," said Middleton.[22] While they wouldn't admit to it, police all over the eastern United States were undoubtedly looking for this mystery man. For the *Herald*, there had to be some connection.

Individuals connected with the case had everyone else speculating. Official expectations were encouraging, as the authorities tried to put the best face on the investigation. Still, people were probably disappointed with the pair of suspects netted by the police. It was like tossing some dry bread to hungry urchins. They ate it up but were unsatisfied and wanted more. Men like Vreeland and Burke were commonplace. They could be found everywhere in New York, part of a surging, struggling, and growing underclass of humanity, much of which engaged in any manner of petty crime. Such people knew nothing of the American dream, but were all too familiar with the gaunt, nightmarish realities of urban life.

Throughout the 1870s all of America was racked by poverty and unemployment, made especially terrible by the economic Panic of 1873. It was a rancorous and violent decade filled with unprecedented political and social problems. The ranks of the poor were swelled every year by immigrants, mostly from Europe. Although many new arrivals went West to settle, there was an imbalance of fresh laborers versus jobs, and in the midst of a depression this tended to keep wages down. By 1876 wages had been cut by as much as one-half nationwide, but there was no decrease in the cost of living. There were an estimated 1 million tramps (ragged, desperate, and unemployed men) roaming the country, including New York. This translated into an army of hopeless adults, many with hungry children at their sides, clinging to life.

The 1870s was also a time of great contrasts, with burgeoning poverty moving alongside impressive developments in railroad building, commerce, and technology. The steel and coal industries also made great forward strides. On May 11, 1877, Alexander Graham Bell demonstrated his remarkable invention called a "speaking telephone" at the Hotel St. Denis on Broadway and Eleventh Street. While an amazed group of notables watched and listened, Bell talked to an assistant in Brooklyn, two miles distant.[23]

Thomas A. Edison was working on the electric light, as were other inventors. During the peak of the Stewart investigation, someone suggested that electricity, "a leading topic of conversation" at the time, be used to protect cemeteries. An anxious contributor to the Herald asked, "Cannot something be done in the electric line that will let the dead rest and the living be relieved of such anxiety?"[24] Grave robbers always worked under the cover of darkness; a lighted cemetery would keep them away. As always, people looked to technology for answers.

Although New York was entering the age of the telephone, electric light, and other great inventions, the city was struggling to shake its economic woes. While the rich lived in effortless splendor largely indifferent to the suffering close at hand, entire neighborhoods were reduced to terrible slums. Occasionally, the rich would scatter some charity, but its impact was negligible. William "Boss" Tweed ceremoniously fed the poor, making a showy display of his generosity, but in reality he was only buying sympathy and support from a constituent group and cared nothing about easing their suffering. Shrewd and unscrupulous, the diamond-studded Tweed found the way to a poor voter's allegiance was through his stomach.

Among its poor, New York featured hordes of scavengers, or "rag-pickers," both men and women, who wandered the streets gathering anything salvageable from rags to bones. Each night, after a day of scavenging, they carted their salvage to whatever hovel they called home. These people often slept with chickens, dogs, and pigs in their rooms, thus, adding to the filth and stench of other rotting debris. While New York had more of this species of poverty than any other city in America, it was a distinction it was forced to share.

Should it surprise anyone that people existing under such wretched conditions would lose sight of those traits that separated men from beasts? Should it shock anyone that there would be among them, in any number of large cities, men who dabbled in the theft and sale of human corpses? Numb to offensive odor and totally unfamiliar with cleanliness, they had, it would seem, sufficient indoctrination in dealing with decomposition.

It was nothing; it could be easily tolerated, especially when it could be converted into life-sustaining money.

Not long after Stewart's casket was lowered into the vault at St. Mark's, rumors circulated that a gang of grave-robbing ghouls, one of many in the city, was seen lingering at the churchyard. Also, the police investigated a plot to steal and ransom Stewart's corpse by the bank-robbing gang of George Leonidas Leslie.[25]

It was believed that at the time of the Stewart mystery, there were "hundreds of grave diggers about the city, many of whom have been accustomed to transferring and re-interring bodies ... buried even for a greater length of time than the body of Mr. Stewart." Some men theorized that among the group that broke into Stewart's vault were professional gravediggers trying to supplement their meager income in very trying times.[26]

It was the time of the tenements, those cramped, infested quarters inhabited by thousands of people, densely packed together amid disease-ridden filth. It was estimated that in 1878 the city of New York had 21,000 tenement houses that sheltered the overwhelming majority of the city's population.[27] The poorly constructed four- and five-story buildings were designed to hold as many people as possible, without regard for ventilation or sanitation. These sad, unsafe dwellings were moneymakers for landlords and hellholes for their tenants.

It was not unusual to find several people living in a single room. The worst of the tenements were, quite literally, open sewers. In these "nurseries of disease and death,"[28] children suffered and died in great numbers from hunger, disease, and maltreatment. The desperation of everyday life was such that it detracted from the threat of storm or fire, both of which were likely to strike random and deadly blows.

The children of the poor who survived beyond infancy were little more than chattel to the business world. Laws prohibiting child labor were a sham allowing children to be freely exploited by industry. The Stewart fortune, for example, was built largely on the backs of women and girls. In fact, the sweatshop assembly-line factory system created conditions in New York that rivaled those found in Charles Dickens' London. Those children who survived the brutal and hellish experience often turned to crime as juveniles and adults.

With criminals produced in large numbers, crime fed on crime in a mad scramble to survive. Those who fell into this deadly spiral could expect little or no mercy. The *New York Times*, for example, admonished the poor for their behavior, believing they should accept low wages without complaint.

Whitelaw Reid, the conservative editor of the *New York Tribune*, was a strong opponent of organized labor, especially when it took to the streets. During the railway strike of 1877, he lambasted the workers, calling on authorities to punish them to the death. One Reid editorial demanded that "authority ought not to rest until it has swept down every resisting mob with grape shot." The strike had to be crushed "though it cost a thousand bloody corpses."[29]

William M. Evarts, a prominent and rich New Yorker, demanded that the workingman revere his employer, from whom all blessings flowed. A friend of A. T. Stewart, Evarts believed the worker should refuse to strike and, instead, protect the workplace with his "life, if necessary."[30] Jay Gould expressed the arrogance of wealth even more succinctly, saying he could hire one-half of the working class to kill off the other half.

Men like Evarts, Reid, and Gould believed that poverty was indicative of personal failure, uninfluenced by outside forces, and therefore not an excuse for crime; hunger was never a cause for violent dissent or even nonviolent unrest. This sentiment was echoed by those in charge of the churches and charities, who considered poverty a moral condition that had nothing to do with economics. Poverty to them was something that had to be "cured" by instilling proper attitudes and values. Others believed it was a personal choice that should be beaten out of the criminally inclined underclass, and they recommended that the authorities bring back the whipping post.

What these comfortable and privileged people lacked was an understanding that a growing underclass tended to destabilize society. The desperate poor were just too distracted to make rational, independent contributions to society. While there was a crying need for social justice, there would be none, for it was an idea whose time had not yet come. Contempt for the poor was policy.

Still the underclass fought back as best as it could, defying the bosses and forming labor unions. The Knights of Labor came into being in the 1870s, but this organization, while significant, was conservative and often sided with business. The Knights were largely ineffective insofar as producing jobs and good wages, so crime remained a viable alternative, with huge numbers of people engaged in theft of various kinds. Young and old, men and women formed legions of pickpockets, shoplifters, sneak thieves, con artists, and others who practiced various forms of covert misbehavior. Fortunately for all, violent crime did not keep pace with crimes against property.

It wasn't as if thoughtful people were unaware of the problem, for many important studies were done and books written. One writer placed blame on the "conformation of the city." New York was, after all, an island, a city of length but no depth, good for commerce but bad for people because of overcrowding and poor public transportation. With so many new people arriving on ships, the population was transient and shifting. The largest city in America was, in truth, a "camping ground," not a city at all; it had no stability or sense of permanence and no room for orderly growth and expansion. Competence and dedication were questionable; honesty and loyalty, including that of the police, were neglected. Everything was up for grabs, giving rise to political corruption and other social ills, such as those described above.[31]

Moral decay was seemingly everywhere. New York had long been a city of eccentricities. Nightclubs permitted dancing, and theaters featured the ballet, activities thought of as damnable. A. T. Stewart's Niblo's Garden Theatre was once referred to as the "bare garden" for the leggy, bare-breasted girls whose nightly performances packed the house and shocked audiences.[32] It acquired a nationwide reputation for revealing too much of the female form. Some people flirted with "free love," meaning casual sex with randomly chosen partners. Prostitution was rampant and very profitable. At least one big-spending brothel madam shopped at Stewart's store. Liquor flowed freely, and opium dens operated openly.

Blood drinking, of all things, had its growing body of devotees. Invalids and others suffering from various ailments regularly visited the abattoirs of the city to drink warm cattle blood, often with a doctor's recommendation. Those whose curiosity was even more perverse drank human blood when it was available. Some of these vampire-like folks satisfied their craving with help from accommodating family members.[33] With all these rampaging oddities, it is no wonder so many called New York a sinful city, a vast playground for the devil's kin.

Outsiders were shocked and appalled at the level of immorality seen in New York. Newspapers in other cities raised the awful specter of a sensual Gotham before their readers with exciting revelations of crime and decadence. Preachers railed against the various forms of evil as fearful moralists sought solutions while trying to restore order to a troubled world that seemed hopelessly out of control.

Labor leaders and others with radical political views were singled out for censure. Immigrants were freely blamed and bashed. Urban America—led by New York—was fertile ground for perspiring, arm-swinging religious crusaders, all of whom felt a longing for a return to some cherished time in the past. While they spoke with dedication and passion, they could not stop the onrushing tide of poverty, crime, and corruption. New York and other cities were strained to the breaking point with urban problems that threatened to blow them apart as they spiraled toward the future that would save or destroy them.

In 1877, after years of discontent and suffering by workers, a series of bloody strikes and riots erupted throughout much of the eastern United States. While it has been said that most people lived their lives in quiet desperation, some of the desperate refused to keep quiet. From Baltimore to Pittsburgh to Chicago, railroad workers and their sympathizers fought a valiant, though crazed and hopeless, battle against their employers and the police. Federal troops were brought in, and pitched battles were fought. Hundreds were killed, including women and children. No place in America was unaffected by these shocking events.

After a summer of bloodshed, the rich and powerful prevailed, leaving the workers deep in misery and back on whatever jobs were available at whatever wages the bosses were willing to pay. By 1878 an uneasy quiet prevailed in most cities, including New York, where pauperism still dominated, as the depression had yet to run its course.

There was a generalized fear, particularly among the educated and privileged, that the gathering of great fortunes in the hands of a few was taking too much money from the public at large. This was producing a permanent underclass that would one day acquire the means and motivation to strike out against the ruling class. Should the immigrants, the ignorant, the indigent, or the chronically unemployed find a leader—a charismatic modern demagogue—America could find itself in another bloody civil conflict. As the nation was making its way to world leadership in an era of emerging democracies, the great inequality of wealth and social conditions were endangering the social stability needed for the United States to be a model for the world.

Out of this deadly matrix it should surprise no one that secret societies were formed from groups of angry, plotting men gathered in dark places, seeking ways to strike out against those who oppressed them, ready to shout their anger at the world and explode in violence. It should be no surprise that a conspiracy was hatched to steal the body of a multimillionaire, who was perceived by many as a cold and heartless oppressor, then offer the corpse for ransom. One should also expect to find men like William Burke and Henry Vreeland involved. From the hordes of like-minded men, the police had an endless array of suspects at their disposal.

With Vreeland and Burke now charged in the crime, the police seemed slightly to relax their efforts—probably because they were tired of the case. This, however, failed to slow down the pursuit of the press. Sleepless cops were hounded for information. In most cases, however, the response was, "I don't have anything to say." One exasperated official said, "No man under God's heavens knows anymore than you do where the body is, except the men who took it."[34] Hilton, too, was especially reticent, locking his doors or ducking into his brougham to avoid reporters. He was anything but his usual pontificating self. A reporter from the *Times* interpreted this to mean that something big was soon to be announced.

As such, Hilton was chased relentlessly by reporters for the *Times*, *Herald*, and *Tribune*. A *Herald* reporter asked him point-blank, "Judge, do you know where Mr. Stewart's body is?" To which Hilton unhesitatingly replied, "No," and then rushed off. It may have appeared to many that Hilton, at long last, was tired of running things.

A reporter for the *Times* went to Hilton's home at 7 West Thirty-fourth Street for a follow-up. Hilton permitted the reporter to ask just one question, probably knowing what was coming. "Judge, to-day, when coming out of the Central Office, a *Herald* reporter asked you did you know where Mr. Stewart's body was. You answered 'No.' Did you mean that?"

Being more weasel-wordy than usual, Hilton replied, "If that was the tenor of the question asked me, I certainly did not so understand it. I supposed it was an appeal for information. I should be sorry to have the *Herald* publish such a question and answer together as emanating from me."[35]

Thus sayeth Henry Hilton. Despite the vagueness and denials, the *Times* encouraged readers to stay calm and stay tuned. Should anything develop, everyone could expect to be informed in due time.

Of course there was concern that if the body was discovered, how could anyone be certain it was Stewart's remains? After all, he had been dead for more than two and a half years. Among those questioned was William Libbey, who emphatically denied the remains were beyond recognition. He said, "All this talk about the difficulty in recognizing the body when found is mere twaddle."[36]

There was more hope and bluster than science in Libbey's assertion. However, his statement was cautiously supported by one of Stewart's personal physicians, a doctor who attended the Merchant Prince on transAtlantic trips and was at his bedside when he died. This man said it might be possible to identity the body by the "peculiar form of the head and teeth," and by examining hair samples that would retain their original, reddish color. Other than that, the doctor believed the features would be decomposed beyond identification.[37]

The notes and letters kept pouring in, some sounding like advertisements for weight-loss products: "A. T. Stewart's remains can be returned. Fair compensation given. Strict secrecy guaranteed. Address H. L., box 146 *Herald* office."

Another party wrote Hilton saying the body of Stewart was "under St. Mark's church. I will see you to-morrow to get $25,000.00 reward." He didn't. "A FRIEND THAT HAS HIS BONES" sent a choppy, angry letter to Hilton complaining about Jews and "them fellows" with "there big mouth to damn wide open." He wanted $100,000, although his letter failed to explain what he would give in return. Another man wanted a mere $50 for revealing the location of Stewart's body. He was willing to meet Hilton, or his representative, at the post office. He would be the man wearing a red scarf around his neck.[38]

A kind-hearted widow wrote to Mrs. Stewart beseeching her to call off the search and cancel the reward, as the matter was better left in God's hands. The widow reminded Mrs. Stewart that "many eminent persons are lost at sea and never recovered" and "many leave home never to return," only to "die among strangers." The widow's advice was to let it be, for it matters not at all where a man's dead body rests. In due time, God will perform his will for the betterment of all mankind.[39]

A pointedly cruel letter came from someone who called himself Rhadat:

To the Editor of the Herald—

The body of A. T. Stewart will never be returned. It has long since been calcined by fire into dust. The thing was long in contemplation and only a befitting opportunity (the excitement caused by the recent election and a drizzling night) was observed. The hour arrived, the blow was struck and the thing accomplished. Five of us were engaged and each sworn. This is the truth. "Vengeance is mine; saith the Lord," his means he places in the hands of his faithful servants on earth.

One of five.
RHADAT.[40]

Not everyone who wrote in was angry, illiterate, greedy, or cruel. Sympathetic people were drawn into sending correspondence, too. One man calmly suggested that everyone connected with the search, except Mrs. Stewart, divest the matter of all sentiment. After all, he said, it wasn't a live person they were seeking. The authorities were making too much of a fuss over a "suit of clothes and the poor and putrefying remnants of a man." Signing his letter "A Citizen," this man said that recovering the body was relatively unimportant and that the Garden City monument would be significant with or without a physical trace in it of the man it was built to honor.

A *Herald* editorial was in accord. It suggested that Stewart's heirs install a tablet over the crypt intended for his remains. The tablet should briefly recite the facts of the case, that the body was stolen from St. Mark's graveyard, and that the police could not find it. In other words, memorialize an admission that the mystery was unsolved.[41]

"A Widow" espoused similar views. While she sympathized with Stewart's widow, this letter writer suggested that offering a reward for the body was something that Mrs. Stewart should never do. "Withdraw your offer … and let the sacrilegious villains know it by public notice." All except the criminals would be served, and Mrs. Stewart would be applauded for her courage.

Mrs. Stewart needed great courage to endure the awful spectacle going on around her. Her husband's missing corpse was the topic of conversation in every parlor and bar in the city, and she could do nothing to silence it. Worse yet, there was no indication that the mystery was about to be solved, so she had to prepare for a long period of misery as her life wound down.

In the last years his life, A. T. Stewart set out to find and destroy all photographs and portraits of himself and refused to sit for any others.[42] It was as if he wanted to leave behind as little as possible for others to remember what he looked like. Yet the image he wanted to destroy was raised to new heights of prominence—and made so very hideous—because of the grave robbery.

CHAPTER 9

The Mystery Deepens

> I drempt yesterday that the remains of the late A. T. Stewart were in Port Jarvis.
>
> A Lady, *New York Herald*, November 17, 1878

Spiritualists and clairvoyants, finding the Stewart mystery to their liking, continued to explore the other world for clues and solutions. Spiritualism was a popular but controversial offshoot of mainstream Christianity. Its adherents were looked upon as eccentric, queer, and dangerous, making it a suspect religion. Nevertheless it provided solace for many who were willing to cross the line and was especially welcomed by women, who found in it spiritual and intellectual relief from their tedious and restricted lives.

Critics were vocal and repressive—some linked it with free love—but spiritualism was quite strong from 1850 to 1870, and its members lived in all parts of the United States. It put a happy face on Christianity, which had long been burdened by rigid, gloomy, Calvinist influences, including the twin pillars of faith: guilt and punishment. Spiritualism was a powerful religious force laced with elements of humanism, and it demanded its place in the pantheon of American religions.

Spiritualists believed that the dead existed on another plane where they could be, and expected to be, reached by the living for mutual comfort and exchanges of information. Bereaved loved ones took comfort in the Spiritualist promise, especially during the Civil War, when young men by the thousands were suddenly cast into the dark abyss of death. Séances by trance mediums were commonplace, and while religious conservatives scoffed, condemned, and sought to outlaw spiritualism, it thrived as a colorful, liberal, and irrepressible belief system. Spiritualism claimed a multitude of eager believers, all searching for something new in desperate, uncertain times. Among the more renowned believers was multimillionaire Commodore Vanderbilt, who regularly consulted his mediums for business advice. Spiritualism was tailor-made for the Stewart mystery.

Clairvoyants were also drawn into the mystery. While clairvoyance, as a form of psychic phenomenon, had a long and storied past, it was not always connected with a religion or any other institution or movement. Nevertheless, many people lumped clairvoyants together with spiritualists because both were out on the frontier of acceptability, constantly probing the darkness, looking for new light.

Simply stated, a true clairvoyant is a person who is gifted with the ability to use his or her mind to perceive—to "see"—beyond the normal range of the senses. Clairvoyants can be mentally aware of events taking place miles away. In other words, they use what is commonly called a "sixth sense" or "second sight."

There are also dream clairvoyants who "see things" happening in their dreams that later are proven to be true. In this regard they are like trance mediums who see things or have an awareness of people and happenings that others in their presence cannot detect. Like the spiritualists, these people found fertile ground for exercising their unique talents while publicizing and promoting their cause in the Stewart disappearance. Should one of their kind provide the information to crack the case, they thought the world would be forced to take a long and serious look at psychic people.

There was a happy and irrepressible optimism about these curious, breakthrough groups as they went about flouting conventional thought and faith. In the Middle Ages the spiritualists would have been persecuted as heretics for daring to go where no form of Christianity had gone before. Unfortunately, the sect was tainted by a noticeable strain of dishonesty.

The same could be said for clairvoyants. They regularly advertised their services in the nation's newspapers, touting their psychic powers and promising money-back satisfaction. Many of them toured the country, stopping at hotels and making public appearances for a fee. An advertisement might say: "Madame So and So, born 'with veil' promises all secrets will be revealed; all worries eradicated." Undoubtedly, most advertising clairvoyants were hucksters.

Spiritualists and clairvoyants—both phony and real—had a powerful impact on the collective psyche of the United States in the nineteenth century. With their sights set on the future, they exercised their power boldly and with intellectual and spiritual arrogance, not unlike the authorities they sought to unseat. The past was tired and needed to be put to sleep; the future was theirs to seize and live to the fullest. Solving a celebrity case would give them enormous credibility.

Thanks to the Stewart mystery, practitioners of spiritualism and clairvoyance were handed the chance to advance the science and ethics of their respective causes. However, attaining credibility was always a problem for them, and the unique opportunity was not handled well.

A woman from Boston wrote to the *Herald* detailing at great length a "communication" she had with the spirit of A. T. Stewart. Her letter begs to be believed, but is utterly lacking in those elements that would convince anyone of its authenticity. This Bostonian lady called herself neither a spiritualist nor a clairvoyant, and she provided no information about past experience in such matters. She was an unknown and gave every appearance of being just another exuberant soul asserting herself in hopes of getting the reward. Nevertheless, she wrote with apparent sincerity—or naiveté.

She explained that her psychic experience was inspired by her young son Arthur, a boy of six, who one day unexpectedly described the place where Stewart's body was hidden. After Arthur left home for school, his mother was "strangely influenced" and overcome by nausea. She slipped into a trance-like state and, in the presence of her husband, visited the spirit world. A voice said, "We are here and will direct you where that of which the little one has spoken may be found."

There was a brief exchange with some anonymous spirits, who apparently lectured her on their abilities and warned her that she risked danger and ridicule if she went public with her account. "The world is not ready to receive it yet," they told her, but soon a "great light" would come over the land, presumably to relieve people of their ignorance and narrow-mindedness.

The lady from Boston, who did not sign her name to her letter, then became very cold and nervous. A voice said, "Oh, I am so anxious you will do what we ask of you; I am here myself. We will protect you from all danger, and reward you too." The lady asked cautiously, "Can this be A. T. Stewart's own spirit?"

"Yes, yes, yes," was the impatient reply. "I tell you, yes! And I am very anxious my remains shall be restored to her who so carefully has prepared the place where they were soon to be placed. Oh tell them what I say." The voice, which she did not bother to describe, then said, "Go secretly to my wife and Judge H., and lay this truth before them. You will be protected and rewarded." The supposed voice of A. T. Stewart said that the lady would be directed to the spot where the body lay hidden. Soon after, the voice expressed exhaustion and would communicate no more.

The next morning, November 15, at another sitting, the spirit of Stewart returned with renewed energy and vitality. Once again the lady from Boston was urged to contact Hilton, but with secrecy and without fear, for she would be protected. With this, the lady closed her letter to the *Herald*. Unfortunately, her wordy, ambiguous manuscript, while a bit spooky, added nothing of importance to the investigation. If she was given specific information by the spirit world to relay to Hilton, she failed to include it in her letter.

It is unlikely that Hilton, or anyone else connected with the investigation, gave the woman's letter any credence under the circumstances. Hilton, the police, and the press had heard far too much of this sort of stuff. After all, why would Stewart's ghost turn up in Boston of all places? Why not somewhere in New York, for instance, at his mansion, Hilton's office, one of his stores, or St. Mark's? What better places to reveal his whereabouts? The Boston letter to the *Herald* was the stuff of skeptics and fodder for wiseacres. It did nothing to promote the belief in spiritualism or clairvoyance.

A man from Chicago was more to the point but equally vulnerable to rejection. He wrote to Hilton to explain that his son, "who is a clairvoyant, saw the night before last the place where the body of the late Mr. Stewart is lying." It was beneath the basement floor of a house at 189 Bond Street in New York City. He admitted, however, that the name of the street might not have been Bond, but could have been Bowery or something similar.

His son "saw" a rough-looking red brick house and four men burying the body in the basement. It was doubled up in a zinc or tin box. The boy also described the leader of the group of thieves, concluding he was an Irishman named Griswold, formerly one of Stewart's employees. This man was said to have been fired by Stewart, and, therefore, the theft of his body was a matter of revenge. The boy could positively identify the leader, but the others wore masks over their faces at all times.

The boy's father gently advised the authorities to check out the location described, and then, should the clues provide results, "I rely on your honor to do what is right in the matter" (meaning the reward, of course). The boy, he said, had been tested in the past and was proven to be accurate. He signed his name William Hopkins and wanted very much to be thoroughly drawn into the mystery, its solution, and the reward.[1] However, he and his son remained on the sidelines, merely a part of the sideshow.

A frustrated and whimsical Hilton tossed the letter aside while remarking that he doubted there was a 189 Bond Street. The man should have first studied a New York plat map. He would get no reward for himself and his clairvoyant son. The problem with spiritualism and clairvoyance was that these movements were loaded with phonies who preyed on the gullible and desperate. Hilton, however, was not ready to fall for it.

While the Stewart mystery hovered over the city like a dark cloud, another grand affair intruded, if only for a day. In what was hailed as the social event of the season, two prominent and old New York families—the Roosevelts and the Astors—were united by marriage. On November 18, 1878, James R. Roosevelt took as his bride Helen Astor, daughter of William Astor and heir to everything that the blue-blooded Astor line stood for. The wedding was front-page news, pumped up in an article that fairly pushed the Stewart story aside. Great mystery or no, a New York society event would not be ignored. After several days of gloominess, it was time for some blissful sunshine.

New York society lived far apart from the rest of the city's population. At times conspicuous and at other times discreetly in the background, its members were a tightly knit, small group of wealthy families. These were old families with ties to colonial times and proud, elite ancestors who were patrons, governors, and the like. They did everything according to old rules of etiquette, moving sweetly and noiselessly in lock step, easily ignoring the groans of the discontented while serving a past whose rigid conventions were handed down through generations, all the while holding society in their soft yet unyielding grip.

The women were well-mannered, stiff, and delicate—tightly wound decorations for their men and their homes, the best of them the crown jewels of society. Much of their time was occupied with planning and executing their structured parties, balls, and annual events, which were followed by the appropriate post-party critiques. The men had their rituals, too, but very little of them involved work. They would spend a few hours at the office engaged in polite discussion or leafing through a newspaper, then it was off to the "club," where kindred spirits waited with expensive liquor, velvet handshakes, and other oblique pleasantries. Like everything else about their lives, the conduct at their clubs was little more than form and appearance.

All New York's gentle, high society people lived in idle comfort, counting on the everlasting blessings of inherited wealth that flowed from their banks, trusts, and land holdings. They viewed themselves as special and privileged, like old-world nobles or great works of art set out to dazzle and humble mere mortals. They created almost nothing, but used as much as they wanted, discreetly covering up each other's indiscretions. They made no contribution to art (except to collect it and keep it where very few could see it), science, or literature, and they were barely a part of the business world. Politics was viewed with abhorrence; a gentleman wouldn't dirty his hands with such vile activity. They added nothing to culture except elevated snobbery and their own stylish, bejeweled selves, who lit up New York whenever they chose to do so.

Except for the need to guard their family graves, the Stewart outrage seemed to have little or no impact on the rich. In their fairy-tale world the ritual events of the seasons had to be honored. Like bees drawn to flowers, they turned out in force with all their finery for the Roosevelt-Astor wedding, which took place at the very fashionable Grace Episcopal Church.

From the long line of elegant carriages to the solemn parade of guests marching two by two into the church and even the extravagant display of priceless gifts, the wedding proceeded magnificently and flawlessly. Gowns and costumes were described in minute and dazzling detail by newspapers covering the wedding. The mother of the bride wore a gown trimmed with 200-year-old lace. Every formality was followed exactly, and everything was perfect—except the weather, something even the rich couldn't control.

Guests included General and Mrs. Philippe DeTrobriand, August Belmont, and Baron Blane and his wife. It was a splashy and powerful display of wealth and prestige the likes of which, from time to time, served to remind New Yorkers that if the United States had a nobility, this was it. It was also a pleasant diversion from the mad pursuit of A. T. Stewart's bones.[2] Of course, had he been alive, Stewart and his wife would probably have not been on the guest list, even though Grace Church stood in the shadow of the Great Iron store.

It wasn't that he went totally unrecognized and ignored. The aristocrats loved to shop in his stores, and Stewart was expected to wait on them personally and with appropriate humility. Aside from that, the Stewarts—like others who attended to needs of the elite—were kept at bay and in their place. Even in the 1870s money couldn't buy everything, for a true gentleman would never introduce a tradesman to another gentleman or a lady. Some honors were bestowed solely by tradition.

The Stewarts and other very rich families rejected by high society had to be content with their own opulent and snobbish lives. During the nineteenth century, in cities throughout the United States, the upper middle class—to which the Stewarts belonged—developed and perfected a rigid code of etiquette that closely imitated the lifestyle of the aristocrats. The money and power of the growing bourgeoisie gave them the ability to spend, build, travel, and party just as lavishly as the New York elite. Indeed, the new rich had everything the old rich possessed except exalted status. While A. T. Stewart chafed and grumbled under these restrictions, most of the new moguls accepted the status quo and enjoyed their wealth.

While the Roosevelt newlyweds embarked on an extended honeymoon trip to Europe, the press and public turned its attention to the court proceedings for Burke and Vreeland, the suspects in the Stewart grave robbery case. The *Times* persisted in its belief that the evidence against them was overwhelming. Strangely, however, when the prisoners were brought before the judge, it was clear that they bore no resemblance to the pair who had appeared the day before. Although this should have prompted some immediate inquiry, the hearing officer, Justice Morgan, had his own agenda. Captain Thomas Byrnes of the New York Police

Department, Fifteenth Precinct, was sworn in and explained the essence of the case against Burke and Vreeland to those assembled.

Byrnes was considered one of the most imposing and skillful detectives on the police force. He immigrated to the United States with his parents, a poor Irish-Catholic couple, and was raised in the Gashouse district of New York. He joined the department in 1863 after mustering out of the army, having fought for the Union (and run in retreat like so many others) in the first Battle of Bull Run. Byrnes' early years were spent patrolling Greenwich Village and lower Fifth Avenue, where he dutifully kept an eye on the mansions of the aristocracy.[3]

Byrnes quickly rose up the ranks because of his success at crime solving. He understood the public's romantic view of crime and its connection to society, and he exploited this fascination to his benefit. Writer Lincoln Steffens called Byrnes "simple, no complications at all—a man who would buy you or beat you, as you might choose, but get you he would."[4] Because of his reputation for using the third degree against recalcitrant suspects, citizens had the right to feel Burke and Vreeland were in big trouble.

Byrnes' first contact was with Burke, who was arrested after he was overheard by a police informant bragging about coming into some money over something that "will astonish the whole country." After some questioning Burke admitted involvement in the Stewart vault robbery, but only after the fact. He was to get a percentage of the ransom for handling the body. He pointed a strong finger of guilt at Vreeland who "was the man who put up the money and did the whole job." He also said he could take Byrnes to where the body was buried. Burke said that Vreeland hired a team and hauled the body from where it had been buried (some twenty miles out in the country) to a place near Chatham, New Jersey.

Burke took Byrnes to Vreeland's home in Brooklyn. Upon entering, Burke told a surprised Vreeland "the jig is up" and they might as well cooperate with the police. Burke was quoted as saying, "This is Captain Byrnes. I guess he's got us dead to rights about stealing Stewart's body."[5]

After some further conversation Vreeland and Burke agreed to take Byrnes to where Stewart's body was hidden. They spoke freely and made several incriminating statements, although they may have actually expected to get the reward. When Byrnes and the suspects were joined by two other officers, Vreeland became nervous. Later he loosened up and remarked that when he was transporting the body "the stiff stunk so that I had to get out and run behind the wagon."

Byrnes and party went first to Orange, New Jersey, and rented a conveyance to take them to Chatham, where Vreeland said the body was buried in a rubber bag near a mill on the Passaic River. They arrived about midnight. Once there and after a cursory look around, Vreeland asked what penalty they could expect for their part in the crime. When told that it was one year and a $250 fine, Vreeland clammed up and suddenly denied any knowledge of the entire affair. Both he and Burke refused to provide any more information, and the party returned to New York without the body.[6]

Byrnes was fudging a bit when he explained the sentence Burke and Vreeland faced for conviction of grave robbery. The actual maximum penalty was five years in prison and a $500 fine for stealing a body to sell for dissection or for "mere wantonness." If a grave was opened and the grave clothes, vestments, or any part of the coffin was taken but the body was not removed, the maximum penalty was a mere two years and a fine of $250. The statute was silent on the subject of ransom or blackmail.[7]

It would be interesting to know what penalty Justice Morgan had in mind when he asked Byrnes whether Vreeland confessed to the actual break-in of the vault. Byrnes unhesitatingly answered no, but was quick to add that Vreeland admitted to having been involved in the crime after the body was taken. Furthermore, the suspects admitted to having the body in their possession at Burke's place, after which it was taken to Chatham. After some ineffectual questioning by the prisoners' attorney, the hearing was closed. Burke and Vreeland were ordered back to jail.

Byrnes, Burke, and Vreeland were among many who tried to steer the search in the direction of New Jersey. Yet knowledgeable people in that state scoffed at the various clues, as some of them were positively ludicrous. For example, the chief of police of Passaic City was induced to dig up a fresh mound of earth in an area frequented by tramps. The reward for his efforts was not the bones of a millionaire but the body of a dog.[8] Most likely there were laughs all around after the disappointment subsided.

The superintendents of the Weehawken cemetery in the village of New Durham and the Hoboken cemetery "laughed very heartily over the idea" that they knew of the body's whereabouts. As for the mysterious Mahoney (also known as Louis Mahon), it was revealed that he had merely made some offhanded remarks about making money with Stewart's remains to his foreman during the course of working at a marble yard connected with the Weehawken cemetery. While Mahoney was a "wild, reckless sort" who had since disappeared, the foreman believed the remarks were in jest and taken too seriously by the New York police.[9]

The aforementioned report was in the *Herald*, which was loath to even mention the *Times* in its columns. (Anyone who read only the *Herald* would be unaware of the existence of the *Times*.) As evidence of the sharp competition between the two newspapers, the *Times* was focusing on a New Jersey solution while the *Herald* was not. There was a strong suspicion that the body had been found there, insisted the *Times*.

There were several cemeteries situated close to Hoboken. In other words, there were plenty of places to a hide the body. A report from Jersey City advised that the body was in a grave "immediately adjoining" the grounds of the Weehawken Cemetery, one of those close to Hoboken, and it was said to be under guard by the police.[10]

This, of course, left people wondering why it was not exhumed and returned to New York immediately. Once again the authorities had the public and the press engaging in more guessing games. The *New York Sun*, like the *Times*, was leaning toward a New Jersey solution, believing that Hilton was tailing Mahoney, planning to make an arrest of the flashy braggart.[11] The obvious question was the one that never seemed to get an answer. Was the body found, in Weehawken or anywhere else in New Jersey?

A *Herald* reporter staked out Hilton's office at the corner of Chambers and Broadway on November 18, where the ex-judge refused to see anyone. His secretary returned the cards of all reporters seeking an interview. The *Herald* reporter stuck it out, however, and cornered Hilton as he was leaving. When asked whether the body had been located at Weehawken and reinterred at the vault in Garden City, as had been reported in the morning papers, Hilton said point-blank, "It is really not true."[12]

The following day, November 19, Burke and Vreeland were brought back to the Jefferson Market Police Court. Before Justice Morgan entered the courtroom, the prisoners chatted freely and eagerly read newspaper accounts of the crime and their alleged participation. They gave the impression they were enjoying themselves.

After Morgan's arrival, Byrnes signed a formal complaint against Burke and Vreeland, accusing them of "acting in concert together, feloniously" to "remove the dead body of a human being from the place of its interment for the purpose [of] selling the same and for the purpose of dissection and with mere wantonness did remove the dead body of the late Alexander T. Stewart from the vault." It further alleged that each man confessed to having "possession of the aforesaid dead body of said Alexander T. Stewart."[13]

Counsel for the defendants, Joseph H. Stiner, was in good humor that day, telling Morgan, "Your Honor, we don't dispute the removal of the body. We simply deny that our clients did the removing." He moved for a dismissal of the complaints because of hearsay testimony offered by Byrnes.[14]

Byrnes seemed determined to pin the crime on Vreeland and Burke, the slick crooks who took him for a useless night ride in the New Jersey countryside. However, under oath and when pressed by Morgan, he was forced to admit that he had nothing to link the suspects to the Stewart crime.

Nevertheless, over Stiner's strenuous objections, Morgan ordered the men held on the charges in the complaint. He denied the motions for dismissal and set bail at $5,000 each, remanding the prisoners to the Jefferson Market Prison.[15] Police records state that Vreeland and Burke were charged with "removing dead bodies from graves."[16]

A reporter for the *Herald* managed to conduct a quick interview with Burke before he was taken away. At first the prisoner said he was warned not to talk to the *Herald*, but then, in the next breath, he spilled his guts. He admitted nothing about the grave robbery, saying only that after coercion by Captain Byrnes, he "acknowledged that we had buried a stiff." However, it was all a gag, as the only "stiff" they buried was a kit of tools, which in a burglar's parlance was called a "stiff." It was all an act, a charade—an angry reaction to the arrest. They were determined to "give him [Byrnes] the kid to his heart's content,"[17] leaving the proud captain and the police with nothing more than embarrassment to show for their efforts.

Unquestionably the whole thing was rather smelly. The grisly crime, the vacant fascination of the public, the irresponsible reporting by the press, and the hapless antics of the police all combined to leave anything but a good impression. It seemed none of the pursuers were up to the challenge of finding the grave robbers.

The press still needed a story, and the celebrities of the moment were interviewed in jail by a reporter from the *Evening Telegram*. Burke proved to be the most talkative. He said he was drunk at the time the police came, and since they were "boring us to death" with questions about the Stewart matter, he and Vreeland retaliated with the ruse about burying a stiff.[18] It may have been great fun, but they landed in jail for their efforts. The authorities were in no mood for pranks.

Believing Vreeland and Burke would soon have company, the *Times* announced that two others had been arrested in connection with the grave robbery, although no names were given. Sticking to its five-man conspiracy theory, this left one man, the so-called "principal," still at large. It was also announced that the reward for the capture of the criminals had been increased to $50,000 for all five and $10,000 for each participant. In doing so, Hilton was giving ground, but it was generally believed that by offering more money, someone with actual knowledge of the conspiracy—if not one of the conspirators himself—would come forth with damaging evidence.

A *Times* reporter, flush with confidence, approached an unnamed man described as one "who has occupied one of the most prominent positions in the chase." The reporter asked point-blank, "Have you found the body?"

After some hemming and hawing, the man said, "Why, of course we have the body, but there are still two men to be arrested." As had happened so many times before, a positive response was quickly followed by a qualifier that raised more questions than it answered. Were the police after one or two more suspects? If the body was recovered, where was it found and why were the authorities so secretive about its location? If the body was safely reinterred, why not just say so?

Henry Hilton was hunted up for yet another round of questioning. He tried to dodge the reporter, saying, "You will have to excuse me. I have made a solemn vow to Inspector Murray not to open my mouth to representatives of the press until this case is concluded."

The reporter knew better and pressed on, advising Hilton of newly gleaned information about suspects still at large. Hilton, on the defensive, said, "Do you know what you are asking me? You say that all the hounds are on the scent, and ask whether they will catch the fox? You cannot expect me to answer!"

"But suppose they fail to catch the fox?" the persistent reporter asked.

Hilton fired back. "What! With the hounds on the scent and the fox in sight, and they near him, and not catch him? There is no such word as fail in this case." End of interview.

It was unusual for Hilton to speak in metaphors, but perhaps he was running low on explanations. Be that as it may, he was not running out of enthusiasm for seeing the great crime brought to a final solution. To that end, Hilton offered generous amounts of money to certain police officials, all of whom reportedly refused; and he had nothing but praise for the work of the department. He paid his own detectives to report to him every day and expended huge sums of money in pursuit of the criminals, with funds that were undoubtedly provided by the Stewart estate.

Despite Hilton's enthusiasm it must have been painfully frustrating to have so much money available and yet not be able to solve this crime. It must have been galling for Hilton and others of high station to be unable to find and jail such hated villains. Hilton probably concluded, to his chagrin, that there was something money could not buy. At this point in the investigation, all he had to show for his efforts and expenditure were two lowbrow suspects with stories of dubious credibility.

Nevertheless, the arrest and testimony of Burke and Vreeland caused another New Jersey sensation. When New York newspapermen arrived at the village of Chatham, New Jersey, on the morning of November 19, citizens of the normally quiet burg were thrown into a state of excitement. Boredom was blasted away as their little town was suddenly the center of one of the great mysteries of the century. Several men with shovels began searching the wooded area by the mill, hoping to find evidence of fresh dirt. The smell of instant fame and reward was in the air, and the rush was on to find the coveted remains of multimillionaire A. T. Stewart. Despite their feverish efforts, all they found was a piece of leather that resembled a portion of a horse harness.

While the excited Chathamites were digging and scouring the land and wading in the Passaic River, the story of the so-called "primary suspect," who was still at large, was coming together in New York. The *Times* would not reveal his name because of a "solemn pledge" made to someone who also remained unnamed. Nevertheless, it was learned that the mystery suspect, apparently a doctor about 50 years old, rented a room about a month before the Stewart incident in a "fashionable" boardinghouse operated by a Mrs. Campbell, which faced St. Mark's churchyard.

The landlady of the third boardinghouse now to come under scrutiny described him as "decently but not extravagantly attired" in a blue flannel suit. She remembered he had striking blue eyes that rolled when he spoke, a fine complexion set off by a silken, brown mustache, and a malformed jaw that he explained was caused by an accidental gunshot. The doctor had the distinctive and strange habit of twitching the left corner of his mouth, a feature that tended to mark his appearance in the memory of others. He claimed to be a native Californian and seemed in every way a gentleman. Immediately after taking the room, he placed an ad in the *Herald* looking for "anybody that will invest $1,000 capital," guaranteeing a "clear profit" of $600 each month.

"Dr. A," as he was called, had several responses to his ad and soon advised his landlady that he was entering a business partnership with one of the respondents, another doctor. Dr. A was a glib talker, fond of anecdotes, and apparently an expert in the use of drugs and medicine. Medical students also boarded at the house, and Dr. A often engaged them in conversation regarding body preservation. He was heard to boast of his ability to deodorize a body no matter how long it had been dead. During his stay he had three regular visitors whom he would meet with in private. His movements on the night of November 6 were unknown, but he disappeared from the boardinghouse sometime before the break-in of the Stewart vault.

Based on sketchy information at best, the *Times* insisted the mysterious Dr. A was the "chief of the entire gang."[19] He was now the focus of the investigation, but was a most elusive subject and not likely to resurface. His ability to remain anonymous and defy apprehension symbolized the entire case. After thirteen days of intense investigation and media pressure, the authorities were, in truth, floundering in the dark, grasping and willing to turn anywhere for any clue and anybody.

A few others were arrested and jailed as "suspicious persons," causing some in the media to speculate that these men were somehow connected with the great grave robbery. Yet, New York had an overabundance of "suspicious persons," so these arrests aroused little attention. Meanwhile, the real grave robbers—whoever they were—remained safe in their hiding places and waited to see if crime would pay, probably enjoying the chaos they unleashed on New York and the nation.

CHAPTER 10

Grave Robber Christian Again

> The alleged chief conspirator and organizer of the robbery of Stewart's grave, was yesterday positively identified as George A. Christian, the notorious Washington resurrectionist.
>
> *New York Times*, November 21, 1878

On November 21 the *New York Times* announced what was considered to be the first real breakthrough in the Stewart case: the naming of George A. Christian as one of the major players. The day before, a *Times* article had focused on the mysterious Dr. A, linking him to the case. Further investigation convinced the police and the *Times* that he was none other than George A. Christian, using the alias "Dr. Douglas." For the first time the police could boast of identifying one of the brains behind the crime.

The *New York Herald* didn't jump on this bandwagon, even though earlier in the investigation it had focused on Christian and his alleged attempt to buy the Allekton concoction from C. N. Middleton. The *Times*, however, thought there was something to the allegations. It said that Christian was one of the suspects in the conspiracy to rob Lincoln's tomb, but failed to elaborate. Nevertheless this added some additional titillation to the story, and Christian's presence in New York at this particular time, coupled with his reputation, could only mean one thing: the notorious Washington Resurrectionist was at it again.

Christian, alias Douglas, alias Dr. A, was "positively identified" by a Miss Thompson, a resident of the Campbell boardinghouse at 306 East Fourteenth Street, and by her gentlemen caller, Dr. George Evans, a Sixth Avenue dentist. Evans and Thompson had frequent contacts with Douglas at the boardinghouse. He was apparently hospitable and chatty and exhibited some superficial knowledge of medicine, but they became suspicious of him because he failed to give a "satisfactory account for himself." Further, he was always at home during the day and away at night, often in the company of strange men of "sporting appearance." This was enough for Evans and Thompson. They decided this was evidence of dubious character.[1]

The landlady certainly harbored that opinion, too. Acting like a proper New York landlady, she became upset when her mysterious boarder took company in his room, insisting that he "receive callers in the parlor and not in his private room." Her other boarders took a cue from his "consequential air" and talkative behavior, and they made Douglas the butt of their jokes.[2]

The suspicious dentist became even more alarmed when he read a newspaper description of Christian and decided that it neatly fit Douglas. It was generally believed that Christian (now called a Cincinnati man) went East in early October. When Evans learned that Christian once worked as a hospital steward and therefore could have picked up some medical knowledge, he concluded that Christian and Douglas were one and the same, down to the rolling eyes and unmistakable twitch of the mouth. Feeling he was on the brink of a great discovery and possibly a handsome reward, Evans consulted with some friends and decided to contact the authorities.

As might be expected, he went not to the police but to Henry Hilton, the keeper of the reward money. There he learned that Douglas was already a suspect, having been seen "on the night of the robbery, leaning against a tree inside the railing of St. Mark's Church-yard." Apparently, Hilton was having Douglas shadowed, perhaps hoping the supposed doctor would lead investigators to other conspirators or to the body.

Evans and Thompson went to police headquarters, hoping to view photographs of Christian, but the police had none. Hilton, however, did have a photograph and sent it to the boardinghouse, where Evans, Thompson, the landlady, and "every other boarder ... positively identified the man in the picture as Douglas." A Pinkerton detective also visited the boardinghouse with two other pictures of Christian, each showing him at a different age. Once again, everyone unhesitatingly identified him as the man they all had come to know as Douglas.[3]

Hilton's son-in-law, Assistant District Attorney Horace Russell, spoke enthusiastically about the mysterious "doctor" and confirmed that Christian, alias Douglas, was a prime suspect. In fact a private detective firm was devoting its entire time and staff toward finding the elusive subject.[4] Russell believed that, though circumstantial, the evidence was sufficient to convict. Expressing a sense of urgency, Russell said, "I wish we had him."[5]

The boardinghouse residents were more than willing to help. Among the faces in the police department's Rogue's Gallery, Evans also picked out two men—one tall and one short—who had frequently visited Douglas at the boardinghouse. The residents also told the police about a strange man known only as "Dr. Blood" (what better name for a ghoul), who was said to have been Douglas' "chief visitor."[6]

The police were given another boost by the landlady's husband, Mr. Campbell, who recalled that an employee of A. T. Stewart was seen in the company of Douglas during the month prior to the vault break-in. This man, whose name was unknown, was also seen near St. Mark's churchyard on the night of the crime. While all this was great news, the police were unable to arrest Douglas or his suspected accomplices because they had disappeared. Nothing could be checked out; nothing could be verified. Another dead end, or so it appeared.

The *Times* continued to hound Hilton, hoping for a scoop, but a weary Hilton was especially hard to get, refusing to talk to the reporter who went to his house. Snubbed, the reporter went to visit a man considered "high in Judge Hilton's confidence" and asked if the body had been located. The man was evasive, refusing to speak factually. He would, however, answer questions based upon his "impressions." When asked if the body had been recovered, Hilton's friend said, "My impression is that the body was found." He further noted that Hilton "has been feeling good for five days," therefore leaving the impression that the body was found five days before.

Sensing a revelation, the reporter pressed. "Was the body found five days ago?"

The man, who was not named, replied matter-of-factly, "Yes the body was found five days ago."

The unnamed informant was quick to add, however, that only a select handful of people knew where the body had been placed. Among them was Mrs. Stewart, who was satisfied that the remains of her dead husband were safe and forever beyond the reach of devious and greedy hands.

"Do you mean that no information will be given to the public of the recovery and burial of the body?" asked the anxious journalist.

"Oh yes," said Hilton's friend, "the public will be fully satisfied, but they will not know of the burial until after it is accomplished."

One could not fault the reporter if he walked away feeling flushed with victory. Still, some sort of corroboration was needed, so he consulted another unnamed man who was also high in Hilton's entourage. This man also asserted that the body had been recovered and could be so reported in the *Times*.

A third unnamed man, also a knowledgeable source, took a different tack by saying, "Matters have been so arranged that Judge Hilton can say truly that the body is not in his possession, and that he does not know where it is. It is in the hands of his agents, and will be produced when the proper time comes." This was yet another serving of tantalizing but contradicting assertions. It was enough to exasperate the most resilient reporter, but it was typical of the fodder that was passed out to the media.

A reporter for the *New York Sun* had different luck. On November 21, 1878, Hilton was interviewed and said point-blank, as if making a painful confession, "We have not found the body; we do not know where it is." The reporter was understandably downcast and concluded that despite the positive rhetoric over the past few days, there was a breakdown of some sort and the trail of the criminals was utterly lost. The massive, well-publicized manhunt, the rewards offered, and the money paid out by Hilton to detectives went for naught. The searchers came up empty, while the schemers and "penniless rogues" were enjoying their notoriety. Men of this stripe had yet to reap the big bucks, but they also had yet to taste the bitterness of failure and disappointment served up to Hilton and the authorities.

The baffled police were described as acting as "dumb as oysters." Other than the mysterious and missing George A. Christian, there was no news about the alleged conspiracy and no information about suspects in or out of custody. While the police had made a number of recent arrests, none were in connection with the Stewart grave robbery. In short, it seemed the police were still very much in the dark—except for the prospect of finding an effervescent man named William H. May.

May was described as a "gigantic Englishman" who, for years, had engaged in the business of making soda water at 30 New Chambers Street. He was a learned man with a glib tongue. He was also a prodigious, habitual drinker, and while in his cups, frequently talked about the Stewart grave robbery and how a man could get rich from it. Patrons of saloons frequented by May recalled that he was greatly affected by the attempt to steal Lincoln's body, causing him to dwell on the topic of grave robbery.[7]

May once told a fellow patron at a saloon that the body could be concealed in an airtight container of soda water and thereby carried away to a secret place. May's credibility, however, was dimmed by his penchant for telling larger-than-life stories.[8] The barroom was his sphere of influence and his pulpit. There he spoke freely and outrageously, enthralling those whom he could entertain or influence and aggravating the rest. Still, the police were interested in talking to him, as someone identified him as one of Douglas' mysterious visitors at the East Fourteenth Street boardinghouse.[9]

While attention was first drawn to May because of stories in New York newspapers, further information emerged from the *Chicago Tribune* that tenuously linked him to the Lincoln tomb break-in and the mysterious Douglas. An article claimed that two men came forward to say that May had approached them with a proposition to join him in a conspiracy to steal Stewart's body, promising that all involved would make a fortune. The men refused.

It was also reported that May subscribed to *Scientific American*, studied chemicals, and bragged about his ability to preserve dead bodies. According to the *Tribune*, he talked so much about grave robbing that his listeners believed he was "out of his head."[10] It was said that the death of his first wife, an Englishwoman who died after making and drinking punch containing carbolic acid instead of brandy, caused him to lose his grip. May talked so much about what he would do with Stewart's body that suspicion was cast upon him after the vault was robbed.

It was revealed that the New York City police first became interested in May on November 13. At that time a couple of detectives were out and about, following up on a letter received by Captain McCullagh. Upon going to the address on the envelope, they questioned two men who admitted knowing May but had not seen him since November 8, a day after the crime. It was ascertained that May left town in a hurry after he transferred all his assets, including his soda water factory, to his landlord to make up back rent. It was believed May had fled to England or Canada.[11]

The police seemed to forget May and instead revived their interest in finding Michael Kelly, the missing hack man, now believed to be alive. They let it be known that Stewart's stolen body was most surely carried away in Kelly's hack. To that end a number of his acquaintances were rounded up and questioned. The jail population was searched, on the possibility that Kelly might have been incarcerated for some other offense. While the search was fruitless, his whereabouts on the night of the crime, combined with his unusual financial windfall and sudden departure, made him a prime suspect. From a variety of leads, the police learned that Kelly had been traced to the Canadian border, where he became another suspect now beyond the reach of the law.

Meanwhile, official interest in the two suspects in custody, Vreeland and Burke, was beginning to dim. The police all but acknowledged that they had arrested the wrong men, for there was nothing of substance to link them to the theft of Stewart's remains. While their statements and the New Jersey escapade tended to incriminate them, the police ruled them out as body snatchers. Burke, it seemed, was especially adept at spinning yarns. He had essentially made a fool out of Captain Byrnes and the New York Police Department, but nothing more. Still, they were retained in the Tombs, one of New York's most infamous prisons, on other charges.[12]

With Vreeland and Burke all but forgotten, the police intensified their search for Christian, the mysterious man "of body-snatching notoriety." Additional leads trickled in indicating that if he was not a grave robber, he was, at best, quite a con man. He claimed to be a graduate of Dublin Medical University, a claim refuted by two medical students at the boardinghouse who actually did graduate from that school. This report appeared in the *Times* on November 23, 1878.[13]

The following day the police announced that they had made another mistake. Douglas was not Christian. They were two distinctly different men, and the mixing of identities and reputations was the result of "boardinghouse gossip." A reputable "gentleman" explained that Douglas, who left the Campbell boardinghouse suddenly at the time of the Stewart outrage, was entirely legitimate, although he bore some resemblance to Christian. To prove it, an indignant Douglas, also known as "Howard" and "Dr. Hatch," surfaced to tell his story.

He spoke to a reporter in Pittsburgh after news broke that a detective named D. M. Terry was looking for him. News "spread like wildfire," and soon everyone in Pittsburgh was talking about the doctor's possible connection with the Stewart crime. It seems that his real name was Hatch, and he used Douglas as an alias, but he was definitely not Christian and was in no way connected with the sordid accusations cast upon him. He denied ever having known Christian.

First, Hatch explained that Terry was not a detective but one of his business partners in a newly formed "patent medicine business." Next, he explained his use of various names while in New York on business. He was trying to raise money for his Pittsburgh-based company. He was party to a business arrangement that included Dr. C. L. Blood, heretofore one of the "mystery men" at the boardinghouse. Hatch's first stop was a boardinghouse on Lexington Avenue, where he placed an ad in the *Herald* under the name of Howard, seeking a "Gentleman" investor interested in taking advantage of "the opportunity of a lifetime."[14]

After about a week of unsatisfactory responses, he aroused the suspicion of the landlady and was asked to leave.[15] Hatch then went to the Campbells' boardinghouse on East Fourteenth Street. He registered as Douglas and again ran ads in the *Herald* to solicit funds for his business. There he met and talked to other guests, including Thompson, who showed an unusual interest in him. As he ignored her, she finally quit talking to him. His regular callers, who others at the boardinghouse assumed were suspicious, were Blood (in no way a ghoul), Terry, and a Connecticut man who was a potential investor.

The clerk at Stewart's store was actually a friend of Mrs. Campbell, and any connection he had with either Hatch or the grave robbery conspiracy was purely fictional. Hatch never saw him. He also denied any connection with Evans—whom Thompson called George—insisting he was never introduced to the man and only spoke to him once in passing. He insisted that he never engaged in conversations about medicine.

When asked by the *Herald*, both Thompson and Evans denied ever having identified Hatch (né Douglas) as Christian. The former merely said that the picture shown to her might possibly bear some resemblance to the man she believed to be Douglas. The latter even denied seeing a photograph.[16] So the story built around their allegations and finger pointing unraveled, leaving another trail of blasted theories. Thompson and Evans were just two more people who would get no reward money, for there was just too little truth to go around.

The proprietress of the Campbell boardinghouse probably had this in mind when she was confronted by a reporter for the *Evening Post*. So bad and widespread was the negative publicity surrounding her mysterious guest that Mrs. Campbell refused to talk to reporters about the sorry episode. The police had instructed her not to submit to an interview, and besides, she didn't want to talk about Christian, Douglas, Hatch, or anyone else connected with the terrible crime. She only wanted to forget the incident and get back to operating a respectable boardinghouse.[17]

Hatch, too, was fed up with it all. He said his departure from the boardinghouse on November 6 was not done by stealth at night but as the result of plans others at the boardinghouse, including Mrs. Campbell, were aware of. It was not until he reached Pittsburgh and received a telegram from Blood that he knew he was a suspect in the Stewart grave robbery. Appalled at such an assault on his character, he wanted desperately to clear his name. In doing so, he exploded the Christian story, blasting it right out of the news.

The *Times*, at least, gave him the benefit of the doubt. Hatch, age 39, was a native New Yorker with piercing blue eyes, an unmistakable twitch in his jaw (the sole feature he shared with Christian), and a stare that seemed to drain the thoughts of the interviewer. He did not, however, "look in the least like a grave-robber." However, the *Times* and, apparently, the police stopped short of an apology.[18] Nevertheless, Hatch openly expressed a willingness to return to New York and talk to the police. They said don't bother, it was a mistake, just leave it at that.[19]

The *Herald* was on to this latest mistake ahead of the *Times*. On November 22, 1878, the *Herald* advised its readers that the police were in error and that its reporters were searching out Blood and Hatch. Although this revelation meant another avenue of the investigation was sidetracked, the reporters apparently thought it would be interesting to get the reaction of these wrongly accused gentlemen. After all, an accusation of this sort at this time was of epic and shocking proportions. It was not the kind of activity anyone wanted on his resumé.

Blood proved to be very elusive, but he left a record of residences all over the city. It was rumored that he had secured the rights to a "system of purifying the blood" through a treatment called "oxygenized air" and was out and about promoting it for royalties. It was believed that this project led him to Hatch, alias Douglas, who was interested in cashing in. A reporter tracked Blood from one boardinghouse to another, only to find that he had moved.[20]

When the reporter finally found a man who admitted he was Blood, it was at a fine brownstone house at 28 East Twenty-first Street in New York. He was large and well built with a "great head, covered with a leonine mane of raven black hair." He spoke freely of Hatch, whom he had known for about five years. He called Hatch a man with an impeccable reputation and a "regular physician." He said Hatch's departure from New York on the night of the Stewart vault break-in was purely coincidental and for business purposes.

Blood laughed a hearty laugh when the reporter reminded him that Evans, the dentist, had identified Hatch as the evil Christian—and he had an explanation for it. He said Evans developed a dislike for Hatch because the latter displayed some undue romantic interest in Thompson. One evening Evans saw Hatch and Thompson "very close together in the parlor." Evans was irked, and in his jealous state of mind, he conveniently concluded that Hatch was Christian. Accuse your rival of being a grave robber—what a novel way of eliminating competition for the hand of a lady. The reporter was impressed with Blood's assertions, and when he left, he was convinced that Hatch was not the notorious Christian and had nothing whatsoever to do with the nocturnal crime in St. Marks' churchyard.[21]

A reporter from the *Evening Post* came to the same conclusion, although he obtained some additional details. Blood told the *Post* reporter that he had known Hatch since 1873 and that Hatch had recently returned from California, where he had been living with his invalid wife. After his wife died of consumption, Hatch left California and returned to New York in October, just in time to be caught up in the Stewart mystery.

Blood was shown a photograph of Christian and quickly pointed out the many ways in which the face of the resurrectionist differed from that of his friend Hatch. The eyes, the nose, the hair—all were dissimilar. If there was any similarity at all, it was in the breadth of the forehead and in the lower lip, which in both men twisted to one side. Blood also pointed out that Hatch was a "perfect walker," whereas Christian was noted for his shuffling gait and lowered head. Clearly, there was no connection between the two men.[22]

If anyone needed any further corroboration, it came from Superintendent Walling in an interview with the *Evening Express*. He knew that Hatch was using the aliases Howard and Douglas. Walling also said he knew a man who was acquainted with both Hatch and Christian, and "I am positive they are not one and the same."[23]

With Hatch and his associates in the clear, where would the police turn for suspects? That question was answered by a group of detectives from Washington DC, who boldly advanced their theory of the case. They settled on a five-man conspiracy consisting of Christian, "a dissolute character named Dr. Crow," Percy Brown (who had assisted Christian in the past), New York soda water maker William H. May, and a professional gambler whom they called "Canada Mack." The last was said to have worked as a salesman for A. T. Stewart and Company.

Most of the suspects were as obscure as they could be, but Christian was more susceptible to suspicion because of his reputation. The odd and illusive Christian was described as an especially daring grave robber, a genuine creature of the night with a raw passion for body snatching. This was belied by his reticent manner, downcast expression, and his peculiar, rolling shuffle with his hands in his pockets.

The *New York Sun* revealed that in 1873 Christian was actually a medical student at Georgetown College, under the tutelage of Dr. John F. Dunphy. Although he never finished, he showed promise as a doctor and apparently relished dissection, yet he stole bodies for excitement as much as for dissection. On more than one occasion he was suspected of robbing graves in Potter's Field in the District of Columbia, and his arrest and imprisonment for body stealing foreclosed any chance at becoming a doctor.[24] He was also linked to the John Harrison grave robbery in Ohio, one of the most daring and outrageous resurrections of the 1870s.[25]

While the *Sun* displayed little faith in a conspiracy theory, the *Herald* was hot on the idea. Christian was an obvious candidate because he was identified as the man who attempted to buy the Allekton body preservative. He was also believed to be the man who bought the lantern and shovel found at the crime scene. Crow was known to be a confederate of the notorious Christian, the pair having teamed up once before in Washington DC. Crow supposedly met Canada Mack in New York, and the two hatched the plan. Years before, Canada Mack was reported to have bragged about a plan to kidnap Stewart and hold him for ransom. Crow brought Christian into the plan to steal Stewart's body because of the latter's skill in this line of work. Then Christian recruited his old brother in crime, Percy Brown, an ugly man who dressed well and was unafraid of handling the dead. The detectives did not mention how May was involved in the conspiracy.

Washington detectives further explained that Douglas (who later turned out to be Hatch) was really Crow. His advertisements for an investor were for the purpose of soliciting funds to promote a new gambling game, like keno, that he invented. Percy Brown was said to be the tall, bald-headed man who visited Douglas at the boardinghouse. As the detectives saw it, he was the one who did the digging atop Stewart's vault. The body was taken away in a carriage by Canada Mack and shipped to Canada from the Forty-second Street depot. The driver of the carriage was Michael Kelly, that mysterious hack man whose reputation as a bad character was just then soaring. Kelly's mysterious visitor at Graham's stable was either Christian or Crow.[26] Find these men and you've got your suspects.

The Washington detectives delivered their loose-knit theory to the *New York Herald*. Upon examination, the *Herald* called it plausible and published the story on November 23, 1878. The *Washington Post*, however, downplayed the notion that Christian was involved. An article in the *Post* revealed that his brother came forth and stated that the "notorious" George Christian was in Iowa at the time of the crime, and besides, he stole bodies for dissection, not for ransom.[27]

Probably because there was never any proof that Christian was in New York, police there were not interested in theories advanced by their Washington brethren. It seemed they were unimpressed with a theory that was weak on supporting evidence, or maybe they looked upon it as an unwarranted intrusion.

While the *Washington Post* made no attempt to connect Christian with the infamous New York grave robbery, it published a horrific report on the theft of Stewart's body—John Stewart's body, that is. This grave robbery was rather routine, but events immediately following the digging and transporting of the body were so shocking that the public and media were aroused and angered.

John Stewart, a black man, age 65, died of consumption and was buried in Harmonial Cemetery, where many other African Americans were interred. His body was taken from the grave by two other black men, whose intentions were to deliver it to the Georgetown medical school. According to the *Post*, the grave robbers were liquored up. In their drunken state they thought they had stopped the buggy in front of the medical school, but, as it turned out, they were one door short of their destination.

Thinking they were at the door to the medical school, they knocked, and when the door was opened, the two men tossed the body inside with the expectation that someone would be waiting to receive it. Unfortunately for them the badly rotted corpse collided with a female tenant who happened to be in the hallway. Her screams aroused other tenants of the apartment building. Hearing this, the body thieves ran off, and soon thereafter the police arrived. It didn't take long for the police to determine that the grave robbers knocked on the wrong door. The mistake caused great consternation among the residents of the tenement, and many of them went screaming into the night, yelling "murder" and "police."

The Washington version of the Stewart grave robbery faded rather quickly, for the *Post* did not expand much space beyond its original story, except to say that the nation's capital was the scene of a "systematic plan of grave robbing." Despite this the *Post* concluded that the police would not likely be too interested in solving this crime because the "subjects" were black people.[28]

In New York the emphasis was, of course, on the other Stewart grave robbery. The press and the police there showed no interest whatsoever in the John Stewart incident, despite its bizarre and almost comic qualities. Nor was there any interest in pursuing the Christian/Crow conspiracy worked up by the Washington detectives.

Had that theory held any interest for the New York police, it would not have been of much use since the men accused were, for all practical purposes, invisible. While others may have agreed that they were the nefarious cast of guilty characters, it did no good, for no one could find them. It was useless to pursue Christian as a suspect because no one could find him, and besides, there was no real evidence, beyond his reputation, to tie him to the crime.

The city was lousy with men who had the nervy, desperate look of a grave robber. The police were stymied, overwhelmed perhaps, by the sheer number of wild-eyed men who were eager for a caper and easily led by the clever minds of a Christian or a Crow. Who were they anyhow?

Amid a shifting mass of scheming men on the brink, gathered in taverns, cheap hotel rooms, tenements, and dank cellars, how could one select suspects from among them?

For the police and others still searching for someone—anyone—who looked "like a grave-robber," it was time to pause and reflect. At this point, the investigation was more a farce than a professional effort, and the police were greatly embarrassed. A few men were arrested without grounds and were quickly released. A twenty-five-year newspaper reporter named Kate Cross was arrested and held as a "suspicious person" in connection with the Stewart grave robbery, but the "fashionably dressed" lady was quickly and quietly released. The *Evening Telegram* said it was a case of "mistaken identification."[29]

In a chaotic spiral of mistakes, names, rumors, reputations, long days, dark nights, false leads, and dead ends, the investigation was wildly and helplessly spinning out of control, looking for a place to crash.

A sense of futility set in, and the police department pulled most of its detectives from the quixotic quest and put them on other assignments. A small contingent was left in the hands of Inspector Murray and Captain Kealy of the central office. The police and Hilton's army of private detectives had failed, and in the process, they boldly and openly lied and misled the press and public. Although they would later claim otherwise, they never had any legitimate suspects and no idea as to the whereabouts of the body.

The *Times* too, seemed exhausted and frustrated but apparently felt no concern for printing unsubstantiated stories, which some may have considered examples of irresponsible journalism. Instead it all but dropped the matter, following a rather garbled and obscure editorial that expressed both anger and shame over the whole sordid affair and took the public to task for its prolonged and intense interest in the matter.

While barbaric in the extreme, the *Times* recognized that grave robbing was an accepted fact of life—like lynchings, poverty, slums, and political corruption. In the age of enterprise, dead bodies were obtained, sold, and shipped like a commodity. In a bizarre spin on the capitalist concept, cemeteries had become the basis for a horrid enterprise. Worse than that, however, it was the public's mixed attitude toward the nefarious activity that was more in need of change. The *Times* concluded that the peoples' attitude had become obsessive, unnatural, and demeaning and that their anger and blame were unevenly applied.

Let the "obscure and friendless" man die in a "charity hospital," said the *Times*, and his body goes straight to a medical college dissecting room. The "prowling resurrectionist" can "rifle the tombs of wretches" (since when were wretches laid to rest in tombs?) and no one is particularly upset, but "woe to the men" who would disturb the "noble dust of Alexander."[30] These men earned a certain high stature, not for what they had done but because of the personality involved. In life, Stewart had attained mythical proportions because of his great wealth and its impact on the American economy and culture. As Stewart was not just another man, his dust was not ordinary dust.

The *Times* was not, however, trying to diminish Stewart's legacy—it would endure although his remains may rot in an unmarked grave. The message was simply this: let there be an end to it. Let there be an end to the search and the public's fascination with it. If the body were not located after an intense, albeit bumbling, search, then in all likelihood it would not be found. Better that all concerned forget about Stewart's body and remember the man. In time every trace of the physical person disappears, be it in a peaceful country cemetery, a magnificent urban vault, the ocean waters, or on a bed of leaves in a remote, wilderness ravine. Recovering Stewart's bones so they could be placed in a lavish monument would not make him immortal, nor would it make the monument more impressive to look at. It would not change anyone's perceptions of the man or affect his role in history.

What the *Times* failed to consider, however, was that people found genuine comfort in knowing their loved ones were securely buried in a grave—a grave that became identified as the deceased person. It was a sense of place, of continuity, where all memories endured without interruption or interference.

The *New York Times* was a proud and confident newspaper long before it adopted the motto, "All the news that's fit to print." In a time when papers were the sole medium for news, it took its leadership role seriously. For nearly three weeks of the investigation, the *Times* staff was steadfast in its search for a solution. Yet one senses that the Stewart case—with its heavy emphasis on the morbid—placed the city in the throes of a mystery so nauseous, atmospheric, and dark as to cause even the men of the *Times* to wish it would all suddenly end.

The staff of the *Herald* had similar sentiments, but in its columns serious reporting gave way to humorous articles that expressed a sense of frustration. After investigating an unnamed cooper who disappeared with a body, a *Herald* reporter discovered that there was some truth in the story. The fifty-two-year-old cooper did indeed disappear with a body, leaving behind a wife and family. The body was that of a young widow of twenty-seven who was "still alive and kicking."[31]

Clearly, those enmeshed in a situation with so much emphasis on the morbid could benefit from some warm, comic relief. The Stewart mystery was like a dark, dangerous storm that raged over the city for so long, leaving everyone longing for laughter and light.

CHAPTER 11

The Investigation Winds Down

> There is absolutely nothing new to communicate in relation to the profanation of Mr. Stewart's grave.
>
> Henry Hilton, *New York Herald*, November 25, 1878

Hilton's quote in the *Herald* was supported by Henry Clair in a short interview with the *Tribune*. Clair, manager of two of Hilton's hotels, was believed to be the mystery man who was sent to New Jersey to claim Stewart's body when most of the focus was on the other side of the East River. Clair flatly denied having anything to do with the matter, saying, "I have never sought for, nor recovered, nor did I know anything about the body of Mr. Stewart, except what I read in the newspapers." Displaying disinterest and irritation, Clair said he was far too busy managing Hilton's hotels to be involved in spooky detective work.[1]

The press was losing interest, too. On November 25, 1878, the *New York Times* gave the Stewart investigation short shrift for the first time since the shocking story broke. Instead of a long column packed with details, a small article was printed under the headline, "Miscellaneous

City News." Much of the article was taken up by a clue from, of all places, Brownsville, Nebraska:

> Mayor New York City: DEAR SIR:
>
> I am personally acquainted with the body-snatchers of A. T. Stewart. I know where body is and all parties concerned. I ask no reward. But A Pardon [sic] and will Expose all as they have betrayed me if a pardon be granted. Telegraph to Omaha Bee, Omaha, Neb., and I will give myself up to the officials of that city or appear in New York if assured no harm may befall me.
>
> AN ASSISTANT OF THE CREW

It was another erratic tidbit to add to the collection of nonsense that fattened the files of the Stewart investigation. While the desire to find the remains and claim the reward was still in the public's mind, people were far less hopeful.

Mrs. Stewart's hopes, too, had all but vanished. A lonely, childless widow, she had suffered in silence, becoming very ill and feeble while her closest friends feared for her survival.

The Stewart's were a close-knit couple, having had only each other for so many years. Though it seemed he was not an affectionate man, he treated her with respect. All in all, she had sufficient reason to miss him. Among her memories she most certainly recalled the early years of their marriage when they lived in one room above their first store. There she worked by his side well into the night, stocking shelves, arranging merchandise, and becoming accustomed to his meticulous manner.

Now she languished in her magnificent mansion, as her luxurious surroundings were no match for her sorrow and the aching in her heart. The loss of her beloved husband's body meant she had to endure his death for a second time. Like other victims of this kind of crime, she was brought down and made helpless and ordinary. She desperately longed for the return of her husband's body and its final interment in the great mausoleum at the Garden City Cathedral of the Incarnation. She may also have longed for her own death.

According to an article in the *Tribune*, Mrs. Stewart had received no information to convince her that the body had been recovered, thus ending the speculative talk about its recovery. Mrs. Rylance, wife of the rector at St. Mark's church—who had close contact with Mrs. Stewart—said the bowed and beaten widow would gladly give up the $50,000 reward if it meant the return of her husband's body. For her, it was a small price to pay for the peace of mind she so desperately needed.[2]

Unfortunately for Mrs. Stewart, neither the police nor the press were able to help her, and Hilton expressed no willingness to make a deal with the thieves should the opportunity present itself. For her it was only money, and she could easily part with it. For Hilton it was money that he refused to part with, probably because it would come out of his pocket, as he had control of the Stewart fortune and treated it as his own.

Hilton's motives were probably understood by the press, although it would be years before he would be taken to task for his selfishness. Instead, the media continued to look for leads as the contest for a solution struggled forward.

In this contest the *New York Herald* seemed to best the *Times* and other newspapers when it came to ferreting out and interviewing people with tantalizing stories to tell. In one such interview, the much sought after Dr. Crow spoke his piece. He readily admitted that he was a resurrectionist and was once in partnership with George A. Christian. Crow said he was available to deliver stiffs for $25 each and seemed to treat the interview as a chance to advertise his services. Still, he would not discuss the Stewart case, except to say that he would undertake to find the remains for a mere $100,000.

Crow openly and proudly boasted of his skill as a grave robber. He had been at it for the past twenty-five years and had "raised fifty or sixty stiffs every winter and [unlike Christian] never got caught." Before that he graduated from the Jefferson Medical College of Philadelphia and was the chief editor for the *Washington Daily News*. Other than that he claimed he invented a gambling game called Centennial that caused him to run afoul of the law. He didn't seem to mind, however. At this point the merry Crow was more of a barroom celebrity than a suspect.[3]

On December 2, Michael Kelly, the hack man, was reprised, briefly. On that day Peter Relyen, an undertaker, visited Inspector Dilks and rather ardently explained why he felt Kelly was the key to the mystery. Relyen insisted that Kelly was a close associate of the grave robbers, that he was "indirectly connected with the removal of the remains," and that he frequently drove the body snatchers about town in his hack. He believed Kelly was not in Canada, the Black Hills of Dakota Territory,

California, or Washington DC, but in New Jersey, in the company of one of the criminals who had sufficient money to support them all.

When Relyen told his story to a reporter for the *Times*, he was asked why he withheld his information for so long. Reylen replied that he had a business to operate and could not afford to travel about the country "playing detective." He expected the police to do that. Dilks declined to give the story any credibility, doubting that Kelly had any connection with the grave robbers. While he was reasonably certain that the slovenly Kelly was a shady character and wanted him arrested, he was of the opinion that the hack man was not smart enough to run with the men who stole Stewart's body.[4] Still, up to this time he was too smart to be detected, even though the Pinkertons were on his trail.

The disappearance of Stewart's body caused cemetery officials in the East to think about security. It seems that in addition to feeling unsafe in their streets and homes, many felt that even in the grave, people were not safe. In Philadelphia, where there was no official policy for protecting the buried, many cemeteries took matters into their own hands. Armed guards patrolled day and night, especially around the graves of the rich. Dogs were let loose within the fences, and in some cases, caretakers, guards, and their families lived in the cemeteries, where their vigilance and alarm systems were counted on to discourage body snatchers. Receiving vaults were checked regularly, especially during the night, and equipped with combination locks or double locks. Newly made graves were watched with extra caution.

At Philadelphia's Woodlands Cemetery, an intricate security system was devised and implemented by the family of recently deceased millionaire Thomas Powers. His grave, and that of his son who died in 1873, were guarded twenty-four hours a day, with two men on duty at night. Their watch was meticulously scheduled and recorded, checked and double-checked. The relatives wanted to leave nothing to chance, as they feared the coming of the resurrectionists.

Another Philadelphia cemetery, West Laurel Hill Cemetery, was located next to a mill that ran all night and cast a bright light on the grounds. The light was such that the superintendent, who lived in the cemetery, could see well enough to "pick up a pin from the porch floor." The doors of the receiving vaults were hermetically sealed. There were nine men and five dogs stationed within the cemetery walls, and attached to the superintendent's house was a wire hooked up to a "gong of sufficient power to startle the whole neighborhood."

Experienced cemetery men generally believed that such detailed precautions were unnecessary in most cases, but they went along with them to placate fearful relatives. Still, they were especially watchful in those instances when someone died of an unusual disease and the family had denied an autopsy. It was feared that doctors would be tempted to steal those bodies. In such cases, the bodies were often stored in receiving vaults for many months.[5]

As December lengthened over New York, the Stewart case was all but forgotten, as if everyone had signaled for surrender. Winter, as usual, brought forth other demands. Some members of the press took to satire, as if to pillory the police and their flimsy theories and disconnected suspects. In one such tongue-in-cheek article, a wiseacre reporter slyly suggested that three well-known men, namely Whitelaw Reid, Reverend DeWitt Talmage, and George Francis Train, were the guilty parties.

The energetic Reverend Talmage was suspected because on the evening of the grave robbery, he was out all night after telling his wife he had to pick up some materials for a sermon. As he left the house, he was whistling, "O, I'm one of the boys." This is probably a reference to his habit of making on-site inspections of saloons and the like.

Although the Stewart investigation was at a standstill, Talmage's very personal harangue against urban evil was moving forward. The reverend's constant finger-pointing and overzealous nature made the lovable sin chaser an ideal candidate for satire.

George Francis Train, a rich author and clipper ship trade promoter, was suspect because, a week before the crime, he was seen in a hardware store buying a spade on credit. Further, on the day before the ghastly business he was seen on a city bench singing lines from the graveyard scene in Shakespeare's "Hamlet."

Train was better known throughout the United States as the quirky, eccentric promoter and financier of the Union Pacific Railroad. Train's overblown view of his importance to the country and his tendency to engage in flowery, cascading speeches must have convinced the satirist to give him a starring role in the farce.

The evidence against Whitelaw Reid was equally powerful. On the evening before the vault was violated he was seen walking out of a saloon carrying a copy of the *Herald*—the same date as the one found at the St. Mark's crime scene—and "when he supposed no one was watching, [he] placed three cardamom seeds in his mouth and walked rapidly away."[6]

Whitelaw Reid was known as the circumspect editor of the *New York Tribune*, having succeeded the late Horace Greeley. His newspaper took other members of the press to task, calling them "romance writers" who offered unfounded, fanciful theories about the Stewart investigation. Reid laid claim to the high road, distancing himself from what he called "*The Daily Slop Pail*" and "*The Morning Screamer*," refusing to publish startling developments until they could be substantiated.[7] Although he was known for his journalistic good taste, not everyone thought he was pure, and now it was his turn to feel the editorial lash.

There was comedy as well as frustration in the article. It indicated how the press and the people felt about the police investigation, which was perceived as an inept and bungling piece of work that left everyone frustrated and unfulfilled. The treasure hunt had yielded no treasure and no reward. There was no satisfaction, only a lingering sense of discomfiture. The ghouls were still out there, and Stewart was not truly at rest. It only remained to make fun of it as a postmortem.

The general impression from among the press was that the police were no match for the body snatchers. With few exceptions the detectives were unqualified for the tasks placed in their hands. Since many were given their jobs by politicians who owed them a favor, they were necessarily hampered by the lack of professional ethics, intelligence, and training. The *Herald* declared that it was "almost impossible for the ordinary detective to steal a march upon a bright bank robber, forger or ressurrectionist."[8] Easily spotted and identified as "ward" detectives, these egotistical but clueless cops were constantly pursuing false leads that sputtered out ingloriously and to their eternal discredit. While they tried to buffalo the press and public, it was the police who fumbled and muddled until the once-in-a-lifetime case—screaming for a solution—gradually sank under its own weight and fell silent.

The newspapers too, were anything but blameless. Jacob A. Riis, the able police reporter for the *New York Tribune*, recalled that many journalists engaged in sensationalist articles with little or no foundation, seeking to prolong the mystery for the sake of selling newspapers. While Riis went on to become one of America's most respected journalists and social reformers, he was not happy with the level of reporting during the vexing Stewart investigation. He called it the "dawn of yellow journalism."[9]

No further arrests were announced, and although Burke was held on unrelated charges, Vreeland was released. There was no further mention of George A. Christian, William H. May, or any other name connected with the events of November. Besides, May had a good alibi, having been seen by several firemen at the scene of a fire on the night of the crime.[10]

Michael Kelly, the hack man, was traced by detectives to Arizona. All chances at questioning him ended, however, when he was killed in a fight.[11] Was Kelly the man with the horse and the hack that carried Stewart's body away that cold and rainy November night? It appears there will never be an answer to that question.

The weird letters stopped coming, and the clairvoyants and spiritualists seemed to lose interest. Henry Hilton turned his attention to managing the Stewart empire, although there were those who believed he was engaged in a massive mismanagement. Aside from another episode of infuriating the Jews, he, too, dropped from public view and probably enjoyed the respite.

Then, while interest was fading in New York City, private detectives in Virginia were reportedly on a mission, feeling confident that Stewart's remains were planted in the "Old Dominion." A short article appeared in the *New York Herald* on December 10, 1878, casting additional suspicion on Christian. Other than pointing a finger at the noted resurrectionist, the secretive correspondent would only say that the body was concealed somewhere along the Rappahannock River. He was "not at liberty to indicate it more closely."[12]

On December 11, 1878, the *Herald* followed this with a story about two mysterious strangers who supposedly buried a box on the banks of the Rappahannock near Fredericksburg, Virginia, site of one of the great and bloody battles of the Civil War. A pair of New York private detectives were smelling out this latest clue.[13] They claimed to be in the employment of some relatives of A. T. Stewart.

The flurry of publicity caused public focus to shift to Virginia. Once again, even the flimsiest evidence was enough to arouse dreamers, eager journalists, and fortune hunters, including the New York private detectives. These secretive men were found by a reporter for the *Herald* at their campsite on Beck's Island, close to the area where some believed a mysterious box had been buried. The detectives were patiently enduring the rigors of the December cold when the reporter, disguised as "an herb hunter, with pick and knife," found them in the woods.

After a short chat with the reporter, the detectives revealed the object of their quest and showed him some documentation that allegedly came from friends of the Stewart family. They were to earn $40,000 should they return with the body of A. T. Stewart. They were induced to come to Virginia because of a corpse carried there from New York City on a strange vessel. They tracked it to the banks of the Rappahannock River. According to the intrepid reporter, the two detectives quit their search and returned to New York after heavy rains washed away evidence of any potential recent burial sites, but the reporter was certain they would return.[14]

The following day, however, cold water was poured all over this story, too, due to the efforts of the *Herald* correspondent. Soon after the December 12 edition of the *Herald* hit the streets of Fredericksburg, an aroused public bought every paper. This sent a group of men scouring the cliffs above Fredericksburg, looking for that mysterious box. The unwanted company caused the two detectives to leave the area, and as the locals were unable to find anything, the matter was quickly forgotten.[15] Folks were left with thoughts of the mysterious box and a strange vessel seen moving in and out of the mouth of the Rappahannock River.

On December 13, 1878, the *New York Times* noted that a Connecticut man was apprehended with a body in a trunk. He was questioned but released, for all he had was ordinary graveyard plunder, probably stolen from a cemetery in Bridgeport, Connecticut. It was not the valuable remains of A. T. Stewart. The tired *Times* called it a "relic of the Alexander case." The man was not arrested.[16]

This and similar stories prove only one thing. The public's attachment to the mystery was so strong and official interest was so intense that suspicion was cast far and wide, and people were willing to go anywhere to hunt down even the most absurd clues. As one newspaperman stated, "Every whisper that could be distorted into a clue was run to earth" by eager participants in this drama.[17]

In Chicago, a small boy sang, "John Brown's body lies a moldering in the grave," as he walked down State Street on a bleak December day in 1878. From the shadows, a sad voice said, "Don't be too sure; it might be in a grave, or on a dissecting table." Nobody can tell, the man advised.

"Look at A. T. Stewart." The boy ceased to sing, and the "dismal-voiced figure disappeared in the darkness,"[18] as if to symbolize the doubt and bewilderment of every man. In the 1870s, both life and death were fraught with terrible uncertainties.

This was especially true in 1878, when grave-robbing activity seemed to hit its peak, topped by the Stewart investigation. So it is only fitting that the year should end with news of yet another grave robbery, this one unusually sad. In the middle of the holiday season a girl's body was taken from the family vault in the Bohemian Catholic Cemetery on the "Milwaukee Avenue plank road" about ten miles outside of Chicago.

The girl, about twelve years old, was known in life as Mathilda Stribing. She died of typhoid fever after it seemed she would recover. After she passed away on a Wednesday, her body was placed in the family vault on the following Saturday afternoon. That night the resurrectionists arrived as if on cue. The dog of the sexton, who lived on the cemetery property, suddenly began barking about midnight, pulling hard against the chain and struggling to get free. The sexton looked outside but saw nothing to arouse his suspicion. The dog persisted, but its anxious behavior was ignored. About an hour later the sexton heard the sound of some type of conveyance passing near his house.

The next morning he discovered that the door of the vault had been "forced open with powerful jimmies improvised for the occasion." Upon entering the vault he saw an open, empty coffin in the company of many others that were undisturbed. The sexton then understood why his dog barked so long and so furiously. Footprints in the snow gave evidence that two grave robbers had entered the vault and carried away the girl's body. It was surmised that they were after the girl only, as there were about twenty other bodies in the vault "in a good state of preservation."

It was also reported that the thieves may have attended the funeral and saw where the body had been placed by the cortege. The article mildly implicated the undertaker and the funeral director, suggesting that one or the other may have, "in some indirect manner," tipped off the thieves. At about 1 a.m. the morning following the body theft, a tollgate keeper saw a one-horse sleigh occupied by two men and a bundle pass by, moving toward the city. The authorities were alerted to this, but as the description of the cutter, its horse, and occupants was so vague, it was of little value.

For the family of the girl whose body was stolen, the holiday season was dismal in the extreme. The child's mother's suffering had been so great that she was not told about the body snatching, for it was feared that she might succumb to death if she learned about the ghoulish business in the cemetery that winter night. The police promised to initiate a thorough investigation and "at all hazards, recover the body."[19]

It was a dull response masked with enthusiasm. The promise seeped out of the sad article and fell flat with an all-too-familiar thud of futility, while the image of the resurrectionst took on a semblance of invincibility as the year ended.

CHAPTER 12

First Contact with the Ghouls

> The story of the theft of the body of Alexander T. Stewart ... has been again brought forward in such a shape that it once more becomes a theme of newspaper discussion.
>
> *New York Times*, August 14, 1879

The search for the remains of A. T. Stewart was renewed in January 1879 after a late-December letdown. Nevertheless, it took the newspapers many months to either get the word or realize the significance of the new clues. By August, when the *Times* and other newspapers finally got around to reporting the events of January, the story was stale and the mystery still unsolved. Yet the reports provide another tantalizing and important chapter in the search for a resolution to the infamous crime.

From the time the police scaled back their efforts toward finding the remains and arresting the thieves to mid-August 1879 when the story broke anew, many believed that the body had been recovered. They believed it would soon be placed inside the crypt of the Cathedral of the Incarnation, which was under construction at Garden City on Long Island.

Although she was still well protected, Mrs. Stewart had appeared in public. She displayed a more cheerful, positive outlook, visiting friends and engaging in other activities denoting normalcy. Hilton had placed four watchmen at the crypt to stand guard twenty-four hours a day. While

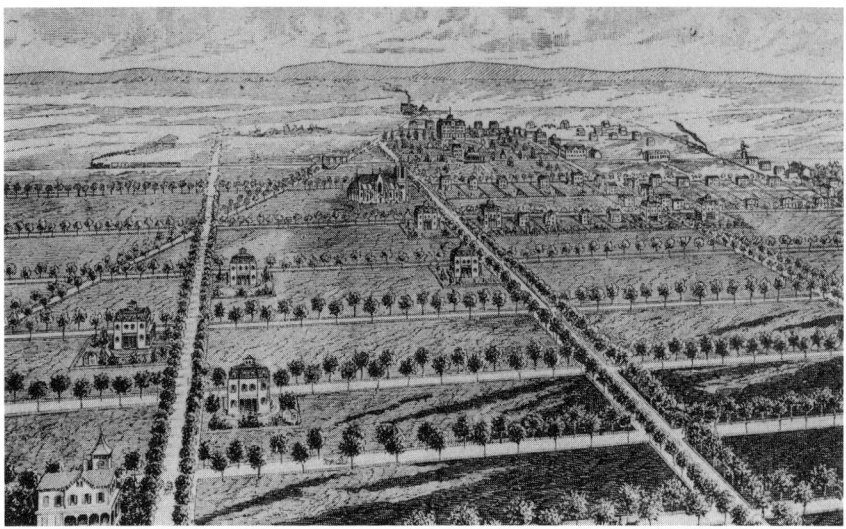

Garden City, New York, looking north, ca. 1880. Image courtesy of Garden City Archives.

these factors were not the best evidence of a solution, many people thought the mystery had run its course. Although none of the grave robbers were brought to justice, Stewart's bones were at peace—or so it seemed.

The public turned its attention away from St. Mark's and toward the cathedral in Garden City. Each day great numbers of people came, as if on a pilgrimage, some from long distances. Their numbers swelled the ranks of guests at the Garden City Hotel, which annoyed the workers who were valiantly trying to finish the "graceful pile" that was intended to house the remains of A. T. Stewart and, in due time, those of his faithful widow.

Some speculated that Stewart's body had already been concealed in the lavish vault, although it was still under construction. What a vault it was! Finely sculpted with white American marble and shaped in the form of a polygon, it was twenty-two feet in diameter and twenty feet high. Placed under the chancel, it was a massive and opulent ornament to immortality, with nine windows and two approaches leading to grand vestibules that connected it to the sanctuary above.[1] Take that, Mr. Astor!

The magnificence alone would have drawn admiring crowds to the open Hempstead Plains. Yet, it was for the Stewart mystery that they came, quietly and in wide-eyed amazement, gazing at the gargoyles and other frills that adorned the church and mausoleum. Others combed the area with the zeal of souvenir hunters, breaking off delicate pieces of stone tracery. The tourist problem got so bad that those in charge came up with a secret password that had to be given to gain entrance to the mortuary chapel. The password was rigidly enforced so that "Judge Hilton himself would find it difficult to gain admittance without giving the word."[2]

Still the visitors came. Being there, in the presence of an architectural wonder, seemed to give many a sense of peace and closure, while others found a deeper sense of mystery. One amazed visitor at the crypt was overheard to say, in reference to Stewart's body, "Where do you suppose

Cathedral of the Incarnation. Photo by John Ellis Kordes.

it can be?" Others speculated that the body had to be nearby because of the energetic pace of the workmen.[3]

Then in July 1879, Police Superintendent George W. Walling made a public statement, saying he now believed the remains of A. T. Stewart had not been recovered.[4] Walling's statement was corroborated by two reporters for the *Tribune* who went to the Garden City Cathedral. They were allowed to go down into the mausoleum, and after a look around, they departed believing the burial chamber was empty.[5]

Next the *Times* interviewed ex-New York postmaster turned lawyer Patrick H. Jones and came out with a sensational story on August 14, 1879, that supported Walling's assertions. According to this story the body had not been recovered. Once again the Stewart grave robbery was deemed worthy of discussion and scrutiny, and the gruesome narrative was reprised. Those who were denied their fill of morbid intrigue got another, wholly unexpected dose of the macabre with Henry Hilton, once again, at the center of it.

Many New Yorkers concluded that Hilton had been deceiving them and that, starting in January, he had engaged in limited but secret negotiations with the thieves, with Jones acting as an intermediary. The guards at the crypt were part of the deception, and among those deceived was the long-suffering Mrs. Stewart. Hilton wanted to create the impression that all was well. He didn't want anyone to know that, even in a small way, he had negotiated and sought compromise with the thieves, as his hatred of the grave-robbing ghouls was deep and personal. Who knows how many times he strangled them in his dreams and private thoughts?

The contact started, according to Jones, on January 26, 1879, when he received a letter and a package at his office at 150 Nassau Street in the city. It was reasoned that he was contacted because the thieves may have worked under him while he was the postmaster, and they were therefore acquainted with his ability and character. The letter was postmarked Montreal, Canada, and it was written in "a scrawling hand." It explained that the body of A. T. Stewart had been taken to Canada and was held there at some place known only to those who possessed it. It was signed "Henry G. Romaine." At this point, another mysterious name enters the story.

Actually, as early as mid-November 1878, a report trickled out to the effect that Stewart's body was in Canada and that a Montreal attorney was attempting to negotiate its return for $100,000 in ransom.[6] This report, however, was quickly and convincingly squelched by the police and Hilton. The New York newspapers also left it alone, until Jones and Romaine forced it to the front pages again.

When Jones opened the letter from Romaine, a $100 bill dropped to the floor. His lawyer-like curiosity now fully aroused, he studied the letter and was baffled more by its appearance than its content. He struggled to read and understand it. The author of the letter, this Romaine, was obviously a careful and clever man who did his utmost to conceal his handwriting. The otherwise polite and business-like letter contained many misspelled words that Jones believed to have been intentional. It was written in a weird combination of large and small letters, all of which convinced Jones that the writer was attempting to disguise himself, trying to thwart any effort by a handwriting expert to trace the letter back to its author.

The letter directed Jones to the package, stating that it contained certain items taken during the robbery of Stewart's underground vault in the early morning hours of November 7, 1878. The letter also stated that the men who held the body in Canada were now ready to negotiate for its release and return. The $100 was meant to be a retainer fee paid to Jones, as a lawyer, to act as a negotiator. If Jones would accept the fee and take the case, he was to go to Hilton and "enter into negotiations for the return of the body." If he did what he was asked to do, he would be paid additional fees.[7]

The revealing letter explained that Jones was singled out for help because, "surprising as it may seem," he was, by reputation, an honest lawyer. Romaine expressed perfect confidence in Jones' ability to carry out the stated tasks. He explained that the thieves had waited until Hilton and his associates had exhausted all efforts at solving the crime. At this point—out of sheer frustration—they were ready to deal.

With a certain undisguised bravado, the letter went on to say that the "press, the people and the police have been beaten from the start." Romaine said he had followed events closely in the newspapers, and he assured Jones that at no time during the harried investigation was success in sight.

Finally, he got to the nuts and bolts of the crime itself, saying:

The remains were taken before 12 o'clock on the night of the 6th, and not 3 o'clock on the morning of the 7th of November. They were not taken away in a carriage, but a grocer's wagon. They were not taken to any house near the graveyard, but to one near One hundred and Sixteenth street. They were then inclosed in a zinc-lined trunk, previously prepared, and left on the early morning train. They went to Plattsburg, and from there to the Dominion; there they were buried. Except that the eyes have disappeared, the flesh is as firm and the features as natural as the day of interment, and can, therefore, be instantly identified.

The letter closed with a firmly worded instruction: "Confer at once with the Reverend Dr. Rylance, Hilton, and Mrs. Stewart."[8]

Thunderstruck at the letter, Jones opened the package and discovered several "screw-heads" that were apparently taken from the coffin. These, however, were unconvincing, but when he saw a scrap of paper cut in an "irregular shape," he believed this represented the same piece of velvet cloth that was cut from the lining of the casket on the night of the grave robbery. It was perhaps the most important piece of evidence next to body itself or the actual piece of velvet that it purportedly represented.

The third item in the package was a small strip of velvet of the type commonly used in caskets. If the piece of paper and the velvet swatch weren't sufficient to convince Jones of the authenticity of the information, he was instructed to place a personal in the *Herald* and the coffin nameplate would be sent. Everyone acquainted with the Stewart story knew of these items, and Jones thought he was on to something big—possibly the final solution to the great mystery.

There was much to be done. Jones was undoubtedly aware that he was up against intelligent opponents who had thought out their moves quite well. They stationed themselves in Canada where they were beyond the reach of New York authorities, and in those days there were no federal criminal investigation agencies.

At this point Jones was probably thinking, "why me?" The answer may have eluded him, but the thieves knew what they were doing. In selecting Jones, a man with a good reputation and a degree of prominence, the plotters displayed good sense. Seeking a less reputable man to act as their agent would have probably caused the authorities and Hilton to dismiss the proposition summarily. Hilton and his associates were already all too familiar with those who wanted to cash in on the crime. They had seen too many cranks come and go.

The thieves must have watched the comic opera, too, waiting for the time to strike. Now they found their man in Jones, a man they believed they could count on. Nevertheless, Romaine was cautious. He warned Jones that should he decline to be their legal representative, "a friend will call for the retainer sent to you."

Convinced that Romaine was either one of the body snatchers or their well-informed agent, Jones knew he had to do something—and he wasn't about to return the $100 retainer. After a consultation with a lawyer friend, he went not to Hilton but to Superintendent Walling on January 27.

Walling was astounded at this development in a case he had devoted so much time and attention to during the past November and December. However, had he checked the voluminous files of letters received by the police, his memory might have been refreshed. Among the many frantic and fragmented messages from the public, there was one peculiar letter put together with words cut out from a newspaper. It read: "In 8 hour I will be in Canada with A. T. Stewart's body. A woman has the remains."[9] Then there was the letter sent to Walling signed "Canada." It simply said: "Farewell and Tell Judge Hilton that the body will never be found unless he pays princely."[10]

Because the police had received so many oddball communications, these letters, which created a link to Canada and not to New Jersey, were cast aside as worthless. Yet, considered in context with the Romaine letter, they rise to a certain level of credibility and importance. It may just be that the ghouls were really trying to reach out to the police, only to be drowned out by the sheer volume of nonsense. Nevertheless, it seems that Romaine managed to get through and get attention. He did so not by sending a letter to the police, Hilton, or one of the newspapers, but by contacting an outsider.

Walling, for one, was impressed with the Romaine message. He needed no other link to Canada. He immediately began thinking about plans to outsmart Romaine, snare the thieves, and close the books on the case once and for all. He instructed Jones to place an ad in the *Herald*, as was suggested by the letter. Then he gave Jones a receipt for the following items: "a package containing one screw, one small piece of velvet, and four screw-caps, supposed and said by letter to be the articles taken from the coffin which contained the remains of the late Alexander T. Stewart."[11]

The personal, placed in the *Herald* under Walling's authority on January 29, 1879, was brief and cryptic: "Canada—Send P.—Counsel."

Three or four days later, another letter and package arrived at Jones' office. In it he found the coffin's nameplate as promised by Romaine. Jones dutifully took the letter and nameplate to Walling. The superintendent read the letter, tossed it aside, and then said rather excitedly, "I can't deal with this man for money. I'm trying to find the culprits. I shall have to refer you to Judge Hilton, who wants to see you at his place of business."[12] By inference, of course, Walling's statement indicated that he had already gone to Hilton with Jones' story and the physical evidence and that in any further investigation, the ex-judge would still be in charge, calling the shots and running things.

Walling gave Jones another receipt:

POLICE DEPARTMENT OF THE CITY OF NEW YORK,
No. 300 MULBERRY STREET, NEW YORK, Feb. 1, 1879,

Received of Gen. Patrick H. Jones, a package containing plate supposed to be taken from the coffin of the late Alexander T. Stewart, and marked as follows: "Alexander T. Stewart, born Oct. 12, 1803, died April 10, 1876."[13]

On February 5 or 6, Jones met with Hilton. After a brief meeting, Jones left feeling ill treated. He had not been taken seriously, felt a bit foolish, and wished he could rid himself of the entire matter. Hilton was "haughty" and somewhat offensive. Instead of treating this breakthrough with enthusiasm, he merely expressed renewed anger at the thieves. Hilton fumed and flatly dismissed the ransom demand as "preposterous." He wasn't interested in paying a ransom; he wanted the thieves, "and I mean to have them," he said.[14]

The meeting terminated with no plans in the works and not a word of thanks from the ex-judge. Hilton must have realized that Jones had come across something important—the coffin nameplate. The engraver who created the piece was contacted and, upon examining it, declared it to be genuine.[15] This was strong evidence that contact with the actual body snatchers had been made.

On February 7 Jones wrote Romaine a brief, business-like letter, accepting the retainer and acknowledging receipt of the piece of velvet, the screws, and the irregularly shaped paper cutout. He reminded Romaine that an attorney/client relationship had been established and requested instructions for dealing with the "haughty" Hilton and the others. He closed saying that Hilton was most certainly "anxious to recover the body of his friend." He didn't let on that his first meeting with Hilton had been most unpleasant.[16]

The equally business-like Romaine was quick to respond in a letter dated February 11, 1879, interestingly postmarked in Boston, not Montreal. After mildly scolding Jones for going to the police, he set forth the "first, last and only terms" for the release of the body. First and foremost, the ransom price was $200,000. For this sum the body would be delivered to Jones and Hilton at a place within twenty-five miles of Montreal. No others were to be present. Then the $200,000 was to be placed in Jones' hands until such time as Hilton was satisfied with his grisly goods. Jones was to deliver the funds to Romaine's designated agent. Finally, all of this had to remain a secret for all time to come. This might explain why the matter was kept out of the press for months.

Romaine stressed that Jones was to deal solely with Hilton. Jones was assured that Hilton would be able to identify the remains of his friend and mentor, for "scientific means" had been carefully employed to maintain the body in an "excellent state of preservation." If these terms were accepted by Hilton, Jones was instructed to place another ad in the *Herald*, saying merely: "Canada—terms accepted. Counsel."[17]

A few days later Jones received another letter from Romaine. This one expressed impatience over the lack of progress, as if expecting fast-paced and fruitful negotiations. To speed things along, Romaine sent another $250, which Jones assumed to be another fee. Jones marched off to see Hilton again, bringing the latest letters with him. Hilton appeared unmoved and unimpressed. Frustrated, Jones said, "Judge, I think the best thing I can do is to close this whole business. I am getting tired of it."

Hilton exploded. "If these scoundrels imagine that they are to get any money from me to compromise their crime they will get tired of the business too. I will hunt them down it if costs a fortune!" Then he picked up pen and paper and wrote a personal ad for publication: "Canada—Terms not accepted. Counsel." This appeared in the *Herald* the following day, and with that, an angry Hilton took himself out of the loop, or at least appeared to do so.[18]

Jones was upset with Hilton over the discourteous treatment accorded him, but told a *New York Times* reporter that he wasn't surprised. Hilton was simply being Hilton—rude, impatient, and overbearing to all but his friends. While Hilton did not insult Jones to his face or charge him with dishonorable motives, Jones broke off communications, feeling that the ex-judge may have suspected the ex-postmaster was one of the conspirators. It was as if everyone connected with the case lived in a foggy atmosphere of suspicion and distrust. For several months thereafter, detectives tailed Jones and watched his office, leaving him thoroughly dissatisfied with having been selected by the grave robbers as their negotiator.

Still, the letters to and from Romaine continued. On February 16, 1879, Jones wrote to Romaine at the Montreal post office, from which most of the previous letters were sent. Jones expressed feelings of disgust and disappointment, confessing he was out of his element. "Indeed, I do not care to have much more to do with this business." As for Hilton, a melancholy Jones told Romaine, "I do not think he wants them [Stewart's remains]. At least he does not evince much anxiety in the business."[19]

Romaine promptly responded with a letter dated February 19. While expressing courtesy to Jones, he angrily took Hilton to task for refusing to negotiate. Acting like a man who had a small fortune within sight but just out of reach, he called Hilton "an ingrate—the vilest of human reptiles." Romaine lambasted the ex-judge, whom he had sorely underestimated, for Hilton stubbornly refused to invest a tiny portion of the Stewart fortune "to secure the prosperity of the living and the peace of the dead." To this condemnation he added a codicil: Hilton would never succeed in finding the desecrators of the tomb. Then easing up a bit, Romaine said he would listen to Hilton's plan. His "first, last, and only" terms were not set in stone after all. Hilton had won this round, or so it appeared.[20]

This letter was taken to Hilton. The results of this meeting were anything but satisfactory to Jones and the Canada-based thieves. Jones could only report that Hilton seemed unwilling to continue their talks unless the demand was something in the neighborhood of $5,000—a far cry from what Romaine wanted. While Hilton believed Romaine had the body in Montreal, he refused to go Canada; he wanted the body delivered to New York. Considering this, the best Jones could do was to meekly advise Romaine not to come to New York, suggesting he would face arrest. Hilton scored again.

Romaine replied in a letter dated February 28, directing Jones to deal no further with Hilton. It was "labor lost." Instead Romaine directed Jones to go to Mrs. Stewart and tell her she could have the body within forty-eight hours, if she so desired. Truly, Romaine faced his daunting task like a man determined to get his money one way or the other.

Jones was then contacted by Dr. Sidney H. Carney, a medical examiner for the New York Life Insurance Company who was said to be Mrs. Stewart's personal physician. Apparently Hilton was working through Carney and another New York man named John Sook, for these two men claimed to have a contract under which Hilton agreed to pay $25,000, the original reward figure, for the return of Stewart's body.[21] Jones sent this proposal to Romaine.

On March 30, 1879, Romaine wrote back. He would not meet with Carney, whom he distrusted, saying that while he was a physician, he was primarily a detective. Then Romaine caved in again, modifying his "first, last, and only terms" even more, suggesting that if Hilton would not come to Canada, he could send his son-in-law, Henry Russell. However, Romaine rejected Hilton's "munificent offer" of $25,000.

Jones was persistent, perhaps clinging to some hope that he might yet be able to successfully conclude this negotiation and assume the lofty role as the man who solved the greatest grave robbery mystery in America. Wouldn't that set New York abuzz? To this end he urged Romaine to reconsider the $25,000 offer and let Carney pick up the body. After all, why should Romaine or the others care who received it so long as the money was delivered? Surely they, too, must long for a solution. They had to be just as weary and sick for having to guard the body as Mrs. Stewart was in thinking that it was somewhere in Canada, still in the hands of the evil grave robbers.

On April 5, 1879, Romaine replied. It was the final letter of the series. He agreed that the selection of the person who picked up the bones was of no consequence, but he failed to mention whether he would accept less than $200,000. Jones did not reply, thus ending his role as a negotiator.[22] Perhaps sensing the futility of it, his correspondent did not write again either. The articulate and mysterious Henry G. Romaine—his powers of persuasion tested to no avail—disappeared and was never heard from again, at least not in the newspapers.

At this point Mrs. Stewart became involved through her attorneys, the powerful and prestigious Wall Street firm of Evarts, Southmayd, and Choatt. No one, not the *Times*, the *Herald*, the *Tribune*, the *Sun*, or Hilton could question their gilt-edged integrity for a moment. Romaine's letters were made available to the lawyers, who examined them and then turned them over to Mrs. Stewart. Jones told the *New York Times* that he copied the letters in a book and sent them to a friend of the widow. It is possible that it was he who alerted Mrs. Stewart's attorneys. Whatever the case, she read the letters but stuck with her belief in Hilton, who had promised her that her dead husband's remains had resumed their eternal slumber and were resting in the Garden City Cathedral crypt. In her heart of hearts, however, she undoubtedly believed otherwise.

The deception of Mrs. Stewart by Hilton was detailed in a short series of articles published in the *New York Sun* beginning on January 16, 1879. In these articles, which were thought to present the truth and therefore not intended to expose anyone, the reporter relates the manner in which Hilton convinced Mrs. Stewart that the remains of her late husband had been secured from the thieves for the sum of $50,000, "no questions asked." This exchange supposedly occurred on or about January 10, sixteen days before Romaine first wrote to Jones.

The *Sun's* source said the negotiations were conducted by a "well-known firm of lawyers" in New York. They were approached by a representative of the thieves (who wanted $100,000) and, in turn, approached Henry Hilton. The deal was consummated for $50,000, and the remains were turned over to Hilton, who saw to it that they were "satisfactorily" identified. The remains were then placed in a "secure vault, well guarded," until such time as the Garden City crypt was ready to receive them. The story was given further credence by two trustworthy friends of Mrs. Stewart, to whom she confided this information.[23]

For the next three days, the *Sun* carefully developed the story, trusting in its sources, and with each well-balanced article, the paper was more convinced in the truth of the matter. Still, it cast a careful, suspicious eye as far as it could see, for a small element of doubt was revealed in each article. While Mrs. Stewart continued to tell her friends the good news, a surly Hilton, when confronted by a *Sun* reporter, refused to talk at all.[24] Anyone reading this and knowing Hilton could see the dark clouds of doubt forming over the story of the recovery.

However, the *Sun* took heart in a startling revelation by Mrs. Stewart. When asked about the matter in light of the wedding of her favorite niece, she said bluntly, "Do you suppose that I could have given my approval [of the wedding] while the body of my husband was being dragged about the country by vandals?"

This kind of profundity had an impact on the *Sun* reporter. Nonetheless, Reverend Dr. J. H. Rylance, the rector at St. Mark's, was hunted up for his views. He confessed that he had not spoken to Mrs. Stewart since news of the recovery broke. However, he did reveal that he had been approached by a man "of the highest credentials" who said that the body could be recovered for a price. At the stranger's request, Rylance promised not to reveal his name, but he immediately turned it over to Hilton and Mrs. Stewart.[25]

In the final installment in the *Sun*, it was revealed that the identification of the body was done by a committee of doctors and others and that it was "identified to the full satisfaction" of Henry Hilton. (One of those conspicuously absent from the company of identifiers was George W. Hamill, the sexton at St. Mark's.) They held council at the Stewart mansion and were convinced by Hilton to keep it all a secret until such time as the body could be placed at the Garden City crypt.[26] One could understand, then, why Hilton angrily refused to talk about it to the *Sun*, for the articles threatened to destroy his little secret.

As it turned out, the *Sun* was following a false trail. It seems that both a sister of Mrs. Stewart and the widow's doctor started a rumor that the body had been recovered and was concealed at Greenwood Cemetery in Brooklyn until it could be moved to the Garden City crypt. Hilton was confronted and backed up the story, getting the reporters to agree to keep silent about it.[27]

A reporter for the *New York Tribune* spoke to some of the same people, surveyed much of the same evidence that the *Sun* considered, and came up with just the opposite conclusion: Stewart's body had not been recovered.[28] Since Hilton would not talk and others in a position to know the truth, including police officers, denied or would not confirm the recovery, the conclusion was obvious. Equivocation does not rise up to the level of confirmation. In a display of good journalism, the *Tribune* insisted that no matter how long rumors are printed, they are always rumors, and a lie remains a lie no matter how many times it is uttered.

The *Tribune* apparently was vindicated and the *Sun*'s theories and articles were completely undermined when Jones and Romaine entered the picture. When the Jones and Romaine correspondence was presented to her by her attorneys, Mrs. Stewart summoned Hilton for an explanation, and he, having deceived her, was on the hot seat and faced with either "undeceiving" her or reinforcing the lie. He chose the latter, arguing that

Romaine's letters were a fraud and unworthy of serious consideration. Romaine was just another bloodsucker, the kind of man Hilton had worked so hard to protect her from. Mrs. Stewart, apparently content with the delusion, returned the letters to her lawyers, who did nothing further with them. Hilton had won her over again.

It was once said that Hilton "seemed to fascinate her [Mrs. Stewart] as a basilisk fascinates a pigeon."[29] The deception in the face of the Jones revelation was a Hilton masterpiece.

However, Hilton had his supporters. Just when much of the public believed Hilton was the greedy, deceptive villain in this affair, Dr. John C. Minor—claiming to be Mrs. Stewart's personal physician—came forth in a letter to the *Tribune* stating that the accusations were not true. First, Minor castigated the press, saying the "recent newspaper flurry" contained "palpable falsehoods" too numerous to delineate in a short letter. Then he said that Hilton did not deceive Mrs. Stewart. Rather Hilton had always been honest with her concerning the details of the investigation, and at no time did he falsely lead her to believe that the body had been recovered.[30]

A reporter for the *Tribune*, anxious for a scoop, located Minor at the Grand Union Hotel. After a short interview the reporter learned that the Jones connection was one of many that Hilton received from men claiming to represent the thieves. Minor didn't really want to discuss the case, but said that "several men now of reputable position in New York were connected with the robbers." He refused to name names, however. All in all, he was about as coy as any other person interviewed by the New York press. Aside from insisting that Mrs. Stewart was strong and assertive and had every confidence in Henry Hilton, Minor added nothing to the case file but titillation.[31]

Hilton defended himself in an interview with the *Herald* that was reprinted in the *Tribune*. Hilton lashed out at Jones, suggesting that Jones was one of the robbers rather than their legal representative. The Romaine letters did not come from Canada, but were written in New York, where the thieves were hiding, "and we are closing in upon them just as fast as we can," said the ex-judge. While he did acknowledge that the letters were turned over to Mrs. Stewart's Wall Street attorneys, Hilton used the interview to deflect criticism while leveling serious charges against Jones and criticizing the New York newspapers that were quick to print articles supporting Jones and his revelations.[32]

So what was the public to believe? Beyond the fact that Stewart's body had been stolen and not recovered, what else was true? With so many twists and turns, accusations, denials, and conflicting stories, it is no wonder that the Stewart mystery was thought of as a dark romance more suited for fiction.

Whatever the truth about his dealings with Mrs. Stewart, Hilton's strategy was to put forth an angry front and halfheartedly negotiate with Romaine, hoping to shake something loose. He tossed out a few crumbs with his $25,000 reward, thinking this might be enough to secure Stewart's remains or perhaps initiate some panic or disruption among the thieves, causing one or more of them to get careless. This in turn might permit the authorities or his detectives to grab them. This did not happen, however, and Hilton appeared to abandon all hope. Then on July 24, Hilton himself reportedly placed another ad in the *Herald*: "Canada: Counsel desires to communicate." About a month went by, but there was no response from Romaine.[33]

From the sidelines Jones surmised that the criminals were gone—in prison, dead, or maybe still at large in New York —and that the remains would never be returned. If the body was buried in Canada, as was stated by Romaine, it could stay in its obscure and nameless grave. It mattered not to Jones; he was finished with the dirty business. It was a connection with history he could live without after all.

For Hilton it was an opportunity missed. He had the first reliable leads in his hands but failed to take advantage of them. He had a chance to redeem himself, to recover the body, and, maybe, the thieves. That he wanted the thieves caught and punished there is no doubt, but he was a stubborn man, unwilling to bargain with criminals or their representative. Money was an object even though he had access to millions. Displaying an arrogance that was peculiar to the wealthy in the late nineteenth century, the miserly Hilton couldn't bear to part with ransom money even when it would be used to secure the remains of his friend. Denying the criminals any compensation for their crime was denying them victory in this contest of endurance. Apparently this was as important to him as finding the body. The rich and powerful were not only different, they also were unquestionably right and didn't have to prove themselves to anyone, including the press.

However, the rich and powerful could be parodied, and none other than the great Mark Twain went after them with gusto. Well known for his fiction and humor, Twain was also fond of mysteries and detective stories, and after following the progress of the Stewart case in the press, he could not hold back. He penned a sharp satire on the police, the Pinkertons, and Hilton, intending to include the story in his new book, *A Tramp Abroad*.

In Twain's story, Stewart's stolen corpse is represented by a "sacred white elephant" that the king of Siam commissioned as a gift to Queen Victoria of England. While on its way to England, the elephant and its escort stop in Jersey City. There, the sacred white elephant disappears, and the great Inspector Blunt (Henry Hilton or Allan Pinkerton) is immediately called upon to find the priceless animal. Blunt confidently sends his entire force of detectives into the field, searching frantically for the missing creature.

Blunt's brigade searches the city of New York and every hamlet and town, ranging into Pennsylvania and Ohio, then down to Washington DC, and up to Canada. Finally, at long last, after considering thousands of clues, analyzing several theories, and paying $100,000 ransom money to the villainous thieves, the white elephant is discovered in a "vast, vaulted basement where sixty detectives always slept, and where a score were now playing cards to while the time." Alas, the white elephant—symbolic of foolish expenditure—is dead. Still, its discovery brings forth a great rejoicing from the public, who heap praise on the brilliant Inspector Blunt.

Twain had great fun with his burlesque of the police and the "infallible" Pinkertons who "never sleep," although he could not conceal his disgust for their egotistical ineptitude. He pounded the press as well, recapping all their exciting stories replete with wild-eyed headlines about the New York "ghouls" and their "ghastly crime." Written in 1879, his tale of "The Stolen White Elephant" was published in 1882 as the title piece to a collection of stories.[34]

The humor magazine *Puck* also had some fun with the grave robbery mystery—at Hilton's expense. In August 1879 *Puck* published a series of cartoons featuring a greedy Hilton and a pliable Stewart as his puppet. Titled "The Story of a Great Advertising Dodge," a cartoonist sketched out key events in the mystery such as Stewart's funeral, the grave robbery, Hilton's quarrel with the Jews, and the Romaine correspondence, with the ex-judge using these events to advertise carpets, clothes, and the like. In other words, Hilton took advantage of the grave robbery to strengthen his hold on Stewart's money while running the business into the ground.³⁵

Patrick H. Jones took a parting shot at Hilton, too, in an open letter dated August 16, 1879, printed in the *New York Sun*. He was responding to the *Herald's* interview with Hilton, wherein the ex-judge suggested that the ex-postmaster was actually one of the grave robbers. Righteously angered, Jones challenged Hilton to explain himself, lest he face a suit for slander. Jones was, however, willing to give Hilton a way out of the mess; he could simply tell the truth. The world was waiting.³⁶

The entire Jones and Romaine episode was given short shrift by the *World*, another New York newspaper. Rejecting all the physical evidence and discrediting the stories taken seriously by the *Times* and the *Herald*, the *World* declared that Jones, a Civil War veteran, was not to be believed. He was a "local politician," an invention of rival newspaperman Horace Greeley along with Miles O'Reilly, both of whom were dead. The *World* firmly believed that Stewart's remains had been purchased from the thieves for $50,000. For this, it relied on Mrs. Stewart's assertions. Jones was another fakir.

How in the world, asked the *World*, could someone of Jones' stature miss the obvious? How could he, an ex-postmaster, fail to notify the postal authorities in Montreal and arrange to have an officer or two stationed at the post office where Romaine picked up his mail? An arrest of Romaine, or whoever of his cohorts picked up the mail, could have been relatively easy. Since Jones failed to recognize this simple expediency, he was a fraud and a charlatan, looking for attention and, perhaps, some easy money. Of course the *World* failed to realize that Jones was acting as the attorney for Romaine and the thieves and would have violated that relationship had he arranged for their arrest. However, the *World* wanted closure and saw in Jones simply another self-serving man who was foolishly stirring the ashes of a long dead fire.³⁷

Jones, who tried hard to effect a settlement between the parties, was apparently willing to fade out of the picture, having spent some time in the spotlight. While Jones had been dealing with the mysterious and elusive Romaine, Inspector George W. Dilks was working quietly on another lead. Like just about everything connected with the case, this aspect was remarkable for its characters and their unlikely roles. In bizarre cases, strange figures always seem to surface with tenuous and tantalizing connections.

On the other side of the coin there was the levelheaded George W. Hamill, sexton of the St. Mark's church and former suspect. In the event that Stewart's body was recovered, it was believed that Hamill's services would be needed to identify the remains. Hamill was willing but skeptical, telling a reporter for the *Tribune*, "When the body is found the fact will either be made public or kept so secret that no rumor will even get out."[38]

CHAPTER 13

The Dream of Mr. Bryson

> In his dream Mr. Bryson saw two men mysteriously digging near the old buildings ... then he saw something removed by them from the earth.
>
> *New York Times*, August 22, 1881

After the brief flurry of media attention in August 1879, the A. T. Stewart mystery lay dormant for two years. The negotiations with Romaine came to nothing—at least nothing that the *New York Times* and other newspapers cared to report. Henry Hilton wasn't talking, and although it was known that some private detectives were still working on the case, all official investigations came to a halt. Once again many people believed the body, or what was left of it, had been secretly recovered and reinterred in the Garden City Cathedral crypt. Little by little, public interest in the ugly business faded, replaced by other scandals, intrigues, and tragedies. New York refused to be bored, and the interval between sensational diversions was usually short.

For others it was an unsolved mystery, leaving a large corps of doubters without a sense of closure. It was yet another case the police could not crack. For those people, A. T. Stewart was not truly at rest, and this meant he had been denied the final measure of dignity accorded others. To them, that was fundamentally wrong.

Then, there were the thieves. Somewhere the most infamous resurrectionists in American history moved about in complete freedom and in undetectable anonymity. Who were they? Where did they live? What did they look like? What were their names? What, if anything, did they gain by this? Someone knew, but no one was talking. Surely one of their number would be unable to restrain himself from claiming credit for the unprecedented crime and would break his silence to claim his deserved notoriety.

It was not to be. Indeed, the silence seemed to suit the body snatchers. Just like ordinary mortals, these men of the barbarous touch attended to the affairs of their lives, mingling with others in undeserved freedom. Lost in the wash of humanity, they freely and casually touched unknowing people with their unclean hands, which were forever stained by their infamous crime. Although biological laws were at work on Stewart's body, those who stole it evaded the punishing reach of man-made laws while they quietly and steadily advanced toward their own graves, as if prepared to bury all evidence of the great crime with their flesh and bones.

Then suddenly, the case was reopened amid a whirlwind of activity that had the press and public all agog once again. On August 22, 1881, the *New York Times* came out with a lengthy article detailing new clues and a renewed search for the celebrated corpse. It was revealed that a group of private detectives from Fuller's New York Detective Bureau were at work on a massive excavation at Cypress Hills Cemetery on Long Island, looking for what remained of A. T. Stewart's body. They were acting on information that convinced them that the discovery of his elusive remains was at hand. Once again the Stewart mystery was front-page news.

This time, however, it had to compete with an even greater crime. President James A. Garfield was shot and seriously wounded on July 4, 1881, by a mad, office-seeking crank turned assassin named Charles Guiteau. In an instant, the United States had both a new martyr and a terrible villain—moreover, a villain with a face. Day after day, the press poured out detailed stories of Garfield's courageous and awful suffering while under his doctors' care in the White House. With the memory of the killing of President Abraham Lincoln still fresh in the minds of many, the shock and the moral outrage that followed the shooting and slow death of Garfield easily overshadowed all other events of that summer.

Nevertheless, the long-dead A. T. Stewart claimed a small share of the headlines.

It all started with a dream. One morning in early August, a Mr. Bryson, the superintendent of the National Grounds (where soldiers were buried) attached to Cypress Hills Cemetery, awoke from an especially vivid and disturbing dream. In the dream he watched intently as some men were digging a hole in section 18 of the cemetery. He found himself moving toward their work, and just as he was about to get an undetected look at what the mysterious men had removed from the ground, he woke up.

At first he thought nothing of it. He was merely one of many who were suddenly and cruelly jolted from their dreams to be left with a feeling of loss and dissatisfaction. Later when he learned that men were excavating in that same section of Cypress Hills Cemetery, Bryson believed his dream was more than an unsettling vision; it was a premonition.[1] He was convinced that he had seen the place where the body of A. T. Stewart had been hidden by those who removed it from the vault, almost three years before.

However, it wasn't Bryson's dream that touched off a new round of activity, arousing the police, private detectives, and assorted fortune hunters. (He worked in a cemetery, what else would he dream about?) The search was resumed after a package arrived at 841 Broadway, the office of Fuller's New York Detective Bureau, a private detective agency, on Saturday evening, August 13, 1881. It was carried up the two flights of stairs by a small boy, acting under the direction of another party or parties. The package, neatly wrapped in heavy white paper, was handed to a clerk by the boy, who said politely, "Please sir, you will give this to Superintendent Fuller right away—give it to him, himself." The boy spoke carefully, as if he was told exactly what to say. In his hand he clutched a silver coin, another fact not lost on the diligent clerk.

In accordance with established procedure, the boy was made to wait in the office while the package was unwrapped. Fuller was absent, so the clerk opened the package. Upon examining its contents, the clerk, his interest piqued, asked immediately, "Where did you get this?" There was urgency in his voice.

"A lady gave it to me down the street," the boy replied nervously.

"Know who she is?"

"No, sir; never see her before."

Becoming more adamant as the discussion progressed, the clerk pressed on. "What did she say to you?" he demanded.

The boy, a hardy ragamuffin from the streets, became increasingly frightened and yet did his best to stand his ground and explain. "Nothing, only give me a quarter and said I must come up in here and give the package to Mr. Superintendent Fuller himself. That's all what she said."

Dissatisfied with the boy's innocent and honest explanation, the clerk summoned a detective, and the grilling of the juvenile messenger continued. Although he was trembling with fear and in tears, the boy refused to vary his story, insisting some lady gave him the package with instructions to deliver it to Fuller. When asked to describe her, he was unable to provide any identification. He had been given a coin to deliver a package and was nothing more than a small boy, unwittingly and unwillingly thrust into the darkest mystery in the history of New York. Still they pressed the lad and took him to Union Square, where they hoped to find his phantom employer, but it was impossible to find her face in the surging crowd of unknowns.

Although the country had broken free of the terrible depression of the 1870s, poverty held its ground in New York. Poor children still roamed the streets in great numbers, desperately trying to earn money. The boy who inadvertently entered the Stewart mystery had lots of company. There were so many children hustling the streets begging and gathering rags, bones, or "cigar stumps" that the New York State legislature was forced to take action at the urging of the Society for the Prevention of Cruelty to Children. A law was passed authorizing the arrest of any child under age fourteen who was engaged in begging, gathering rags, or collecting cigar stumps. Those apprehended were turned over to the Catholic Protectory. Their parents or guardians were charged with misdemeanors and fined from $25 to $100.[2] In 1881 the desire to punish poverty still ruled the day.

The Fuller detectives didn't want to punish the poor messenger boy; they only wanted to find the mysterious woman. Failing to do this, they focused on the package. Upon cursory examination they concluded that it was significant. It contained some tantalizing information about the disappearance of A. T. Stewart's remains, summoning old thoughts about the awful mystery and bringing to the fore, in an instant, dreams of its final solution and perhaps, above all else, the winning of the reward and the recognition that would come with it. The clerk recognized the grand possibilities and sent a message by wire to Fuller: "Come home; big case; you're needed right away." The sequel had begun, and new excitement was brewing.

When he arrived at his office, J. M. Fuller was quickly drawn into the intrigue. The package contained a cryptic note, not unlike the many others that had surfaced during the early days of the investigation. It read:

> The violet bed was removed the middle of April, 1881. Do not make inquiries of the man about the grounds or allow the painting to be seen. You will be followed if you are seen making special observations.
>
> COR.

Had there been nothing more than the note, it would have been tossed away immediately, but the package also contained an oil painting, well executed and richly framed. It was this painting that provided new insight into the old mystery. On a one-foot by one-foot canvas, someone had painted a peaceful, cemetery scene with roads and trees, including a mature, double-trunked weeping willow and an oak. At the base of the oak were two flat stones. In the background stood a picket fence and two buildings: one wood and one stone. So far, it was a painting of scenic solitude and nothing more.

However, there was more. What caught Fuller's attention was a "narrow, white mound" drawn opposite the oak tree at the juncture of two roads. On the mound in bold letters, were the words: Cypress Hills. Stewart is buried here.[3] Both the inscription in the painting and the note were written by the same hand, which was believed to be that of the woman who hired the boy to deliver the package.

What could be the meaning of all this, wondered Fuller. While the painting said only "Stewart" and not "A. T. Stewart," the assumption was readily made that it referred to the lost Merchant Prince. Why else would anyone go to such pains? Fuller leaped to this conclusion, and the New York press jumped in with enthusiasm.

While the name "A. T. Stewart" still aroused curiosity, there had to be something of substance to warrant a reopening of the case, and Hilton would have to be sold on it. Was this just another crank looking for notoriety? If so, why so long after the grave robbery? Was it another attempt by Romaine or some other agent of the body snatchers to work out a deal? Was one of the thieves, at long last, breaking ranks? Or was it the work of some well-meaning person who, out of good conscience, wanted to help out but remain anonymous? Perhaps most important of all, if this was truly a reference to Stewart's body, dead and adrift for more than five years, how could the body be identified and verified?

Fuller had a theory of his own that he aired in the *New York Herald*. He reasoned that one of the thieves had broken ranks and had, in effect, squealed on the rest of the gang. Why else would the note point out the location of the body without asking for money? Fuller may have believed he was dealing with a repentant or angry grave robber who decided to reveal the whereabouts of the body and thwart the ransom plans of his former colleagues, assuming they still had any such plans.

Fuller told a reporter for the *Herald* that he was acquainted with "the man known almost positively to have been the principal actor in the robbery." He also said that the "wife of one of the most notorious of the robbers recently fell out with him." Strangely, the reporter did not press Fuller on these assertions, leaving readers with more ambiguity. There were no names, no identification, and no indication that the police or the media, other than the *Herald* and the *New York Times*, took any serious interest in Fuller's work.[4]

Why Fuller was chosen to receive the package is not clear from the *Times* or the *Herald*. It is likely that his firm was one of many that worked for Hilton and was involved during the early stages of the investigation. At any rate Fuller was considered a rather astute man for a New York private detective, not easily drawn into a phony scheme. Yet he leaped into action and placed a personal ad in a city newspaper, addressed to the mysterious Cor:

> If Cor, who mysteriously sent an oil sketch of an important event will communicate additional particulars, we will undertake to solve the mystery. Should we succeed, and if you care to reveal your identity at any time, you will be considered a "good samaritan" in the truest sense. Call or address day or night, J. M. FULLER, Sup't Fuller's New York Detective Bureau, 841 Broadway.

Obviously a man who loved intrigue and pursuit, Fuller was off and running.

A reporter for the *Times* paid a visit to Fuller at his well-appointed and luxuriously furnished "private sanctum" at 841 Broadway. The reporter was well acquainted with Fuller and apparently had no reservations about asking questions. He got a good story out of the interview, for Fuller was fond of talking about his cases. When describing the note and the painting, Fuller mentioned that he had "evidence of a startling character" that would "create a bigger sensation than New York has known for a long time. This evidence purports to be nothing less, indeed, than the absolute solution to one of the gravest mysteries of the age, a mystery on which much of the very best talent of America and Europe has failed."

However, Fuller was quick to add that the entire thing might just be another hoax, however sophisticated, that was concocted to extract a few dollars from Hilton or Mrs. Stewart. Nevertheless he was sufficiently tempted and had decided to see it through. To his friend of the *Times*, he said, "there is no reason that I should not give you the story now and get your opinion of it." He was always more than pleased to oblige the *New York Times*.

Fuller, known to be cautious and conservative, had two major hurdles to overcome in his search for the truth. First, he had to draw Hilton back into the mystery. Second, he had to seek out additional facts and test the authenticity of the painting.

Trusting that the ex-judge had the stomach—and the money—for more adventure, he wrote to Hilton on August 16, 1881, outlining the latest developments. Fuller did so with certain reservations. There was the "semi-official report that has prevailed in detective circles during the past year to the effect that the body has long ago been recovered." Fuller doubted the truth of the report, but his detective instincts told him to consult with Hilton. He wanted confirmation or denial of the reports. It would be futile, of course, to search for a body that had been found. Fuller was bold, but he was no fool and didn't want to be made to look like one. His detective agency was one of the best known and most reputable in New York.

Fuller laid out the facts for Hilton, explaining the manner in which the package had been delivered. He sensed Hilton would be hard to convince and admitted that he doubted the veracity of the note and painting. If Hilton did not reply, the logical assumption would be that the body had been recovered. Then the note and painting would be nothing more than an artistic hoax—just a bit more A. T. Stewart trivia. If, on the other hand, Hilton responded, it would be taken as a signal to go forward. He would wait for forty-eight hours.

"Succeed and there's a mint of money for you," said the *Times* reporter.

Fuller calmly said, "Money? Yes, possibly. But, Sir, I am not after a mere reward in dollars and cents. There is something higher and better in this case."[5] Of course, he would not turn down a fee from the estate or Hilton. It was just that he placed himself above such material aspects. Here was a trophy he could hang from his wall for all time to come. He would be satisfied to march into history as the man who solved the mystery of the Stewart grave robbery.

Within twenty-four hours, Fuller received a communication from Hilton, requesting further information. Hilton had taken the bait; this was a sign that the "semi-official report" was just that and nothing more. On August 17, Fuller wired Hilton, saying he had provided everything "except locality, which is within 15 miles of New York." He asked Hilton to send a representative for further discussion. This was probably the biggest thing that had ever popped into Fuller's life, and he didn't want to take any wrong steps.

Hilton wired back that same night saying there was no one in New York whom he could send to represent him in such an important matter. Still he was interested and asked for a full narrative report from Fuller. This is precisely what Fuller wanted to hear. Early the next morning, the eager private detective swung into action. He had a plan.

On the morning of August 18, five days after the delivery of the package, Fuller and four other people arrived at Cypress Hills Cemetery. Included in the party was Fuller, the *Times* reporter, two detectives from Fuller's staff, and a pretty young girl dressed in "blue ribbons and [a] primply starched linen dress." They were searching for the clues so exquisitely featured in the oil painting, but to throw off suspicion they conducted themselves like a party from the country who had come to the city to engage in an innocent cemetery ramble.

The Cypress Hills Cemetery was founded in 1849 when a group of investors purchased several hundred acres on the Queens/Brooklyn border. During the first year of operation, about 35,000 bodies were moved into the new cemetery from Manhattan's crowded churchyards. The location appealed to middle-income people because the lots were affordable. The graveyard possessed a commanding view of the Atlantic Ocean and the surrounding countryside. It was charming, quiet, and rural.[6]

It was commonplace for people to visit cemeteries and casually walk among the tombstones, read names and dates, and admire the style and age of the markers while taking notes or sketching. By the 1880s large, sylvan, park-like cemeteries had replaced the small, gloomy, and cramped churchyards of colonial times. Many cemeteries featured winding roads, finely landscaped grounds with flowers, shrubs, and trees, as well as massive vaults and other grand examples of sepulchral art.

Because of a changing attitude toward death, there was nothing unusual about strolling through a cemetery and visiting the dead while blithely and silently conceding one's own mortality. It was a part of the beautification of death. So Fuller felt certain he could pull off his investigation without drawing the attention of anyone who might be watching.

The girl, who was dressed to look like "the exact ideal" of the "pretty country girl of Queens County," smilingly drew the attention of cemetery workers as the party casually roamed among the graves. She looked innocent enough—that was the plan—but according to the *Times*, she was one of the best private eyes in New York.[7]

The curious group strolled through the main part of the cemetery and then turned north up Lake Road, following a picket fence like the one in the painting. After a jaunt of about one-fourth of a mile, where Lake Road was intersected by West Dolorosa, a narrower street, they came upon the terrain that closely resembled the area in the oil painting: it was section 18, owned for many years by the superintendent of the cemetery, John Runcie.[8]

Just as in the painting, they looked upon the old frame stable building surrounded by trees and shrubs. Opposite that was the stone building, which was described as "a tumble-down conservatory," and beside it a pile of wood. Both buildings were close to the picket fence. Midway between them stood the large, double-trunked weeping willow, and close by was the oak tree with the heavy flat stones at its base. Looking upon this in unison, all were astounded because they found what they were looking for.

Still, they were puzzled, as there was no sign of the mound that was featured so prominently in the painting. Then looking about the area, they noticed a secluded spot beyond the picket fence, near a seldom-used road to the town of Williamsburg. The Fuller group studied the area and decided it was an ideal place to hide while secretly burying a body.

A wagon could have waited there for hours, undetected. A coffin could easily have been lifted over the picket fence and carried to a hole dug in advance. The old conservatory and stable added to the seclusion and also provided a place to hide, should the need arise.

The area under scrutiny by the party of five was unimproved and overgrown by shrubs, weeds, and brush. It had been used in the past for dumping excess dirt and rocks. The area was essentially set aside for future growth, and no one would suspect that a body was hidden beneath such rough ground. Said Fuller to his reporter friend, "A body would be safer here than in a Garden City crypt; yes, indeed, safer by long odds."[9]

While making these observations and still trying to be nonchalant, the girl noticed that a cemetery laborer had been watching them intently while pretending to be busy. "There is a man over there studying us," she said quietly. The man, who for all appearances was just a worker, seemed anxious, casting furtive glances at the group from beneath a wide-brimmed white hat while he pounded the ground with a rake. Fuller observed the man's smooth hands and fancy, alligator-skin shoes and concluded, "That is no common style of man." Believing the man was on to them, Fuller approached with a ruse at the ready. Offering the man a cigar, Fuller engaged in some small talk, but the man was especially reticent and uneasy.

Soon the worker was called to another part of the cemetery, but before leaving he made an effort to get Fuller and his associates to accompany him, urging them to see another part of the cemetery where they could continue their discussions and copying of epitaphs. They followed for a short distance and then meandered back to the spot that supposedly concealed the body of the millionaire Stewart. After some further discussion they moved toward the main gate, and the wary worker bade them a good-bye.

The reporter interviewed another detective who had substantial connections to the investigation during the early stages. This man said he believed "all along that Cypress Hills Cemetery was chosen by the thieves for the burial place of the body, after the excitement had virtually subsided." He had paid many visits to the cemetery, in one guise or another, but was "utterly at sea" and got nowhere. He was also shadowed by a man who bore an uncanny resemblance to the man seen by the Fuller party. The detective quit his search when he gained "reliable information" that Hilton had worked out a deal with the thieves and Stewart's body had been placed in the crypt at Garden City. Now, however, he was out of the business and would leave further investigation to men like Fuller.[10]

Fuller was in good spirits after the cemetery meander. His suspicions were confirmed. Brimming with confidence, he immediately wired Hilton at Saratoga Springs, saying: "Have investigated and found everything as stated. Promptness now means complete success. Will you come at once and settle the matter?"

The next day, Hilton sent the following dispatch:

Saratoga, August 19, 1881
Superintendent J. M. Fuller, New York:

If you will write and fully explain what you claim to know, and what you propose doing, I can then answer your inquiry.

HENRY HILTON

One might conclude that Hilton was playing games, for in three dispatches he was quizzical and noncommittal, but Fuller was not worried. He was so thoroughly involved in the case that Hilton's ambiguity was not an issue or obstacle. To protect his reputation Hilton had to be circumspect, but Fuller—armed with a few facts and unburdened by social constraints—had the luxury of plunging headlong into the mystery. He would go forward with or without Hilton's help, for to delay would merely give his competitors a chance to "carry off the laurels."

Of course he was pleased to receive Hilton's dispatches and was quick to respond. Shortly after receiving Hilton's latest, Fuller sent this message:

FULLER'S DETECTIVE BUREAU
Hon. Henry Hilton, Saratoga, N. Y.

Letter of 16th shows what I claim, and I propose to dig. If information is correct I alone shall reap. Shall proceed today or tomorrow. Will you come?

J. M. FULLER

Hilton was finally impressed by Fuller's confidence and straight talk. He shot back a reply that would indicate he was very much interested in these latest developments.

Saratoga, Aug. 19, 1881.
Superintendent J. M. Fuller, New York

Telegram received. Edward D. Harris leaves here this afternoon and will be at my store tomorrow morning. You may confer with him on the subject and he will act as I would.

HENRY HILTON

That night, Friday, Fuller paid a visit to cemetery superintendent John Runcie and requested a permit to excavate the portion of the cemetery where clues indicated that Stewart was buried. According to the *Times*, Stewart's name was not mentioned during their brief conversation; Fuller merely said that a "crime has been committed" and proof of it lay hidden in the cemetery dirt.[11]

The *Herald* had a different slant on their conversation. After the detective asked for permission to dig, Runcie politely asked Fuller, "What do you wish to dig for there?" Fuller answered promptly and melodramatically, "For the body of A. T. Stewart."[12]

Runcie was taken aback by the request but expressed a willingness to cooperate in the investigation. After all, he reasoned, section 18 was an ideal place for someone to dispose of a body, and it wouldn't surprise him at all if the dead millionaire was found in that isolated and neglected ground. After suggesting he had some important knowledge to share, Runcie said, "You shall have your permit tomorrow and I will assist you all I can, for I believe it is in a good cause."[13]

The following morning, August 20, Fuller met with Hilton's man Harris at the Stewart store. After a briefing the two left for Cypress Hills Cemetery. At one o'clock in the afternoon Fuller and his staff, along with Harris and Runcie, were prepared to dig holes and trenches in section 18. Runcie had ordered the entire work force to perform duties at the opposite end of the cemetery, except for three men whom he selected to join in the excavation. Police Inspector William Murray, an old hand in the investigation of 1878, made an appearance too.

The area featured in the painting was sounded with a rod to locate disturbed, soft, ground, but as the soil was rocky, a deep probe was impossible. Nevertheless the decision was made to dig. As work was about to begin, Fuller and Harris noticed a group of men approaching quietly from the trees in the background, making their way slowly toward the crew.

One of their number was selected to go forth and confer with Fuller and Harris.

Harris was reluctant to proceed in the presence of so many spectators and wanted to delay digging until they were gone. They were like hungry vultures and had no business there. Fuller, however, understood that these men, who were self-styled detectives, had learned of his investigation and were anxious to be a part of any great discovery. The representative of the intruders insisted they had every right to be present and Fuller should not expect to keep everything to himself. The outsider explained that his group had also been working the same clues, developed independently. Fuller had no objection to having witnesses present. While they watched, Fuller's crew commenced digging.

Harris left for Manhattan on "urgent business" at two that afternoon, not long after the diggers had broken ground. He asked Fuller to wire him in the event that anything of importance was uncovered. After an afternoon of digging somewhat randomly in the plot, they excavated a trench five feet deep, two feet wide, and several feet long, yielding nothing more than cobblestone-type rocks. While the workers wielded their picks and shovels, "hundreds" of people passed by in carriages or on foot, looking on with questioning gazes. Maybe at long last, the Stewart mystery would provide a glimpse of the unforgettable.

Those who asked about the entrenchment were given "thoroughly satisfactory replies." The day ended with Fuller placing guards around the area of trenches. While he had unearthed nothing but rocks, Fuller left the cemetery that night in high spirits, prepared to resume his search the following day.

The story in the *Times* and the *Herald* revived the public's interest in the Stewart mystery. Everyone, it seems, was talking about the dead millionaire again, freely offering opinions: he was either entombed at the cathedral in Garden City or in the dirt in section 18 in Cypress Hills Cemetery. The trains from Brooklyn and New York to the cemetery were crowded with curious folks who wanted to watch the digging. As if on a holiday, entire families packed picnic lunches and made a day of it. Wandering around the cemetery in wide-eyed amazement, many of them engaged in speculation over the exact location of Stewart's body.

Two children stood on a small mound of dirt. "He is here, mamma," shouted one of them.

A fat woman enjoying the frolic said, "Bless his soul, he's buried on a hill. I read it in the papers." Another suggested, jokingly, that he was hidden in a hollow.

Three young women were overheard talking about Stewart and his wealth and how awful it was that his body should be the subject of so much ghoulish speculation. "Richer than anyone in the country," one of them said sadly.

At that point a clergyman, overhearing their conversation, interjected his own thoughts. "My dear young ladies," he said pointedly, "you seem to think that money should have helped the departed Mr. Stewart. You should know that money cannot buy ..." Just as he was about to say "happiness," a mosquito landed on his nose, causing the pastor to slap his nose and say "damnation" instead. The horrified young ladies moved on as the embarrassed pastor departed the cemetery.

The excitement took another humorous turn when a "burly German" spotted a tombstone with the name "Stewart" on it. He studied the name and in badly broken English lamented, "Vell, uf dat don't beat all the dings what I see. Dose peeples dat hef got de sheek to put a stone over him. Dot looks as if dey vanted to give de thing away."[14]

With so many people celebrating the macabre, it should be no surprise to learn that a few ghost stories were floated about the cemetery as evening set in. With clouds of mosquitoes doing their best to divert attention, some of the "oldest inhabitants" of Long Island, who had spent their boyhood days in the cemetery and knew every foot of it, regaled the visitors with ghost stories. They recalled seeing human forms "flitting to and fro about the place" along with occasional "sheets of flame" that seemed to shoot up from the ground. Oh yes, they warned, the ground that supposedly held Stewart's bones had a long and haunted history.

One man said, "I was passing this very spot" (pointing to where Stewart's body was supposedly buried) "when just from that very place there seemed to issue a lot of flame sufficient to light the place all about. I had to shut my eyes. When I opened them it was dark."

Superintendent Runcie, one of the listeners, asked lightly, "Where had you been that night?" This evoked a ripple of laughter from the crowd.

"I wasn't drinking," was the man's quick and serious reply, "and as true as I am here I saw what I told you. I was staggered for an instant, but

I am sure of what I saw." It was a day and a night to remember at Cypress Hills Cemetery.[15]

Fuller was not one of those brushing away mosquitoes while listening to tales of phantoms and fire. When he arrived for work that day with a tintype of the cemetery painting he was immediately surrounded by reporters, all eager to learn of any new developments. Fuller was basking in mosquito-free prominence.

Loving his newly found celebrity, Fuller answered questions freely and unhesitatingly, quick to tell all that it was he, not Hilton, who was in charge of the investigation. "Judge Hilton does not bear a single penny of the expenses," said a beaming Fuller. He acknowledged the cooperation of Hilton's man, Harris, but said, "Every move of importance in this case has been my own." He spoke like a confident man, but when asked if he was certain that Stewart's remains were about to be uncovered at long last, Fuller backed off a bit, saying the whole thing could yet prove to be a hoax. One can be certain that reporters were standing by for further updates on the hot story.

The New York Police Department stationed three men at the diggings just in case a body turned up. One of the police officers questioned said that the department had been "working on the same clew for some time." Although he admitted that he was not optimistic, he thought it worthwhile to "watch the case" because he was certain that Stewart's body had not been recovered.[16]

The story of the digging was widely circulated with great enthusiasm. For some this was taken as a sign that a great discovery was at hand. Fuller also relied on the metaphysical, seeing signs of success in the recurrence of the number thirteen. While he emphatically declared that he was not superstitious, thirteen was his lucky number, a figure he could rely on. He was born on the thirteenth of the month, began his detective business on February 13, 1876, and the street number of his Broadway office, 841, added up to thirteen.

In the past, whenever the number thirteen appeared in his investigations, Fuller was successful in solving the case. In this case, the number thirteen was prominent. The mystery package and note were delivered on August 13, a day that exactly thirteen men were employed in his office. When Fuller and his party did their cemetery trip, the streetcar on which they rode to the grounds was number thirteen, as was the conductor's cap. Another car he traveled on that day, from the Grand Street ferry to East New York, was also number thirteen. Perhaps most significant, the gravesite indicated in the oil sketch was in lot 175, the numerals of which added up to thirteen.

With good signs galore, there was excitement in the air. Fuller was brimming with confidence while his crew was readying itself to deepen the four-foot trench to six feet. Meanwhile, at the cemetery office, the curious bought souvenir maps of the grounds for twenty-five cents each, attracted no doubt, by the initials "A.T.S." marked in red pencil.[17]

Henry Hilton himself, showed up on the twenty-first to take a look at the excavations,[18] but little digging was done on that day. There were, however, plans in the works to excavate until every foot of ground in the sketch was overturned. Meanwhile the targeted area was kept under guard. On another front Fuller was still seeking out the mysterious lady who was responsible for these latest revelations. She was the key to the mystery. He wasn't overly concerned with finding her, however, as he reasoned that she would soon communicate with him in some way, especially if he was unable to locate the Stewart remains on his own. When this happened perhaps she could be persuaded to tell all her secrets.[19]

On August 22, digging at the site was vigorously pursued. The trench was deepened and extended in all directions. There was a moment or two of excitement when one of the workers struck soft dirt. Yelling, "I found it!" the digger drew a large crowd. After a few scoops, however, he hit hard ground again.

When asked how long they would dig, one of the workers replied, "Until we are satisfied the body is not here." He expressed great confidence despite the lack of results.

A reporter mockingly suggested they "dig in the road," as "some of his [Stewart's] bones may have dropped as they were carried to this spot."[20] It seems that some observers considered the work of the digging party to be a fool's errand—futile and a bit funny.

The cemetery employee whom Fuller and his friends believed to be a spy because of his alligator-skin shoes was identified as James Dagner. He also joined those doing the digging. Dagner—who lived nearby—was overheard to say that if he found the person who implicated him in the affair, "I'll break his head with my dinner can."[21] Hard at work and tickled at his brief notoriety, Dagner narrowly escaped arrest. Still, cemetery officials were quick to defend him, insisting he had nothing to do with the Stewart conspirators. After a full day of digging, nothing of consequence was located.

On the twenty-third, digging was resumed with a view of shutting down the operations should the remains not be discovered. Only three men threw dirt, while fourteen spectators looked on. Among those not digging were eight reporters and three detectives; the rest were cemetery officials. Enthusiasm was waning with each meaningless scoop of dirt. Fuller failed to show up and supervise his dwindling crew.[22]

About 10:30 a.m., a newspaper carrier rode in on horse, approached the diggers and the watchers, and said, "I think I can find that body if it is anywhere in this neighborhood." He dismounted and walked around the area until he found a place where the earth was soft. Then, as if entranced by the boldness of this man, the reporters stood by and cheered while he dug with great vigor until he was standing in a hole about four feet deep. Then, just as quickly as he came, the man quit digging and left those in the area disappointed.[23]

A cemetery trustee visiting the area of the dig said he doubted that Stewart's remains were actually buried in Cypress Hills. He was quick to add that he believed the body was conveyed to Long Island because, at 4 a.m. on the morning of the robbery, his son saw a couple of suspicious men cross Hunter's Point Ferry in a wagon that contained a "long wooden box." Hearing this one of the detectives at the site said, "That makes three thousand and thirteen persons who have seen that mysterious box and two suspicious looking men on the morning of November 8th, 1878."[24]

The search was suddenly and officially abandoned on the twenty-fourth, called off by a sad and disappointed Fuller, whose enthusiasm sank as quickly as it rose. While workmen refilled the trenches, Fuller announced to the press that he had been fooled and felt bad about it. Aside from a large black snake that slithered out of an excavation and the discovery of a coffin screw, the digging was dull and uneventful. Fuller concluded that it was a hoax after all, designed to irritate Hilton and Mrs. Stewart while creating some "big sensation" for purposes known only to the perpetrators. Somewhere in New York, someone was enjoying a big laugh at the expense of Fuller, Hilton, and hopeful newspaper reporters.[25]

A few days later Fuller was visited by Cor—the mystery lady who paid the boy to deliver the package containing the clues that set in motion the Cypress Hills excavation. She explained that on the night of the vault break-in she saw "an undertaker's wagon with a trunk in it going toward the cemetery." This occurrence and a couple of other strange incidents caused her to believe she could solve the entire mystery.[26] She accomplished nothing other than to add an additional layer of disbelief and frustration to the long-running investigation.

So it ended, another phase in the investigation for the ages, not with a sensational headline but with a small piece buried among other articles in the *Evening Post*.

While Cypress Hills was forgotten after its brief notoriety, the incident gave skeptical newspapers a chance to exercise their critical faculties. The *Sun* made fun of the spectacle, comparing it to the energetic but aimless digging in New Jersey that occurred during the week following the grave robbery. The *Daily Eagle* snickered at Fuller's quixotic quest for a "soft spot" in the ground, noting that the real soft spot was on his head.[27] The *World* called it the "silly season" story, contending that the matter was done up by Fuller solely for the purpose of advertising his detective agency. The *World* believed that Hilton recovered the body and that Fuller was foolishly searching for something that had already been found.[28]

It was an embarrassing twist for such a great mystery. It called to mind memories of the St. Mark's grave robbery and the unpaid reward, and it revived familiar feelings of doubt and bewilderment. It was, in every sense, an unsolved mystery, stranger than fiction.

Yet there were, undoubtedly, many people who fervently believed they had not heard the last of it. The theft of Alexander T. Stewart's body was not simply another crime—not at all like a killing du jour. In a bold stroke the rich man's body was stolen in the dead of the night in a city that never sleeps. Nearly three years later someone concocted an elaborate plan, or hoax, to revive interest in the mystery and then quickly vanished. The spectators in this sleepless masquerade waited quietly for something else to happen, as if gazing at a horrible mask of death that looked back in derision.

CHAPTER 14

A Footnote to a Grave Robbery

> The thieves who stole A. T. Stewart's body were not half as contemptible as Hilton, the robber of Stewart's widow, who seeks to crawl into the empty coffin to hide his own infamy. We mean you, Henry Hilton.
> *New York World*, May 1, 1890

With those words, the *New York World* and Joseph Pulitzer mercilessly took Henry Hilton to task. Not satisfied with just one blast, the *World* hit him with a series of scathing articles—a torrent of vicious, mean-spirited verbiage, the likes of which was exceptional, even in late nineteenth-century America.

In 1890 newspapers were still terribly biased and made no pretense toward objectivity. Publishers and editors had agendas that included more than providing the news. They were attack dogs for business and political interests—weapons of war in the cultural struggle for the wealth, morals, and future of a nation. They picked targets from the vast array of the rich, the sleazy, the popular, the unpopular, and the powerful, then they blasted away with a mixture of carelessness, anger, and self-righteous zeal. While New York was blessed with journalistic talent, the newspaper enterprises were often out of control and on a rampage, practicing free speech as if there were no limitations.

Born in Hungary in 1847, Joseph Pulitzer came to America during the last year of the Civil War and served the Union in the cavalry. He was a headstrong, intelligent, fairly well educated, and restless lad. After the war he went west in search of his fortune. Following a series of menial jobs, he worked for a newspaper in St. Louis, and from that point launched one of the greatest journalistic careers of all time.

Pulitzer was hired by the *Westliche Post*, an important German-American immigrant newspaper. He was described as tall and lanky, with a long neck and "bulbous head with an unusual beak of a nose" that stood in sharp contrast to his receding chin, which was decorated with a short red beard. He was energetic and worked hard. When he was on an assignment he cut an unflattering figure, running down the streets of St. Louis with coattails flying. However, there was nothing funny about his writing and news-gathering talent.[1]

In 1883 Pulitzer went to New York and purchased the decrepit *New York World*. Within a short time his newspaper was a blazing success, and by 1892 it was the circulation leader in New York. The *World* was vibrant, energetic, and remarkable for the quality of its illustrations. While it featured its share of sensationalism and scandal, it also contained hard-hitting news written with flare and color, so reading it was a rip-roaring good time. Pulitzer was like the second coming of *Herald* publisher James Gordon Bennett, although he lacked Bennett's original genius. Pulitzer's enormous success invited the envy and criticism of other publishers, while he marched on fearlessly, praising the good in people, as he saw it, and attacking the villains.[2]

Pulitzer's *World* became known for its stunts and crusades, both of which were largely responsible for the popularity of the paper. Among the big targets he pursued were Standard Oil Company, New York Central, the Bell Telephone monopoly, the Louisiana lottery, and white slave traffic. The paper's reporting was crisp and colorful, and its editorial page was of high caliber, earning Pulitzer a reputation as a "leading spokesman for liberal ideas in America."[3]

The powerful and prominent Hilton—a celebrity cast in the role of a villain—was not a popular person. People disliked him because he was perceived as undeserving and greedy, having gathered in all of "old Stewart's money" to the detriment of the widow, heirs, charities, and potential public works. People who hit the jackpot often incite the bitter envy of those who do not. Fate sometimes sets people up so they can be knocked down.

Henry Hilton, *New York Herald*, August 25, 1899.

Pulitzer obviously hated Hilton and had an ax to grind, and he did so in front of a vast audience of Hilton haters. When he was finished, the talented and caustic Pulitzer—who later in the decade became one of the twin giants of yellow journalism along with William Randolph Hearst—turned a powerful, haughty man into a tattered and helpless rag doll. Hilton the influential and noteworthy businessman was, in a matter of weeks, reduced to a sniveling caricature of his former self.

For a flattened Hilton, that was the awful price of fame and fortune. It reflected a painful, dark side of his longtime relationship with Stewart that was as terrible as—or worse than—those distant days following the most infamous grave robbery in American history. Not only had he failed to find and arrest the grave robbers, he also presided over the steady degradation of A. T. Stewart and Company. For all this, he gained riches. It was a terrible contradiction, hard to bear in the late nineteenth century, when only self-made winners were rewarded. Hilton may have, indeed, felt the world was against him.

Hilton, the loser, came to symbolize what remained of the dry goods empire of the Merchant Prince. Overshadowed by usurpers who eagerly profited from his example, Stewart's vast enterprises gradually sank beneath the weight of incompetence and greed, leaving in their stead the image of one avaricious, self-serving man. Most would have agreed that a man of Stewart's stature deserved a better legacy.

For the drum-beating Pulitzer, Stewart's legacy was summed up in two words: Henry Hilton. He was as much a part of the Stewart legacy as was the Marble Palace, the Great Iron store, the art and book collection, and the cathedral on Long Island. Also, the Stewart grave robbery lingered in the collective memory of New York and the rest of the United States. However, as curiosity about the whereabouts of the body and the identity of the thieves waned, the *World* made certain that serious and scathing scrutiny was focused on Hilton.

It didn't have to happen that way. Hilton could have taken his million-dollar inheritance and then faded gently and comfortably into the rich tapestry of New York history had not it been for an event that occurred shortly after the death of Stewart. This event, at first lightly publicized and subject to little criticism, was the passing of control of the vast Stewart empire from Mrs. Stewart to Hilton. On April 14, 1876, just a few hours after the great merchant's funeral, Mrs. Stewart granted Hilton a power of attorney in exchange for the sum of $1 million. She also entered into a partnership with Hilton and William Libbey, but it was the power of attorney that, in effect, put the fate of her late husband's business affairs into the waiting hands of the ex-judge.[4]

Mrs. Stewart could not be faulted for this, even though the decision was fatally flawed. For along with his will, her late husband penned a letter advising her to rely on the honesty and judgment of "our friend," Hilton.[5] While she lived in material comfort for the remainder of her life, she could not have failed to see and lament the deterioration of the great enterprise that was once the envy of the world, which occurred despite Hilton's boast that the business would proceed as usual. Finally, in May 1882 Hilton—$10 million richer—pronounced A. T. Stewart and

Company dead after firms from all over the United States cancelled hundreds of orders.[6]

It was another sad death for Mrs. Stewart, a prisoner of perpetual grief, locked within the walls of her marble mansion. First she lost her husband, then her husband's body, and after that, everything they spent their lives building. One can pity her suffering, but one can ever gauge its depths.

The spectacle of Hilton's arrogance, greed, and mismanagement no doubt compounded her sorrow. He essentially stepped into the shoes of his former mentor and controlled every aspect of the business, raking in money, with Libbey in tow and taking a cut. However, Hilton utterly lacked the Stewart moneymaking magic. He was as underqualified as he was overconfident, all the while making decisions that weakened the company and contributed to its gradual demise, doing everything except what Stewart would have wanted.

Stewart once confided in his friend and business associate, Richard Lathers, that he was preparing Hilton to take over A. T. Stewart and Company. Stewart told Lathers that "the art of trading is simple" and Hilton was "an apt scholar." Lathers expressed skepticism, saying there was more to running a company than being a clever lawyer.[7] Lathers was right. Placing so much confidence in the honesty and judgment of his "good friend" Henry Hilton was one of the few bad business decisions Stewart ever made.

It was, however, good theater for New York, and for years a vast audience watched it with a mixture of humor and contempt. Among them were many veteran New Yorkers who smugly predicted that Hilton would most certainly and speedily ruin all that Stewart had created.[8]

Pulitzer watched the spectacle, too, although by 1889 his eyesight was poor and worsening. He noted over the years how Hilton dominated the business affairs of A. T. Stewart and Company, fighting off the claims of alleged heirs. Pulitzer watched as a devouring Hilton fattened on the wealth of his great benefactor, while the sorrowful widow lived as a virtual shut-in and claimants were turned away by the probate courts. The journalist with a love of sensationalism and a reputation for exposing greed and corruption gathered about him a vast array of fact and rumor and shaped it into a plan. He made a first strike on April 14, 1890, nearly four years after Mrs. Stewart died and almost twelve years after the body of Stewart disappeared.

It's fair to conclude that Pulitzer had been at work on this project for a considerable period of time, considering the sheer volume of information and the excruciating detail pursued in its display. If it was his intention to wait a decent interval after the death of Mrs. Stewart before printing his story, it was the only decent thing he did. When he decided it was time to print, the man who was described as somewhat introverted let loose with both barrels.

It started with the word HILTON. In simple bold, block letters that cried out with long overdue condemnation, Pulitzer began his public lashing. The opening salvo was as loud as anything that ever emanated from a New York newspaper. Like any sneak attack, it was shocking and vicious, loaded with sly and salacious suggestions about the "mystery of Hilton's influence over A. T. Stewart" that had been "at last discovered." Pulitzer had found men who "can and will talk." He boldly claimed that the "motive for the grave robbery" would be "made clear." Column by column, line by line, Hilton was meticulously stripped and left cringing, as if naked in front of all of New York.

The attacks on Hilton were as domineering and loud as the horror stories that followed in the wake of the robbing of Stewart's vault. This was vintage Pulitzer. He believed that crime, dishonesty, and scandal had to be conveyed to the public extra loudly and clearly so that the gravity of the offense was not lost in the details.

The front-page article, long and merciless, promised shocking revelations were in the making. It appears, however, that Pulitzer was more interested—for the moment, at least—in taunting his target and tempting his audience. For aside from a suggestion that Hilton's influence over Stewart was "founded in a crime" that would have destroyed the dry goods business in its infancy, the article was mostly fluff. While it delivered a telling blow, it did not illuminate "the darkness that shrouds the relations which existed between A. T. Stewart, Mrs. Stewart and Henry Hilton,"[9] but there was more to come.

The next day Pulitzer's paper struck again, sending another verbal cannonball across its front page: "HILTON!" It was a single word that stood out as if the entire staff of the newspaper suddenly pointed angry fingers of guilt at their cornered and cowering prey. We mean you, Henry Hilton!

The writer of the article described Hilton's legal career and a few of his pet projects. It mentioned he was once a member of the infamous

Tweed ring, as if to impute the unrivaled crimes of the ring to Hilton. It revealed that Hilton liked to be in charge and that Stewart often allowed him to run ahead and be a front man—like a prancing puppet—especially at social functions where the older man felt uncomfortable. The piece suggested that Hilton was at one time very close to taking control of the great enterprises when Stewart was nominated to be Secretary of the Treasury under President Grant.[10] This second article—like the first—toyed with Hilton, using innuendo and suggestion intended to merely soften him up, so to speak, and to leave readers asking, what's next?

The *World* continued to blast and belittle Hilton. Pulitzer's paper made it clear that Hilton was in no way responsible for helping Stewart make his millions. He was not a key player or decision maker in the business, and he was merely a go-between in Stewart's relationship with President Grant. He was paid a relatively small salary by Stewart and kept busy with legal matters and other business of small importance. Hilton became a sort of hatchet man for his aging boss, doing dirty work, intimidating employees, and keeping everyone in line. Stewart allowed Hilton to think and act like he was a "big" man. The *World* even claimed that Stewart disliked his right-hand man.[11]

What, then, was the hold Hilton had over Stewart? The *World* was especially coy about providing an answer, and when the revelation was at last made, it was almost lost in a morass of words. Working its way up to the great denouement, Pulitzer's paper said that Hilton was good at managing Stewart, something no one else could do at all. Hilton had a certain crude but effective magic that worked on Stewart even if it left everyone else unimpressed.

Hilton was skilled at appealing to his employer's vanity, always at the ready with the right words of praise or appeasement, easing the pain of decision making. This was especially true in Stewart's later years, when he had lost his congenial attitude and become a lonely, isolated man unable to enjoy his wealth. Hilton understood this and knew what to do. After years of standing beside his boss, whispering encouragement and lawyerly advice, Hilton gained certain secret knowledge—knowledge so potentially devastating that if it had been revealed, Stewart would have been ruined and held up to public ridicule.

It was knowledge of a "crime," said the *World*, that Hilton used to cement his relationship with his benefactor. Then, at last, after three lengthy articles, Pulitzer's paper got to the heart of the matter. Even then, however, it was stated somewhat obliquely, suggesting only that Stewart fathered a child out of wedlock some thirty years in the past and that Hilton became privy to this knowledge and kept it secret—for a price. The "secret ... involved a charge of the birth of a child the entanglements growing out of which Hilton compromised for A. T. Stewart."

The *World* never revealed the sources of its information about this "crime," saying only the accusation was based "on authority of one of the best known and most reputable citizens of New York." Having exposed a long-hidden secret and believing absolutely in the veracity of its sources, the *World* fearlessly pressed on.

Hilton, the ex-Tweed man, covered up this crime. For this he was rewarded with position, power, and money. This kept Hilton quiet while Stewart lived, but what would happen after Stewart died? Could Hilton be controlled from beyond the grave? The paper's assertions, if believed, indicated that Stewart had a plan for that, too.

In 1873, when Stewart fell ill, it was Hilton who made out the great merchant's will. It and the codicils were in Hilton's handwriting.[12] So in a sense, it was Hilton who gave himself the incredibly generous gift of $1 million, believed to be the largest bequest ever made to a nonblood relative up to that time. Hilton may have drafted the will, but Stewart still had to sign and approve it. A man as sharp and shrewd as Stewart certainly would not have overlooked a million-dollar gift. This suggests that Stewart knew he had to keep Hilton silent and that the price of that silence was $1 million.

Subsequent events, however, indicate that Hilton wasn't satisfied with a mere million. He wanted more and would not be controlled or restrained by a dead hand. According to the *World*, Hilton used the secret information as leverage against Mrs. Stewart to gain complete control over the business empire. He purportedly confronted the widow in her home and said, "I hold in my hand your husband's reputation and can blast it, if I wish."[13] In other words, blackmail. The implication is that she understood the potential for disaster and gave in.

Having penetrated to the heart of the matter and perhaps sensing it had brought down Hilton, the *World* shifted the focus of its attack to Stewart himself. The next three articles surveyed his long and illustrious career. They noted his genius for marketing and his unparalleled success, but criticized him for his greed and his unwillingness to acknowledge his relatives and share his wealth with them.

Stewart was even accused of snubbing his own mother (and stepfather as well) to the extent of refusing to introduce her to his friends and his society. While he did not deny her money for material comforts, he kept her in the background for fear of possible detrimental effect on his business and social status.[14] Indeed, he hid her so well that for the last twenty years of her life it was thought she was dead.[15] She lived with him from 1838 to 1847, and at her death, she was interred in the St. Mark's vault.[16]

While acknowledging Stewart's ability to conceptualize and carry out great plans, the newspaper counterbalanced those traits with stories about his greed and unwillingness to brook competition. To have accepted the *World's* view of the Merchant Prince, one would have to have concluded that Stewart went to sleep at night dreaming of how he could have all the money in the world. He looked at competitors as obstacles to this goal, seeing their success as an insult to him. Whatever they sold belonged to him; their money was his money. They were encroaching on his sacred turf. Only A. T. Stewart belonged. Like a pirate on the high seas, he pursued his competitors until he found them and destroyed them.

Unmoved by human suffering, his idol was gold; his goal was the destruction of all those who stood in his way of acquiring every last nugget. A rapacious exploiter of his workers, Stewart rode the waves of the oppressive factory system to great riches. This was the image conjured by the *World*.[17] This was the real Alexander T. Stewart "whose bones are supposed to lie beneath the Cathedral arches" on Long Island.[18]

Plotter and criminal! Pirate and highway robber! The *World* shouted its message aloud. The pursuit and destruction of other merchants and tradesmen by Stewart was "unequaled save by that of the savage Sioux towards his victim at the stake." Finally, as if to drive a stake into the heart of Stewart's reputation, the *World* said that during his halcyon days of the 1850s and 1860s, "there was a dinner party at his house and *among his guests were two of his mistresses.*"[19] This last accusation was as powerful and damning as any that could be made in Victorian America. Better a rich and famous man be called a murderer than an adulterer.

This image of Stewart as a greedy, dark sinner stood in stark contrast to his public persona, for he was well known for maintaining the dress and decorum of a man of the cloth. In his store he was always a gentleman, respected by the ladies. While he lived he used this image to his best advantage, although like other men of power and wealth, he was not always above suspicion or beyond temptation.

There was temptation galore in New York, especially in the 1830s and '40s when Stewart was a young man. Brothels operated openly and freely, owing to lax laws and public indifference. Many such businesses were located in fancy houses in respectable neighborhoods. They were staffed by well-dressed and attractive young women, creating ample and discreet opportunities for restless young men willing to cross the line into marital infidelity.

Among the many letters sent to Stewart that somehow were not destroyed, several were from desperate women begging for money, favors, or other assistance. For example, there was a suggestive letter from a New York girl named Carrie Stevens dated December 7, 1871. She called Stewart "My dear lover." Her message was brief and to the point: "Come and see me immediately. I want to see you very bad. Forever your beloved girl."[20] Then there was the letter from a widow who claimed that she met Stewart in St. Louis in 1857 and he asked her to accompany him to California. She declined because she was about to marry a St. Louis attorney, but now she was in dire straits and pleaded with Stewart for help. She closed by saying she would "wait in suspense."[21]

In 1866 Stewart hammered two newspapers that printed articles accusing him of adultery. He had two journalists from the *National Police Gazette* arrested and tossed into New York's Tombs prison for "gross libel" in connection with a scandalous article that linked him to a woman whom "he never knew or saw." After their arrest the reporters denied that their article was about A. T. Stewart, but the aggrieved party wanted his pound of flesh.[22]

Another newspaper, the *Daily Missouri Republican* of St. Louis, also accused Stewart of marital infidelity. The offending article said that he "allows one of his mistresses a house and five thousand dollars a year pin money" and called his marital relationship "dreadfully infelicitous." The stinging article said that Stewart was a miserable, uncharitable man who was totally obsessed with the aggrandizement of wealth, unable to take recreation like a normal person, and willing to pay his wife the sum of a half a million dollars if she would divorce him.[23]

Stewart retaliated by having the editor and the reporter arrested for criminal libel, and then filed suit. All charges were dropped, however, when retractions were printed.[24] However, the *World* was under no such constraints now that Stewart was dead, and Pulitzer and staff pressed on confidently and freely.

While the series of articles steadily climbed to a shocking crescendo, there was an attempt to assign some perspective to it. The *World* reminded its readers that this was New York, raising the image of a big and sinful city where scandals and mysteries abounded, where schemers and plotters without number hatched out their nefarious plans for blackmail, thievery, murder, and cover-up behind the walls of brownstones and great mansions. The Hilton/Stewart scandal was but one of many, a single link in a long, heavy chain forged over the years by numberless sinners.

Had the *World* limited its attacks to Hilton there might not have been a counterattack. After all, the ex-judge could have absorbed the blows in silence, having reached his objective (the bulk of the Stewart fortune). Say what they might, they could not take it away from him. Others in his position had felt the pain of a free and unfettered press. Whatever the First Amendment gave to an individual American by way of free speech and personal liberty, it took away by giving a corresponding right to the press to publish freely. However, newspapers published at their peril, and indictments and lawsuits for libel were frequent and nasty. Before long, the *World* was drawn into that ambiguous net.

On April 23, 1890, a grand jury issued indictments for criminal libel against Joseph Pulitzer, John A. Cockrell, Julius Chambers, and James F. Graham of the *New York World*. An aging Hilton still had some clout.

The indictments were the direct result of a letter from Hilton to the district attorney for the city and county of New York. In it, Hilton complained of a series of "libelous" articles directed at Stewart and "upon myself," published in the *World* from April 14 to 19. Hilton somewhat tepidly called the articles "grossly libelous on their face" consisting of "groundless insinuations, assumptions and conclusions" that were "conspicuously barren of allegations of fact."

He grew angrier as he wrote, calling the popular *World* an "infamous sheet" that was not worth the trouble of a civil suit for libel. Besides, it was not his own reputation that concerned him, rather that of Stewart, "my dead friend and benefactor." Hilton sharply denied any "dark secrets," crimes, or dinners with mistresses present. Compared to Pulitzer and his allies, the men who robbed Stewart's grave "were gentlemen of refinement and character."

Pulitzer was in Europe when the charges were brought. Those whom the law could reach posted $1,000 in bail for their release. Swords had been crossed and the fight became far more bitter as time went on.[25] The "gentlemen" who robbed Stewart's vault must have been watching with special glee.

"COWARD! Hilton Basely Hides Behind the Corpse of the Dead Merchant Prince," the *World* shouted back in anger and indignation. There would be no apology or retreat. The indicted parties seemed reenergized and, in this powerful mood, heaped on more abuse. Bringing up the awful specter of the grave robbery, the paper called Hilton a "woman despoiler" who "crouches hyena-like, upon the ravished vault of his old patron."

Hilton was attacked with even greater vigor and stronger language. The *World* said more pointedly than ever that Hilton "defrauded and plundered the widow, Mrs. Stewart." He was lambasted for his refusal to spend money to find the robbers of the vault simply because, in doing so, there would be less to squeeze out of the widow.[26] All his newspaper interviews and everything else he did during the investigation were window dressing and subterfuge.

The next day, in an editorial, the *World* proudly proclaimed that its "mission" was to "expose and combat all the shams, frauds, hypocrites and rascals, high or low," and the higher the better. Hilton, it seems, was on the high side of the list, and it was with special pride and a sense of duty that the *World* attacked him.

While the *World* backed away from further pounding of Stewart, denying any libel of the dead man, instead hinting that if anyone was libeled it was Hilton. It dared Hilton to press his case. Come on, the paper seemed to imply, let's go to court and put our hands on the Bible and testify under oath. Feeling certain there would be no challenge, Hilton was likened to the outlaws Robin Hood and Jesse James. By comparison, they were decent fellows. The ex-judge, on the other hand, was a coward and a thief. He "skulks behind the unburied corpse of Stewart and wraps himself in the grave-clothes of the man who made him."[27]

Other newspapers around the country weighed in on Hilton, siding with the *World*. The *Washington Chronicle* said that all of Stewart's blood relations and his wife were "ignored while Hilton plundered and absorbed" his former employer's wealth and property. The *Newark Standard* raised the specter of an evil Hilton, a "mean cur ... grinning behind the skeleton of [the] late A. T. Stewart." The *Columbus Press* chided Hilton for bringing charges in the name of Stewart only, thereby avoiding cross-examination as a witness. This created the appearance, at least, of cowardice.[28]

The public had long been mystified by the close relationship between Hilton and Stewart. The theft of the Stewart's body, Hilton's prominent role in the attempted recovery, the aggrandizement of wealth, and the vigorous defense against purported heirs—all of this enhanced that curiosity. It was a mystery with no solution in sight and therefore one without end.

On May 8, 1890, just a week after the criminal libel indictment, Graham, the city editor of the *World*, filed suit against Hilton, charging the beleaguered ex-judge with civil libel. He sought $50,000 in damages, charging Hilton with "verbal and written statements" that damaged his "fair fame and credit." The complaint quoted freely from Hilton's letter to the district attorney, using his own words against him.[29] All in all, Hilton had a rough week.

Next, Pulitzer pulled the owner of the *New York Sun* into the picture. Charles A. Dana—known to Americans for his service to the Lincoln administration during the Civil War—was accused of defending the Tweed ring in the past until the scandal stunk so much that he, too, was forced to join the opposition. Now Dana was defending Hilton. Referring to a short editorial in the *Sun* that complimented Hilton for refusing to pay "blackmail" to the *World*, Pulitzer's paper called Dana—who was one of the most artful and charming journalists of his time—a liar who should know better. A self-proclaimed fighter for the truth, the *World* declared boldly that the "trail of the widow-robber, Hilton, leads directly into the rickety old *Sun* building."[30]

It seemed that Pulitzer and his staff had an insatiable appetite for revenge, and each man wanted to enjoy it hot and in full view of the public. Each new article of condemnation seemed to be in competition with the previous one. After Hilton was flushed from cover, each article pounded him without mercy. The *World* would never undo what Hilton had done, but it would never let him forget that there was power in a free press—power to expose wrongdoing and dishonesty. There was also the power to be mean and inflict pain and misery. The pages of nineteenth-century American newspapers proudly featured villains and victims. Henry Hilton was both.

Hilton was powerless to stop the crusading Pulitzer and his staff. Doubtless, he understood this. After all, Hilton was a shrewd and gregarious man of manipulative skills. He could only wait for the runaway train to run out of steam, and he was smart enough to know that there would be a limit to the assault and an end to his humiliation and suffering.

He was right. The criminal libel charges against Pulitzer and company were dropped, and the Graham lawsuit fizzled. Pulitzer's crusade was over. Because of his failing eyesight, Pulitzer gave up day-to-day control of the *World*. Nevertheless, he was still very much in charge and remained so until his death in 1911.[31]

Diminishment of public interest in the pursuit of Hilton must have paralleled the fading of the fixation on the Stewart body mystery. Yet, nine years later, when writing Hilton's obituary, the *World* couldn't resist one final jab. "Is there any stranger story, any greater mystery than that of Henry Hilton's power over hard-fisted A. T. Stewart of whose millions he gained sole control?"[32]

Many would have said that the greater mystery was that of the grave robbery and the greater outrage was the lack of a solution or Hilton's refusal to reveal details he knew about efforts to recover the body. However, the great crime slowly lost its allure. With the death of Hilton in 1899, answers were put out of reach—as if hidden by a gentle, unseen touch, like the earth that quietly covers the dead and holds the mystery.

CHAPTER 15

Was Stewart's Body Recovered?

> It is certain that something was lowered down into the crypt which was built for the body of A. T. Stewart, but there are men in this city who assert that it was not the body of the merchant prince of Manhattan.
>
> *New York World*, April 19, 1890

In the dark, predawn hours of a winter morning in early 1879, the violated vault of Alexander T. Stewart was opened again to admit another inquisitive man on yet another mysterious mission. This time George W. Hamill, sexton of St. Mark's Episcopal Church, was involved. According to secret plans, Hamill met the visitor at St. Mark's and, after a brief discussion, willingly dug down and uncovered the vault. Then, with lamps in hand, he and the visitor quietly entered the chamber and descended slowly into the dark, acrid atmosphere of death. The short walk could not have failed to remind them of that horrible November morning when the crime was discovered. Both emerged in a matter of a few minutes, relieved and satisfied that they had found what they were looking for.

The man who went into the vault with the sexton was a high-ranking official with the New York City Police Department. He took with him a piece of irregularly cut paper to see if it matched the section of fine velvet cloth cut from inside the lid of Stewart's empty casket. According to a report in the *New York Sun*, it was a match.[1] It also helped to fuel speculation that Stewart's body had been recovered, although no one knew any details of the recovery. On that issue, everyone was still in the dark.

So what was there to go on besides rumor and speculation? During this same time period, Mrs. Stewart made comments to faithful friends, saying confidently that the body of her beloved husband had been recovered. This led to reports in New York newspapers in support of this contention. If Mrs. Stewart—this courageous, upright lady of faith—said so convincingly and in public, then it must be true. For some, no corroborating evidence was necessary.

For the skeptics there were the words of one William T. Blodgett, a well-respected resident of Garden City on Long Island. He reported seeing men carrying an oblong box into the cathedral at or near the time of the official visit to the underground Stewart vault at St. Mark's. After that, a guard was posted around the Garden City crypt, and men, supposedly in the confidence of Hilton, said the body had been recovered and safely reinterred.

Another highly placed man, however, disputed this information. W. R. Hinsdale, the manager of the Stewart estate at Garden City, said that the mausoleum was not yet ready for an occupant and that every day men carried oblong-shaped boxes in and out of the construction site. Furthermore, the night watchmen were employed by contractors, not the Stewart estate.[2]

In light of this confusion, many people gave strong consideration to the fact that Mrs. Stewart's happy messages to her friends were spoken during the same time that ex-postmaster Patrick H. Jones began his communications with Henry R. Romaine of Montreal. While the exchanges between Jones and Romaine were apparently not public knowledge until several months later, there were those who believed that Hilton was involved in low-profile negotiations with the criminals. It is not too much of a stretch to conclude there was some connection between Hilton's negotiations and the Jones/Romaine correspondence.

After all, it was Jones who produced the piece of cut paper sent by Romaine, and it was Jones who took it to the New York City Police Department. Therefore it is logical to conclude that the visit to the St. Mark's vault by the high-ranking police official was prompted by Jones' efforts. Taking this line of logic further, the piece of paper that matched the velvet cutout from inside the casket lid must have convinced the police and Hilton that Romaine and his cohorts were the thieves or their agents. Knowing this, Hilton entered his secret negotiations that allegedly led to the recovery of the body. (Is it also possible that Hilton engaged in bargaining sessions with another, unknown group, totally outside of media coverage?) Whatever the answer, Hilton himself supposedly identified what remained of the corpse by examining the teeth.[3]

So the brief report in the *New York Sun*, along with Mrs. Stewart's credible utterances and Jones' hard work—all this taken together along with who knows what else might be in the mix—led to the widespread belief that somehow Stewart's body had been recovered. Admittedly, the facts lacked the desired clarity and continuity, and reports that Jones broke off his negotiations with Romaine cast doubt on the matter. Nevertheless the majority opinion among the outside world held that the thieves (while not identified) had successfully negotiated for the release of their plunder. They got their money, and Mrs. Stewart regained her peace of mind.

New York newspapers were largely responsible for the theories that were circulated. While the news media could be wild and vicious, it could also be influenced or manipulated—or bought and tamed by the rich and powerful. Just how much of this type of influence was imposed on the New York media during the Stewart investigation can never be known. However, it is interesting to note that at no time did Henry Hilton—who had the power to influence the media—make a public statement regarding the recovery of the body. For those who waited for Hilton to produce hard proof and for those who distrusted his pronouncements and motives and doubted the credibility of news media, there was no closure. They waited for further developments and promoted rumors without number.

These folks were undoubtedly impressed when, in August 1881, private detective J. M. Fuller began extensive digging operations at Cypress Hills Cemetery in Brooklyn. The matter was resurrected again. While many people thought Fuller an utterly foolish man for launching the project, the New York City Police Department stationed a trio of detectives at the site, just in case the private detective's crew found the body.[4] This alone, indicates that the police, at least, believed the body was still missing, notwithstanding Hilton's secret negotiations. Also, Hilton sent a representative to talk to Fuller. Was this because the body was still missing, or was it to throw everyone off?

For years following the futile digging at Cypress Hills, the insiders—Hilton, the widow, the thieves, and the police—weren't saying all that much, leaving room for doubt. Jones and Romaine failed to resurface, and George A. Christian, the Washington resurrectionist, was forgotten, as was Michael Kelly, the hack man. In the wake of all this tantalizing ambiguity lay years of doubt and speculation that paralleled a gradual loss of interest in the unsolved mystery. As it died away, it haunted New York until all those who tuned in to the macabre events were gone or simply lost interest. There was really no closure, only a fading out.

With the end of the 1870s came the end of the grave-robbing era. News of this sordid crime diminishes greatly with the beginning of the next decade. In Ohio, the state where both medical schools and body snatching predominated, the legislature passed a law in 1881 permitting unclaimed bodies to be used for dissection.[5] Lawmakers wisely acknowledged that this horrible crime could only be eliminated by making bodies available to medical schools. By creating a legitimate supply to meet the demand they were killing an illegitimate enterprise. It was not only a simple application of a business principal but also a significant victory for both science and the shifting mass of the bereaved.

Yet the fear and memory of the grave robber lingered. If the Stewart grave robbery had any lasting impact on society, it was embodied in the men who stood guard in the cemeteries of eastern cities, day and night. Because grave robbery was still viewed as a very real threat, guarding rich men's graves became a necessity. The peace of mind of wealthy families had to be served. Well armed and with orders to shoot, the guardians of the dead paced around the great vaults during the night or stood in the dark shadows near "immortelles and roses and branches of palm" with an uncanny devotion to duty. Depending upon the wealth and prestige of the family, the graves were guarded for weeks or months—all because of the disappearance of Stewart's body. If nothing else, it proved that the wealthy feared something other than the devil and hell.

Occasionally, a newspaper would print an article about Stewart. He was just too famous a man to leave alone for too long. In one such instance, a reporter for a New York newspaper hunted up an "intimate friend" of the late merchant who was eager to talk about Stewart's superstitions and powerful seller's instinct. Toward the end of the interview, the informant said, pointedly, that Stewart's body had not been recovered, blaming Hilton's refusal to deal with the thieves. This interview took place in 1881,[6] before the farcical Cypress Hills Cemetery excavations.

A small ripple of excitement appeared in 1882, coming from a prison cell in Chester, Illinois. The stir was caused by Lewis C. Sweigels, who was serving a term in the Illinois state prison for robbery. He was also reputed to be a grave robber, and it was said that he was "concerned in the attempt to rob the grave of President Lincoln." Chicago Chief of Police McGargile and a couple of detectives interviewed Sweigels, who supposedly told a "very complete, circumstantial and consistent story of the robbery of A. T. Stewart's grave by himself," and two obscure men named Larry Gavin and a Mr. Coffe (first name unknown). The latter was the keeper of a saloon on Fourteenth Street in New York.

The story of the attempted robbery of President Abraham Lincoln's tomb in 1876 was recounted in Chapter 4. A man named L. C. Swegles (note the similarity to the name above) was then an agent for the U.S. Government and was sent to infiltrate the conspirators and convince them to take him in on their plans. While seemingly more a con artist than a faithful ally to the government, he did endear himself to members of the Lincoln conspiracy and was the direct cause of its ruin. Owing to his dubious character, however, it should surprise no one that he ended up in jail. The similarity of the spelling of the names, along with the story just related, is more than one could expect from coincidence. They are undoubtedly one and the same man.

Sweigels (or Swegles), the inmate, convinced officials that, if pardoned and given part of the reward, he could "restore the body." As the story goes, he was released and formed a syndicate with—of all people—the chief of police, two detectives, and a man named E. J. Lehman, all of Chicago. Their scheme was to "work up a case" and present it to Hilton along with promises to deliver Stewart's body for $100,000.

The syndicate allegedly made two or three trips to New York and conducted negotiations through a Mrs. Johnson, who was a New York police detective formerly connected with the Chicago police. According to the story, the meetings resulted in the body being returned to Hilton for the sum of $25,000. (Could these be Hilton's secret negotiations?)

When sought for an interview, McGargile admitted that he was instrumental in getting Swiegel released and hinted that there had been certain negotiations in New York, but he denied forming a syndicate, saying only that he and the other detectives lost faith in Swiegel. McGargile said that Swiegel conned them into releasing him and that their negotiations ended before the body was recovered. All this came from the *Chicago Inter-Ocean* and was squeezed down into a ludicrous article in the *New York Times* that added nothing but confusion to whatever dialogue remained.[7]

A couple of other stories were lightly circulated, but since they dealt with more inconsequential efforts, the reports never aroused much newspaper attention. In one such report Hilton supposedly received information that Kelly, the hack man, knew where the body was concealed, having carried it away as a hireling for the thieves. The purveyor of this information claimed to have known Kelly's movements from the time he left New York until the time he reached San Francisco, where he worked in Sutter's Market.

Hilton was sufficiently impressed with the story and paid a detective to cross the continent to San Francisco in search of Kelly. When he arrived in San Francisco, the detective learned that Kelly had moved to Tucson, Arizona, where he worked as the superintendent of a mine. The detective dutifully followed the trail to Tucson, only to learn that Kelly had been murdered by some of his workers because of a dispute. So at long last all interest in Kelly was put to rest.[8]

After this another group of unknown people surfaced with alleged information about the location of Stewart's remains. Trusting they could earn the $25,000 reward, they sent word to Hilton via a go-between, asking him to send the cash with a trustworthy agent to a designated meeting place. Other than that, they asked for immunity from arrest and prosecution. Hilton, ever wary, met this demand with a suggestion that they return the body first and trust to his honor that he would come forth with the reward after the remains were identified. He promised that, if satisfied with what they had to offer, he would give them the money and forty-eight hours head start before attempting any arrest. This counteroffer was refused and all further contact was ended, after which Hilton conceded that he had done everything he could do and would terminate all further efforts.[9]

While these stories did little to stir public interest in the Stewart mystery, a crime occurred that must have reminded people of the Merchant Prince's after-death experiences. It was an attempted grave robbery of yet another wealthy man. As it turned out, money motives were at the heart of the matter, but unlike the Stewart sensation, it was wrapped up in short order with strange, wholly unexpected conclusions.

This crime occurred at the Spring Forest Cemetery in Binghamton, New York, on October 23, 1884. By the mid-1880s wealthy East Coast families commonly hired heavily armed night watchmen to guard the vaults and graves of their dead. Night after night for months after interment, these hired guns stood guard from dusk to dawn, lest the cemetery be visited by grave robbers. The theft of Stewart's body placed the wealthy on alert.

However, there was no guard on duty at the Phelps family vault at the Spring Forest Cemetery when a team of grave robbers broke into the massive and lavish vault in an attempt to get at the remains of Robert S. Phelps, who died about three years previous. As with the Stewart outrage, the thieves made two attempts to carry away their prize. In the first attempt, sometime previous to October 23, they left evidence that crowbars had been used on the door. Sheriff Foster Black, one of the "keenest detectives in the state," also discovered that the lock on the vault had been replaced. He traced the purchase of the new lock back to a "prominent man" and laid plans to intercept the thieves, should they return.

Authorities were also intrigued because of a lawsuit against the estate of Robert S. Phelps by a doctor, H. O. Ely. He had sued the estate to recover fees of $5,000 for embalming the body and $4,500 for medical treatment, seemingly outrageous amounts for the time. Expecting a lawsuit to lead to exhumation, the sheriff believed that the doctor's adversaries, perhaps even members of the Phelps family, might be interested in denying Ely and his lawyers the opportunity to get their hands on the body.

On the night of October 23, Black placed two deputies in the graveyard to await the much expected second coming of the resurrectionists. At about midnight, the deputies—struck by fear—hesitated and considered their options, while the thieves quickly forced their way into the vault. Then, instead of stealing up to the vault to attempt an arrest, the deputies fled the cemetery in a panic. They ran through town shouting for help, awakening the townspeople and causing dogs to bark. This was not without effect, however, for the grave robbers, on hearing the dogs, were frightened off. When the sheriff returned with his weak-kneed deputies, they discovered an open casket and a partially removed body.

The sheriff was upset with his deputies and outraged at the brazen attempt to steal the body of such a prominent man. In his anger, he locked himself inside the vault and spent the night in the quiet company of the dead. The next day he left, still angry, saying only that he was not dealing with ordinary grave robbers.[10]

The general consensus probably was with the sheriff. Many people believed that, like the theft of Stewart's body, a group of clever men conspired to steal Phelps' corpse and hold it for ransom. Others felt that men of a different stripe were interested in procuring it to see how well Ely's embalming techniques preserved the body.[11] If Ely actually had to prove that his techniques worked and were worth the high cost, what better proof than the body he embalmed?

After some weeks it was announced that the father-in-law of the deceased man was indicted along with his attorney, Daniel Richards. Richards' eldest son, Robert, a promising law student, was also charged. These prominent men were implicated in a plot to steal the body of Robert S. Phelps in an apparent attempt to obstruct justice in the lawsuit brought by Ely. If the story is to be believed, they wanted to get the body out of the $8,000 vault before Ely obtained it by legal process.[12] After this report the matter died away rather quickly and was forgotten, while the Stewart mystery sustained some interest.

Then, in 1887, New York City Police Superintendent George W. Walling came out with a startling story, explaining in some detail how Stewart's remains were finally recovered, not through the efforts of Hilton, however, but by direction of Mrs. Stewart. Walling's story was one chapter in a book he titled *Recollections of New York Chief of Police*. It was a tell-all book about Walling's forty years spent investigating some of the most sensational crimes in the history of New York. Not surprisingly, he numbered the Stewart grave robbery among them.

According to Walling, Mrs. Stewart decided to take matters into her own hands. Once, "after a wakeful night," she boldly decided to deal with the body snatchers without the advice and consent of Hilton. She ordered her "representative" to offer $20,000 to the thieves in exchange for the body of her late husband. While Walling's story does not reveal when and how Mrs. Stewart contacted the thieves—or who it was she contacted—the plan was to have one of her relatives, possibly a Clinch nephew, deliver the money. The thieves consented, and the plan was put in motion.

The thieves instructed Mrs. Stewart to send her messenger with the money in a one-horse wagon out into the night. The messenger was to drive on until he came to the place of exchange and delivery. He was to come alone and surrender himself to the thieves, trusting in their honor. He didn't have to be concerned about where he was going. He wouldn't find the thieves; they would find him.

The messenger was instructed to depart New York at 10 p.m. and drive to Westchester County along a "lonely road" shown on a map provided by the thieves. He was to travel an indefinite distance until the early morning hours, and if the thieves were satisfied he was alone, he would be intercepted at some unknown place and given further instructions.

According to the story, Mrs. Stewart's kinsman bravely ventured forth alone in a one-horse carriage, driving through the night, not knowing where he was going or who he would meet. On two or three occasions, he sensed he was being followed. At about 3 a.m., a masked rider approached and gave a signal the messenger recognized. Further following instructions, he turned his buggy onto a lonely lane. After about another mile, he was confronted by another buggy, blocking the narrow road. There a masked man appeared with a bag and said, "Here 'tis. Where's the money?"

While the bag was loaded onto the messenger's wagon, he asked rather boldly, "Where is the proof of identity?"

The masked man handed Mrs. Stewart's kinsman a piece of velvet, saying only, "Here." By the light of a bulls-eye lantern, the messenger carefully compared the piece of velvet to a piece of irregularly cut paper and was satisfied there was a match. The thieves moved aside and counted the purchase money by lamplight. Then both parties departed in opposite directions, apparently satisfied in the fairness of the exchange.[13]

According to Walling's book, the bag loaded in the messenger's wagon contained the body of A. T. Stewart that, over the years, was pathetically reduced to bones. Since these events allegedly transpired between 1882 and 1884,[14] there would have been nothing left of the vagabond corpse but bones. Those the messenger transferred to a trunk. He accompanied the trunk on a train to Garden City, where the trunk's contents were emptied into a waiting coffin inside the magnificent crypt far beneath the dome of the Cathedral of the Incarnation and forever safe from grave robbers.

The *Times* dutifully reported these events but with generous grains of allowance. According to the *Times*, the story was told with the "imagination necessary to form a proper literary conclusion" to a mystery that had more twists and turns than an Edgar Allan Poe horror story. Apparently the *Times* considered Walling's fragmented account to be as unreliable as the past investigatory efforts of the then-superintendent and his fellow police officers. Walling wrote with all the "gloomy style" that characterized the "penny horribles in literature." Other than that, the *Times* would only state that "whether the remains were or were not actually returned, those in possession of the facts still refuse to say."[15] There were too many secrets and too many people determined to keep them. Truly, this was not an open-and-shut case, and there was apparently insufficient motivation for people to come forth with the truth.

Other New York newspapers including the *Herald* and the *World* were also harshly critical of Walling's book. The general consensus was that Walling shed no light on the mystery, although he could certainly have done so. Aside from venting his frustration on the rich and poor alike and laying the groundwork for numberless libel suits, Walling accomplished nothing. His intense personal views inserted in the chapters of his book dimmed his credibility as a writer.

Yet there were those who bought into his explanation and others who augmented Walling with their own revelations. An old manuscript in the archives of the Cathedral of the Incarnation repeats much of what Walling wrote. It states that Hilton refused to negotiate with the thieves who were acting through Patrick H. Jones. Then, in 1881, Mrs. Stewart decided to act and appealed to a young relative for help. An agreement was struck with the thieves, who promised to return the remains for $20,000. Instructions were sent to Mrs. Stewart that read, "A single man must leave New York at 10 p.m. and drive into Westchester by a lonely road." The young relative ventured out, the body was exchanged for the cash and brought back to New York and then to Garden City.

The curious manuscript further asserts that the entire arrangement was handled by the law office of Alexander and Greene of New York. The young relative who retrieved the body was a member of their firm. He was Prescott Hall Butler, a nephew of Mrs. Stewart.[16]

The Walling explanation was repeated in a book titled *The Gangs of New York*. It states, "Late in the winter of 1880, Mrs. Stewart ... approached the ghouls on her own account through General (Patrick H.) Jones." Romaine said he would turn over the remains for $100,000, and Mrs. Stewart was willing to pay. Jones, however, negotiated Romaine down to $20,000, and a deal was struck. The rest of the story flows like Walling's account. It even includes an illustration showing the thieves delivering the remains to a man who appears to be scrutinizing a piece of velvet from the coffin.[17]

An interesting piece of Stewart folklore grew out of this scenario. In 1936 an old man recalled that in his younger days, when the Stewart mystery was in the public mind, folks near the small town of Perrys Mills spoke of "A. T. Stewart's grave." The alleged grave was a shallow hole located by a big hemlock tree beside the Big Chazy River in upstate New York, close to the Canadian border. The hemlock tree bore the initials "A.T."

On May 7, 1936, an article appeared in the *North Countryman* in Rouses Point, New York, explaining the discovery of the grave by two boys fishing in the river. The boys saw a pile of dirt by the tree, an empty hole, evidence of a campfire, and the freshly carved initials. Because Stewart's stolen body had been the talk of the land, local people long referred to the spot as the place where it had been hidden pending Romaine's negotiations with Hilton and, later, Mrs. Stewart.

The reporter ran with the story and reasoned that the spot was, indeed, the temporary hiding place of Stewart's remains, deposited there in a zinc-lined trunk as the thieves made their way into Canada. When Mrs. Stewart worked out a deal for the return of the body, the thieves came back, dug up the trunk, and hauled it into Westchester County, where they made contact with the family member. The reporter triumphantly declared, "That all available information points to the fact that for weeks, a shallow grave beneath a hemlock tree near the little village of Perrys Mills held the key to a mystery that baffled the police of an entire nation."[18]

This fanciful solution fits nicely with Walling's story and shares with it a lack of credibility. It seems unlikely that the thieves would hide the body in plain sight on the bank of a well-traveled river where the fishing was good and then mark the tree with the letters "A. T." Why, after laying elaborate plans and pulling off a daring grave robbery, would they risk losing their bargaining chip? While the thieves probably did bury the body pending receipt of the ransom money, any such burial would have been close to their hiding place where it could be watched at all times. Thieves such as those would not have let their plunder out of their sight and control.

Mrs. Stewart, who religiously shunned publicity, made no public comments on the supposed recovery or her relative's role in it. It seems unlikely given her passive, secretive personality and Hilton's hold on her that she would have struck out on her own with a plan to rescue Stewart's much traveled bones. It was enough that she would spend the remainder of her days shut up inside her lavish mansion, utterly dependent on Hilton for advice and counsel. Alone with her memories and enshrouded by the shame that singled her out as an object of pity, she lived as a shut-in. It was a life of self-imposed exile that was broken occasionally by carriage rides around the city and visits from sympathetic friends.

So it was appropriate that Walling's story was released after she died. This lady was above reproach. She sat and suffered so long on a lonely pedestal that no one from among the press would disturb her. Nor would anyone who might harbor thoughts of publishing a book about the disappearance of her husband's body consider doing so while she was alive. While the news media often operated without restraint and with light regard for the truth, it had its limits. There was a perception among some

Cornelia Stewart giving the deed to the Cathedral of the Incarnation to Bishop Littleton in 1885. Henry Hilton stands at her left. Image courtesy of Garden City Archives.

newspapermen that Mrs. Stewart lived the life of an unhappy woman, one who shared her husband's wealth and goals but was denied any tenderness and affection by a loveless man. After his death she was allowed to suffer and age in private, burdened by certain terrible knowledge that every newspaperman in America coveted.

Finally, after spending the summer at Saratoga Springs, Mrs. Stewart died on October 25, 1886, of pneumonia, after a two-day illness. She was 84 years old, ancient by nineteenth-century standards. While her death was a front-page event, it couldn't compete with the arrival and dedication of the Statue of Liberty, France's gift to the United States. The magnificent statue and the long-running Buffalo Bill's Wild West Show were causes to celebrate. While much of New York was reveling in these pleasures, a small circle of friends and relatives was quietly shedding tears for Cornelia Stewart.

Cornelia Clinch Stewart, 1803–1886. Image courtesy of Garden City Archives.

Her funeral was low-keyed and simple, just the way she wanted it. It would have pleased her that her demise was overshadowed by public display elsewhere in the city. She never tried to draw attention to herself and purposely stayed out of the way during the investigation of the grave robbery.

Hilton, of course, took charge, running things and giving orders to Mrs. Stewart's private detective to admit no one to the mansion except close friends, including Mr. and Mrs. William Libbey. Mrs. Stewart was interred in the now famous Stewart mausoleum in the Cathedral of the Incarnation at Garden City, Long Island. Her casket was placed in the crypt, covered by a marble slab. An urn weighing 3,000 pounds was placed on top of the slab.[19]

There was no mention, of course, about the possibility of an attempt to steal her body, and yet all of New York must have thought about it. The presence of the heavy urn could only mean that her family was not taking any chances. It was a message to those daring or desperate enough to try: forget about it. The *Times* did, however, state that she was laid to rest "beside the grave wherein Mrs. Stewart had always supposed that the remains of her husband reposed." His name was inscribed on the slab next to her name,[20] and to all appearances, it looked as if a husband and wife were reposing side by side. Together forever—so it appeared.

So what if it was form over substance? Appearances were very important to the wealthy in the Gilded Age. The wondrous Stewart burial chamber, with its sculpture, marble, and inscriptions, gave off a rich, warm, Victorian glow that concealed all elements of an ugly, old crime and provided an attractive, artificial closure to the case. This artful arrangement was apparently satisfactory with the cathedral officials and the people of Garden City.

The *New York Sun* printed a long, touching obituary along with a small likeness of Mrs. Stewart, drawn from a photograph taken when she was eighty-three. Along with the expected eulogistic remarks, the *Sun* mentioned that she was placed in a sarcophagus next to one prepared for the body of her long-dead husband. "Whether or not it holds that body now is a secret with Mr. Henry Hilton ... who has never affirmed nor denied" reports of the recovery of Stewart's body.[21]

The *New York World* also used the occasion of Mrs. Stewart's death to briefly reprise the story of the theft of her husband's body almost eight years before. Looking over the history of two intertwined lives, the *World* quantified one as a life of sorry self-aggrandizement and the other as one of futility for having so little in the midst of so much. The ill-fated pair left behind "an immense estate and a perfect maelstrom of rumor and gossip." Abandoning the position it held in 1879, the *World* boldly stated that Stewart's body had not been recovered, suggesting that Romaine had destroyed it with quicklime after negotiations with Hilton failed.[22]

With Mrs. Stewart gone, a key player in the mystery most assuredly was silenced. While it is unlikely that the secretive lady would have made any revealing public statements had she lived longer, there were others still alive who were capable of exciting and definitive revelations. Among them were the men in charge of the cathedral, who most certainly knew whether a body had been secretly entombed there. There also were the thieves, of course, assuming they still lived, and Hilton, whose assorted, self-serving strategies many believed were to blame for the lack of a definitive solution.

Hilton reigned supreme, though uneasily, over the Stewart empire, subject to public criticism and, as noted in the previous chapter, vulnerable to editorial attack. Pulitzer's cruel vendetta, however, did not remove Hilton from power and failed to extract any new information about the truth of the recovery of Stewart's body. The assumption of many was that Hilton was satisfied with his work toward bringing the investigation to a close.

While he enjoyed the benefits of the Stewart fortune, Hilton was not able to keep the dry goods business profitable. After several entities tried and failed to run the business, A. T. Stewart and Company became Hilton, Hughes and Company. His partner was John Hughes, a son-in-law.

Hilton also entrusted his sons with managing the business, but they were not up to the challenge and were said to be "fond of amusements." While he pumped money into the business from the estate, his sons spent money freely. Accustomed to a carefree, good life, they were prone to chasing pretty, young actresses while dangling expensive gifts and were thus unable to handle executive responsibilities. One of his sons, Henry G. Hilton, a married man, carried on a positively scandalous and expensive affair with the famous actress Sylvia Gerrish, a California beauty.[23]

While the enterprise went steadily downhill, it did stand out in one way. Hilton, Hughes and Company purchased and operated what were surely some of the first motor vehicles in America. Called the Rogers Horseless Wagons, the French-built "automatic petroleum wagons" were put into operation in New York by Hilton on August 29, 1895, amid great fanfare. The inventor, Emile Rogers of France, launched three of the primitive horseless vehicles at Washington Square to the delight of the large crowd. It was said the rubber-tired, self-propelled wagons "ran well on the cobblestones and had no difficulty in going up the slight inclines."[24]

While Hilton was not interviewed on the subject, his futuristic experiment was called a success, probably the only stroke of genius he ever exhibited, assuming that it was his idea. No one knew it, of course, but New York was about to transform itself again, and Henry Hilton was at the wheel with the chance to run things as he had never run them before. All this was lost to him, however, for he was essentially an 1870s businessman with a mind for connivance and self-aggrandizement that was ill suited for science, invention, or even the management of a great enterprise. His vision extended no further than his next scheme to solidify his grasp of Stewart's money. Then, in 1896, one year after the grand motor-vehicle experiment, Hilton's company collapsed, and with it came the final fall of the House of Stewart.

The failure of Hilton, Hughes and Company made front-page news in the *New York Times*, a newspaper that was generally favorable to Hilton. Yet on September 27, 1896, the *Times* was forced to report that after twenty years, Hilton's company had lost $5 million of Stewart's money. Worse yet, creditors were banging at the door, demanding payment. The business was in the name of Albert B. Hilton, the youngest son of the ex-judge, but it was Henry Hilton himself who pulled the plug, allowing the great enterprise to collapse and die a quiet, public death in the streets of New York.

Over a twenty-year period, Hilton exploited the wealth of A. T. Stewart. He vainly attempted to run the dry goods business empire while luxuriating in mansions and resorts, rusticating on his farms, spending freely, and warding off attacks against Stewart's fortune and reputation. His Saratoga Springs mansion sat on a 2,000-acre estate called Woodlawn Park.[25]

He had far more than people thought he deserved, and the ease with which he acquired the fortune baffled many envious observers. Therefore his post-Stewart life amounted to a galling spectacle that left many shaking their heads. Then suddenly in the summer of 1896, it was over. Stores were closed, notices were posted, and employees were paid off. In the interest of protecting creditors, Hilton executed a general assignment to George M. Wright.[26]

It was said that Stewart's unique style of management included his habit of keeping vast amounts of critical data stored in his head, not on paper. It was he alone who understood the secret to success in dry goods—a secret he apparently did not share with his confidant. If he did, it was to no avail, as Hilton utterly failed to manage the huge business that he gathered unto himself. He was forced to quit, retreat, and retire with his riches. He was old and his money was safe, but his days of running things were over.

The collapse of such a lucrative business was caused by, in large part, Hilton's lack of the Stewart attention to detail and moneymaking magic. In the end, Hilton was good at self-aggrandizement and little more. It was a quality he shared with other wreckers and looters of the Gilded Age—men who gathered great wealth unto themselves at the expense of others.

The business collapse was also caused by Hilton's rabid anti-Semitism. As noted before, in 1877 Hilton issued a proclamation barring Jews from vacationing at the Stewart-owned resort in Saratoga Springs. Stewart, himself, would not have done anything to insult a group of people with money and influence. Following Hilton's prejudiced blunder, however, Jewish merchants began canceling orders from A. T. Stewart and Company. While Hilton failed to recognize the damage this caused, it was said that the Jews—whom Hilton willingly made his enemies—pulled away sufficient business to deliver blows that eventually proved fatal to the company with which they had long enjoyed a mutually profitable relationship.

So it came to pass that by design and deception or by the lack of talent, Hilton failed Stewart, his friend and mentor. He did this first by convincing Mrs. Stewart to hand over the company to him, next by alienating the Jews, who were some of his best customers, then by dominating and botching the investigation for Stewart's body, and finally by presiding over the steady decline and ruin of what was left of the great merchant's business empire. If Stewart had any special reason for holding so much trust and confidence in Hilton, it was lost on New York observers. This lapse of judgment by the otherwise astute Stewart was almost as mysterious as the disappearance of his body.

More secrets were lost with the death of Hilton on August 25, 1899, after a long illness at his great mansion in Saratoga Springs. The *New*

York Times took the occasion of his death to bring up Hilton's relationship with Stewart and to track the demise of the merchant's empire. The article was exceptional in that the Times dared to openly criticize Hilton, a task previously untaken by other papers. Hilton's career, said the Times, was built on the ruins of the "splendid fortune accumulated by his patron, A. T. Stewart." Echoing popular sentiment, the Times wanted to make certain everyone knew that Hilton did not earn and did not deserve the beneficence.

Summing up his life, the Times took the position that Hilton was a secretive, clever, selfish man who used his considerable manipulative skills and uncanny friendship with Stewart to assume control of a fortune and live life as a millionaire.[27] Then there was little else for the Times to write about, for Hilton, like Stewart, kept the events of his youth to himself, and no one, it seems, was willing to fill in the blanks. Instead, many indulged in spinning romantic yarns about the enigmatic Hilton, who, like Stewart, emerged from obscurity to a life of wealth and power.

Like his father figure, Hilton died a bitter and lonely man. He was estranged from some of his family members, haunted by failure, and essentially friendless. Despite his continuous, high-profile prancing, his public image was never one that earned respect. It was said that even his former associates from the Tweed days refused to attend the funeral.

Hilton was buried in Greenwood Cemetery in Brooklyn, the largest and most prestigious cemetery in New York and the surrounding area. Begun in 1840, Greenwood Cemetery features many elaborate and expensive statues, monuments, and tombs. It was often said that an ambitious New Yorker desired to live on Fifth Avenue, stroll through Central Park, and upon dying, rest with the elite at Greenwood Cemetery. Hilton joined many luminaries, including Horace Greeley, Peter Cooper, Henry George, Samuel F. B. Morse, and William "Boss" Tweed.[28]

He was buried in an ordinary three-by-seven grave. Some thought it unusual that "the only man who knew the full truth of the ghoulish raid upon the tomb of A. T. Stewart, would go to his long rest unprotected." Disappointed tomb builders expected the family to erect a fortress-like mausoleum for Hilton to protect the body from grave robbers. Others believed that some type of sophisticated electric alarm was placed in the ground to alert cemetery personnel should anyone commence digging.[29]

Surely the burial ceremony must have reminded mourners of the great mystery surrounding the theft of Stewart's body so many years ago. While friends and relatives stood beside Hilton's casket savoring memories of the man and contemplating the sad, uncertain adventure of death, many among them must have included his long-dead friend in their thoughts. Did anyone shudder and think of the possibilities at hand? Would the ghouls who took Stewart's corpse—still angry at Hilton's handling of the investigation—come in the night with a vengeance for the ex-judge's body? After so many years, would the terrible shadow of the grave robber appear over New York again?

The day could have been sunny and bright, or it could have been cloudy with rain, but it was not an ordinary summer day. That was no ordinary funeral, and those in attendance were burying more than a body. With the death of Hilton, the likelihood that anyone would come to an understanding of his long friendship with Stewart was greatly diminished. Moreover, Hilton's death meant that those who hoped for a definitive resolution to the most sensational grave robbery of the 1870s would get no satisfaction. Of the many hundreds of people who played a role in the mystery, Hilton was the one man who knew for certain whether Stewart's body had been recovered and, if so, the circumstances of the recovery.

In the Hilton obituary, the *Times* had little to say about the Stewart grave robbery. Recalling those frenzied days in 1878 and 1879, the *Times* merely stated that "energetic efforts" were made to find the body but that no one "ever admitted that it had been recovered." The paragraph ended by saying that most people believed that the body had been found and then reburied secretly to prevent others from stealing it. The *World* was far more quizzical. It said that the transaction for the return of the body was botched, scaring off the robbers, and as a result, "the body was never returned. Or perhaps it was returned—who knows?"[30] Who knows?

That was in 1899. Forty-two years later, when *The New Yorker* magazine briefly reprised the Stewart mystery, it was revealed that there were no records at the Cathedral of the Incarnation to show that he was reinterred in the lavish crypt beside his wife. There was, however, the word of old Adam Fleging, a Civil War veteran who had served as a night watchman at the cathedral while it was under construction and for some years after.

Fleging recalled that one day when he was at his post two men came in with a package and placed it in the crypt without ceremony. The old veteran—who proudly bore the scars of that tragic war—assumed, and then later in life asserted, that the package contained the remains of A. T. Stewart.

Fleging said the reburial took place in 1885, after the body had been concealed in the Marble Palace, Stewart's oldest store. He recalled that it came to the cathedral in a box marked "Bronze Statue from Galveston, Texas." The box was concealed in a "dark closet" under the north transept entrance. Fleging said that late one afternoon Mr. Cumliffe, the manager of Garden City, and E. D. Harris placed the remains in the crypt, unbeknownst to the bishop.

Another man, Horace Staples, who succeeded Fleging as a cathedral watchman, claimed he knew of a secret passage in the Marble Palace (then the *New York Sun* building) where Stewart's bones were concealed from the time they were turned over by the thieves until the reburial.[31] The official position of the cathedral is that Stewart's remains lie in the crypt.

The accounts of Fleging and Staples were carried forward into the twentieth century along with another tale about an elaborate alarm system supposedly installed in Stewart's crypt. According to an oft-told story, the crypt was wired with electricity so that any attempt to break and enter would cause the cathedral bells to chime. This burglar alarm was intended to rouse the community of Garden City and prevent the escape of the thieves. Since the bells never broke their silence in this manner, the assumption is that no one ever tried to break into the vault. *The New Yorker* called this a fabrication and nothing more.[32]

Thoughts and feelings not committed to writing; questions not asked and many others not answered; and reports, letters, and diaries—all were gone. Weakened memories, elaborate stories stemming from small remnants of truth and spun out of control, and of course, death all contributed to a deterioration of the great A. T. Stewart mystery.

The great Stewart mansion—the formidable marble mausoleum—was destroyed, too. Despite its artistic magnificence and splendor, it was torn down prematurely and unceremoniously in 1901 after serving as the headquarters for the Manhattan Club following the death of Mrs. Stewart.[33] Although built like a fortress with an enduring quality, it failed to stand the test of time. Strangely, most of the marble from the demolished house was converted into gravestones for the city's cemeteries.[34]

The body thieves, hunted for so long, kept their distance and their silence, dying anonymously, one by one, with their notoriety intact. While they caused one of the greatest sensations in American history, none of them stepped forward to take credit for it. One might conclude that they were satisfied for merely having pulled it off. One might also admire the bond that held them together in a vow of secrecy—surely one of the strangest elements in this mystery. Interestingly, Mrs. Stewart's will did not provide a pool of funds to be used in the continued pursuit of the body snatchers. This suggests that she was satisfied that her husband's bones had been recovered or wanted to leave the impression that they had come home at long last.

Other players faded quietly, too, over time, including George A. Christian, hack man Michael Kelly, St. Mark's sexton George Hamill, the Hiltons, the Clinches, Henry R. Romaine, and Patrick H. Jones. Henry Hilton and Cornelia Stewart are still resting in peace; no one came for their bodies. The spiritualists and clairvoyants—two groups that were badly discredited by the end of the century—added nothing toward a solution. Aside from Superintendent Walling, no one from the New York City Police Department made any public revelations.

For the participants in this long-running drama of the macabre, time literally ran out. No one took a bow because no one emerged triumphant. The spectators from among the public were forced to deal with their bewilderment as best they could. Their hunger for the truth or further embellishment went unsatisfied. If the chain of events proved anything, it was that not all great New York theater took place on a stage.

It was, however, theater that was not easily forgotten. At least, it was not forgotten until the nineteenth century ended and the next century burst on the scene with an energy and a modern outlook that made grave robbery seem so evil and repulsive that it could not have existed at all and was, therefore, not a part of the racial memory. The sunny, progressive politics of the new century set it apart from the dark and desperate economics of the 1870s, when grave robbery was very real and emblematic of a terrible, pessimistic time. That was a time so desperate that certain, extraordinary people would flout ancient taboos and dig up the dead—like a root crop—to sustain the living.

In 1904 a veteran grave robber came forth, broke his vow of silence, and told the story of a band of grave robbers that operated in central

New York State in the 1880s. Orville A. Manzer of Camden, New York, revealed that "hundreds of bodies" were stolen from graveyards in the New York towns of Camden, Herkimer, Richland, Watertown, Rome, Utica, and Syracuse, then sold to medical colleges or held for ransom.

The gang was led by Harvey W. Kendall, a young man who was mysteriously murdered on May 18, 1883. Kendall and all twelve gang members, except Manzer, were students attending a Syracuse medical school. It was always suspected that Kendall was shot and killed while attempting to rob a grave. His body was found in a cemetery with an empty six-shooter along with "burglar's tools and appliance used for opening graves." Manzer's announcement confirmed long-held beliefs.

Manzer spoke about the gang's solemn vow of secrecy, given in a secluded ritual during which he made a "blood curdling oath not to divulge anything he might have seen or heard." He explained, "After the ceremony each of the students and myself bared our right arms. From the vein of the arm of each a little blood was drawn into a human skull. Into this mixture of blood whiskey was poured and from an orifice in the skull each of the thirteen men drank in sequence." Each man was then a "full member of the Body Snatcher's League."

That was long ago. Now the repentant resurrectionist said he had nothing to hide and nothing to fear by talking about that which was once forbidden, indicating that his fellow gang members were no longer alive to harm him. For many years after he broke ranks with the grave-robbing enterprise, he lived the life of a well-respected man. He had been an associate manager of the *Camden Advance-Journal* and a member of the First Methodist Church, and he was known throughout the state for his support of the Prohibitionist Party and its crusade against alcohol. It would seem that he had long been involved in good works, as if trying to undo the evils of his past.

While the exciting revelation smacked of exaggeration and shed no light on the Stewart mystery, it did reveal, in stark detail, something of the dark, secret world of the resurrectionists, perhaps the most unique combine of kindred spirits to inhabit the planet. It may never be possible to understand the strength of such an alliance and the inner workings of its collective psyche, lingering, as it does, outside the reach of everyone but those with the wildest ability to imagine. It competes favorably with tales of ghosts, werewolves, vampires, necromancers, and other beings of high legend.

Was Stewart's body found? Considering the lack of a convincing report from the authorities, a newspaper, or a corroborated contemporary account, the weight of the evidence suggests that it wasn't recovered. Harry Resseguie, a leading authority on Stewart, doubted the veracity of Walling's account and those that followed it.[35] Other Long Island historians concur. Richard Lathers, who knew Stewart and followed his mercantile career, was of the opinion that the body was not recovered and so stated in his lengthy *Reminiscences*.[36]

Of all the wordy pronouncements made by Henry Hilton, the one most conspicuously lacking is a positive, forthright public statement about the recovery of the body. It seems oddly inconsistent with his character and his behavior during the investigation that he would accomplish his purpose and keep it a secret. It seems logical that Hilton, who led the investigation with so much vigor and determination, would have wanted to let the world know that he succeeded if, in fact, he had. A man who was enthralled with running things would certainly want to revel openly in his successes. A man whose entire life was spent in the pursuit of gain had nothing to gain by keeping his mouth shut.

Does this mean that the sketchy reports of a reburial in the crypt at the Cathedral of the Incarnation were false and were the result of yarn spinning, speculation, confusion, or a desire to deceive, much like other incidents in the historic investigation? Did Hilton actually recover the body, reinter it, and choose to keep it a secret? Or did Mrs. Stewart find the strength to circumvent Hilton, take steps on her own volition, and later convince Hilton to keep it a secret?

There are many questions. We are left with uncertainty and a cold, defiant stare from the sad, blank eyes of Henry Hilton as they look out at the world from a photograph. If the body was not recovered, why not? If it was found, how and when was it reclaimed, and what was the price? Pick out an explanation from the many possibilities or create your own theory. Better still, take the position of Herbert Anstey, Hilton's trusted private secretary. In 1890 he was asked by a reporter point-blank, "Tell me Anstey, what is there in these reports about the recovery of the body?" Anstey replied, "Nothing. The body has not been recovered."[37]

Many years passed after Anstey's forthright statement—many years with no credible news of a solution. Then early in the evening on July 14, 1956, a terrible fire broke out in Stewart's Great Iron store, then called the Wanamaker Store. It burned for twenty-five hours, destroyed

Bust of A. T. Stewart created in 1969 for Garden City's 100th anniversary. Image courtesy of Garden City Archives.

the historic building entirely, caused injury to 187 firemen, and disrupted subway traffic for a week. The large fire inspired more articles about A. T. Stewart and the mysterious disappearance of his body—a mystery that still confounded "whodunit" fans of the macabre.

The *New York Times* merely mentioned that the Stewart grave robbery was unsolved,[38] but Ruth Reynolds, a reporter for the *Daily News*, went much further. She wrote in detail about the death, funeral, and resurrection of the Merchant Prince, events that took place long ago, beyond the memory of all but the very oldest of New Yorkers. Her account agreed in most respects with the newspaper record of 1878 and 1879, but there was more. In addition to old news, she located and talked to Bernard Cowen, a veteran attorney with a long memory and a willingness to digress.

About twenty-five years previous, Cowen had a client named Terence H. Forrest, owner of the Forrest Shirt Laundry at 430 West Forty-fifth Street in New York. Cowen recalled that Forrest was a "spry 95 years old" and "given to reminiscences." Among his memories were the many graveyards of old New York, some of which were abandoned as the noisy metropolis grew and, like a hungry giant, indiscriminately chewed up land in big chunks. By the mid-nineteenth century, some cemeteries began to look like real estate, too valuable for the quiet neighborhoods of the dead.

Forrest talked to Cowen about the cemetery next to the Grace Episcopal Church on Broadway between Tenth and Eleventh streets. Grace Episcopal was an upscale church, frequented by New York society types who paid up to $1,600 per pew for the privilege of sitting through weddings, baptisms, and funerals. This Gothic masterpiece was just to the north of the property Stewart bought to build his Great Iron store. During the excavation of the ground, some of the graves in the church cemetery collapsed and fell away. According to Forrest, bones and pieces of coffins were simply loaded up and hauled away with dirt and debris.

In about 1874, two young Irishmen returned to New York from the West and went to the cemetery at Grace Episcopal Church to visit the grave of their father. When they discovered their father's grave was among those that were destroyed during the excavation of Stewart's property, the angry and saddened young men sought out the Merchant Prince for an explanation. They were summarily dispensed with by Stewart, who had more important things to do, so they went to the building contractor. The contractor merely said he was following Stewart's orders when he hauled the human remains away, so the angry young fellows went back to Stewart. According to Forrest, Stewart kicked them out of his office.

They left as ordered, but before they departed, the two young men (whom Forrest did not name) made an awful promise: "Mark you Stewart, your bones will never rest. You'll get the same treatment!" Forrest then told Cowen that the two young Irishmen, with the fire of vengeance in their hearts, pulled off the great grave robbery at the St. Marks churchyard on November 7, 1878.

Cowen recalled that he was shocked and amazed at this revelation and grilled Forrest for further explanation. Forrest stubbornly stuck to his story, insisting the two young men were telling the truth because they were his relatives and he trusted them. He even allowed them to bury

Stewart's remains on his Long Island farm property at Amityville. Cowen was curious as could be expected and intended to explore the farm for evidence of a body, but never got around to it.[39]

There is some fragile support for this story. Articles in the *New York Herald* and *New York Times* at the time reported that cemetery property was disturbed when Stewart's Marble Palace was under construction, causing public outrage. It was believed that the desecration of so many graves at Stewart's order caused some of those affected to retaliate and steal Stewart's body. However, the idea was never given serious consideration by the police or the press, and Hilton scoffed at it. Furthermore, the newspaper articles referred to the Marble Palace and the cemetery at Amity Street Baptist Church, not the Great Iron store and the Grace Episcopal Church cemetery.

Still, it might be tempting to believe the story of the two young Irishmen seeking revenge for their father. After all, it is a sympathetic—even heroic—explanation. This writer, however, doubts the veracity of this grave-desecration theory, for aside from location inconsistencies, it seems highly unlikely that two men acting alone could have pulled off the crime no matter what their motives might have been. There are always elements of luck and coincidence in any risky enterprise, but to conclude that just two people planned and stole Stewart's body stretches all random elements beyond the point of restraint. So with some more twists and turns, the mystery came to another dead end seventy-six years after its inception.

In 1956 a terrible fire destroyed a New York landmark, rekindling old memories of a great mystery that Gothamites were never able to bury. The spectacular fire on Broadway brought A. T. Stewart back from the darkness and into the limelight like a second resurrection embellished with flames and horror, but with no definitive answers to the questions raised by the great mystery of America's most infamous grave robbery. Like a secret passageway running through history, allowing the truth to hide, there is something out there that has escaped everyone.

Notes

Chapter 1: The Life of a Merchant Prince

1. *New York Times*, April 12, 1876.

2. Doane Robinson, *History of South Dakota* (Logansport, IN: B. F. Bowen & Co., 1904), p. 243.

3. Jay E. Cantor, "A Monument of Trade, A. T. Stewart and the Rise of the Millionaire's Mansion in New York," *Winterthur Portfolio* 10 (1975): 165–198.

4. *New York Times*, April 11, 1876.

5. *New York World*, June 6, 1890; James Bell disappeared at sea in 1818. According to Vincent F. Seyfried in *The Founding of Garden City, 1869–1893*, (Uniondale, LI: Salsbury Printers, 1969), p. 6, Stewart's half-sister was named Minnie.

6. *Harper's New Monthly Magazine*, December 1866 to May 1867, p. 522.

7. Harry E. Resseguie, "The Folklore of A. T. Stewart," *New York Folklore Quarterly* 18 (2) (Summer 1962): 128.

8. *New York Times*, April 12, 1876.

9. Ibid., April 11, 1876.

10. Ishbel Ross, *Crusades and Crinolines* (New York, Evanston and London: Harper & Row, 1963), p. 13.

11. *New York World*, April 14, 1890.

12. *St. Paul Pioneer and Democrat*, October 29, 1862.

13. "New York Letter" in the *Rochelle* (Illinois) *Register*, February 12, 1881.

14. *New York Times*, April 12, 1876; according to Resseguie in "Folklore of A. T. Stewart," p. 135, she sold shrimp, not apples.

15. Stephen N. Elias, *Alexander T. Stewart: The Forgotten Merchant Prince* (Westport, CT: Praeger, 1992), p. 5.

16. William Addison Clarke, "A. T. Stewart the Merchant Prince, a Story of His Business Career," *The Counter* 4 (3) (June 1901): p. 8.

17. Harry E. Resseguie, "The Decline and Fall of the Commercial Empire of A. T. Stewart," *The Business History Review* 36 (3) (Autumn 1962): p. 257.

18. Elias, *Forgotten Merchant Prince*, p. 61.

19. *New York Times*, December 30, 1878, interview with Henry Hilton.

20. Harry E. Resseguie, "A. T. Stewart's Marble Palace, the Cradle of the Department Store," *New York Historical Society Quarterly* 48 (42) (April 1964): pp. 137–138.

21. Cantor, "Monument of Trade," pp. 171–298.

22. Marquis James, "The Corpse of A. T. Stewart," *The New Yorker*, December 6, 1941.

23. Resseguie, "A. T. Stewart's Marble Palace," p. 160.

24. Dumas Malone, ed., *Dictionary of American Biography*, vol. 18 (New York: Charles Scribner & Sons, 1936), p. 4.

25. *St. Paul Pioneer and Democrat*, October 29, 1862.

26. Elias, *Forgotten Merchant Prince*, p. 51.

27. Ibid., p. 49.

28. *New York World*, April 17, 1890.

29. William Leach, *Land of Desire* (New York: Pantheon Books, 1993), p. 21.

30. *St. Paul Pioneer and Democrat*, October 7, 1868.

31. Jean H. Baker, *Mary Todd Lincoln, a Biography* (New York: W. W. Norton & Co., 1987), p. 185.

32. Author Unknown, "Stewart's," *The Nation* 34 (332) (April 20, 1882).

33. William Perrine, "A. T. Stewart's Nice Young Men," *Ladies Home Journal* 21 (10) (September 1904).

34. Elias, *Forgotten Merchant Prince*, p. 50.

35. *St. Paul Pioneer and Democrat*, January 22, 1862.

36. Richard O. Boyer and Herbert M. Morais, *Labor's Untold Story* (New York: United Electrical Radio and Machine Workers of America, 1972), p. 19.

37. Elias, *Forgotten Merchant Prince*, p. 90.

38. Baker, *Mary Todd Lincoln*, p. 185.

39. Ishbel Ross, *The President's Wife, Mary Todd Lincoln* (New York: G. P. Putnam's Sons, 1973), p. 209.

40. Elias, *Forgotten Merchant Prince*, p. 104.

41. *New York Times*, March 6, 1869.

42. Elias, *Forgotten Merchant Prince*, p. 172.
43. *New York World*, April 15, 1890.
44. *New York Times*, March 12, 1869.
45. Edward K. Beale, ed., *Diary of Gideon Welles, Secretary of the Navy under Lincoln and Johnson*, vol. 3 (New York: W. W. Norton & Co. 1960), p. 548.
46. *The Business History Review*, p. 263.
47. *St. Paul Pioneer and Democrat*, May 5, 1869.
48. Elias, *Forgotten Merchant Prince*, p. 138; *New York Times*, March 10, 1869.
49. *The Business History Review*, p. 264.
50. Richard O'Connor, *Gould's Millions* (New York: Ace Books, Inc., 1962), p. 65.
51. Andy Logan, "That Was New York, Double Darkness and Worst of All," *The New Yorker*, February 22, 1958.
52. *New York Times*, August 27, 1896.
53. Roger A. Wines, "A. T. Stewart and Garden City," *Nassau County Historical Journal* 29 (1) (Winter 1958): 9.
54. Elias, *Forgotten Merchant Prince*, p. 184.
55. Ibid., pp. 185–186.

Chapter 2: The Death of a Merchant Prince

1. Michael Klepper and Robert Gunther, "A Ranking of the Forty Wealthiest Americans of All Time," *American Heritage*, October 1998 (they erred in one respect, using a photograph of another man to represent Stewart), p. 58.
2. *St. Paul Pioneer*, August 10, 1866.
3. Elias, *Forgotten Merchant Prince*, pp. 147–148.
4. Malone, *Dictionary of American Biography*, p. 4.
5. *New York Times*, March 6, 1869.
6. M. H. Dunlop, *Gilded City, Scandal and Sensation in Turn-of-the-Century New York* (New York: Perennial, An Imprint of Harper Collins Publishers, 2000), p. 51.
7. *New York Times*, April 12, 1876.
8. Vincent, *Founding of Garden City*, p. 6.
9. "New York Letter," in the *Rochelle* (Illinois) *Register*, February 12, 1881.
10. *New York Times*, April 14, 1876.
11. Maxwell F. Marcuse, *This Was New York!* (New York: Carlton Press, 1965), p. 348.
12. Marquis, "Corpse of A. T. Stewart," p. 56.
13. *New York Times*, April 14, 1876.

14. *New York Herald*, November 8, 1878.
15. *New York Sun*, November 9, 1878.

Chapter 3: Violation of the Tomb

1. *Cincinnati Gazette* in the *New York Evening Post*, November 7, 1878.
2. *New York Herald*, November 8, 1878.
3. Richard Wheatley, "The New York Police Department," *Harper's New Monthly Magazine*, December 1886 to May 1887, pp. 498–499.
4. *New York Times*, November 8, 1878.
5. Moses King, ed., *King's Handbook of New York City 1893*, vol. 1 (Boston: Moses King, 1893; New York: Benjamin Blom Inc., 1972), p. 351.
6. Michael Norman and Beth Scott, Historic Haunted America (New York: Tom Doherty Associates, 1995), pp. 243–244.
7. *New York Sun*, November 8, 1878.
8. Ibid., November 9, 1878.
9. *New York Herald*, November 8, 1878.
10. *New York Times*, November 8, 1878.
11. *New York Herald*, November 12, 1878.
12. *New York Weekly Tribune*, November 13, 1878.
13. *New York Herald*, November 8, 1878.
14. Ruth Reynolds, "The Merchant Prince and the Grave Robbers," *Daily News New York*, August 12, 1956.
15. *New York Times*, November 8, 1878.
16. Ibid., August 27, 1896.
17. *St. Paul Pioneer*, March 6, 1868.
18. *The National Cyclopaedia of American Biography*, vol. 10 (James T. White & Co., 1900; Ann Arbor, MI: University Microfilms, 1967), p. 401.
19. *New York Evening Post*, November 7, 1878.
20. *New York Herald*, November 8, 1878.
21. *New York Weekly Tribune*, November 13, 1878.
22. *New York Tribune*, November 8, 1878.
23. Wines, "A. T. Stewart and Garden City," p. 11.
24. *Washington Post*, November 9, 1878.
25. Alexander B. Callow Jr., *The Tweed Ring* (Oxford: Oxford University Press, 1969), p. 127.
26. *New York Times*, April 16, 1882.
27. *New York World*, April 14, 1890.
28. Elias, *Forgotten Merchant Prince*, p. 158.
29. *New York World*, April 16, 1890.
30. *New York Times*, August 25, 1899.

31. *New York Herald*, November 8, 1878.
32. *New York Times*, November 8, 1878.

Chapter 4: The Resurrectionists

1. Patricia Cline Cohen, *The Murder of Helen Jewett, The Life and Death of a Prostitute in 19th Century New York* (New York: Vintage Books, a Division of Random House, Inc., 1998), p. 108.

2. T. S. Sozinsky, "Grave Robbing and Dissection," *Penn Monthly* 10 (206) (1879): p. 216.

3. *New York Times*, November 28, 1878.

4. *National Police Gazette*, January 3, 1880.

5. *Dakota Pantagraph*, June 18, 1878.

6. *New York Times*, November 13, 1878.

7. *National Police Gazette*, May 8, 1880.

8. Ibid., May 22, 1880.

9. *Sioux Falls Argus-Leader*, April 4, 1904.

10. Pittsburgh Dispatch in the *Dakota Pantagraph*, April 30, 1879.

11. Cincinnati Commercial in the *Dubuque Daily Times*, March 4, 1859.

12. Lloyd Lewis, *The Assassination of Lincoln, History and Myth* (New York: MJF Books, 1957), pp. 265–266. The monument was dedicated on October 15, 1874.

13. *Chicago Tribune*, November 18, 1876.

14. Lewis, *Assassination of Lincoln*, p. 269.

15. *Chicago Tribune*, November 18, 1876.

16. Dale Carnegie, *Lincoln, The Unknown* (New York: Dale Carnegie and Associates, Inc., 1932), p. 249. The reader is cautioned that the Carnegie account differs somewhat from the newspaper reports at the time of the crime.

17. Carnegie, Lincoln, *The Unknown*, p. 251.

18. *Chicago Tribune*, November 18, 1876.

19. *New York Times*, June 1, 1877.

20. Lewis, *Assassination of Lincoln*, p. 282.

21. *Chicago Tribune*, November 18, 1876.

22. Harry J. Sievers, *The Harrison Horror* (Public Library of Fort Wayne and Allen County, 1956), p. 8.

23. Sievers, *Harrison Horror*, p. 8.

24. *New York Times*, May 31, 1878.

25. *Cincinnati Times* in the *New York Times*, June 5, 1878.

26. Sievers, *Harrison Horror*, pp. 22, 27.

27. Yankton Press and Dakotaian (Yankton, Dakota Territory), June 27, 1878.

28. *Bismarck Tribune* (Bismarck, Dakota Territory), April 23, 1880.

29. *Columbus Journal* (Columbus, Ohio) in the Dakota Pantagraph, September 11, 1878.

Chapter 5: Middleton, Allekton, Dr. Christian, and Other "Clews"

1. *New York Weekly Tribune*, November 13, 1878.
2. *Daily Iowa State Register* (Des Moines), September 2, 1871.
3. *New York Evening Express*, November 13, 1878.
4. George W. Walling, *Recollections of a New York Chief of Police* (Montclair, NJ: Patterson Smith, 1972), p. 229.
5. *New York Herald*, November 9, 1878.
6. *New York Sun*, November 9, 1878.
7. *New York Evening Post*, November 9, 1878.
8. *New York Times*, November 9, 1878.
9. *New York Sun*, November 9, 1878; *Evening Telegram* (New York), November 9, 1878.
10. *New York Times*, November 9, 1878.
11. *New York Sun*, November 10, 1878; *New York Herald*, November 9, 1878.
12. *New York Evening Post*, November 14, 1878.
13. *New York Herald*, November 9, 1878; *New York Evening Post*, November 9, 1878; *Newark Morning Register*, November 10, 1878.
14. *New York Evening Post*, November 11, 1878.
15. Ibid., November 13, 1878.
16. *New York Herald*, November 10, 1878.
17. Ibid., November 11, 1878.
18. Ibid., November 14, 1878.
19. Ibid., November 11, 1878.
20. Ibid., November 14, 1878.
21. *New York Times*, November 10, 1878.
22. *Chicago Tribune*, November 9, 1878.
23. *Newark Morning Register*, November 9, 1878.
24. *New York Herald*, November 10, 1878; *Newark Morning Register*, November 12, 1878.
25. *New York Herald*, November 10, 1878.
26. Alvan, F. Sanborn, ed., *Reminiscences of Richard Lathers, Sixty Years of a Busy Life in South Carolina, Massachusetts and New York* (New York: The Grafton Press, 1907), p. 46.
27. *New York World*, October 26, 1886.
28. George H. Douglas, *The Golden Age of the Newspaper* (Westport, CT: Greenwood Press, 1999), pp. 29–34.

29. Frank Luther Mott, *American Journalism, A History: 1690–1960* (New York: The MacMillan Co., 1962), p. 420.

30. Douglas, *Golden Age of the Newspaper*, pp. 39–43.

31. Michael Schudson, *Discovering the News, A Social History of American Newspapers* (New York: Basic Book, Inc., 1978), p. 68.

32. John Tebbel, *The Compact History of the American Newspaper* (New York: Hawthorn Books, Inc., 1963), p. 125.

33. *New York Herald*, November 11, 1878.

34. *Chicago Tribune*, November 9, 1878.

35. *New York Times*, November 11, 1878.

36. *New York Evening Post*, November 11, 1878.

Chapter 6: In Search of the Ghouls

1. *Baltimore Gazette* in the *Washington Post*, November 26, 1878.

2. *New York Sun*, November 12, 1878.

3. Patrick F. Palermo, *Lincoln Steffens* (Boston: Twayne Publishers, a Division of G. K. Hall & Co., 1978), p. 26.

4. Jacob A. Riis, *The Making of an American* (New York: Grosset & Dunlap, New York, 1901), p. 219.

5. *New York Evening Express*, November 15, 1878.

6. Ibid., November 18, 1878.

7. *New York Times*, September 18, 1878.

8. *New York Evening Post*, September 23, 1878.

9. James Lardner and Thomas Reppetto, *NYPD, A City and Its Police* (New York: Henry Holt & Co., 2000), pp. 24–26.

10. *Evening Telegram* (New York), November 6, 1878.

11. *New York Herald*, November 11, 1878.

12. Ibid., November 12, 1878.

13. Ibid., November 13, 1878.

14. *Evening Telegram*, November 13, 1878.

15. *New York Times*, November 12, 1878.

16. Ibid., November 14, 1878.

17. Resseguie, "Folklore of A. T. Stewart," pp. 138–139.

18. *New York Times*, November 14, 1878.

19. Ibid., November 12, 1878.

20. *New York Herald*, November 12, 1878.

21. *New York Times*, November 12, 1878.

22. *New York Evening Post*, November 8, 1878.

23. *New York Times*, November 13, 1878.

24. Ibid., November 14, 1878.

25. Ibid.
26. *New York Herald*, November 12, 1878.
27. *New York Sun*, November 14, 1878.
28. *New York Herald*, November 20, 1878.
29. Ibid., November 14, 1878.
30. *New York Evening News* in the *Washington Post*, November 15, 1878.
31. *New York Times*, November 15, 1878.
32. Douglas, *Golden Age of the Newspaper*, pp. 57–58, 120.
33. *New York Times*, November 16, 1878.
34. *New York Herald*, November 16, 1878.
35. *Evening Telegram*, November 15, 1878.
36. *New York Herald*, November 17, 1878.

Chapter 7: Hackman Kelly

1. *Evening Telegram*, November 15, 1878.
2. *New York Sun*, July 6, 1879; *New York Times*, November 23, 1878; *New York Herald*, November 24, 1878.
3. *New York Herald*, November 15, 1878.
4. *New York Sun*, July 6, 1879.
5. *New York Tribune*, November 26, 1878.
6. *New York Times*, November 16, 1878.
7. *New York Sun*, November 14, 1878.
8. *New York Herald*, November 16, 1878.
9. *New York Times*, November 15, 1878.
10. *New York Herald*, November 16, 1878.
11. *New York Evening Post*, November 14, 1878.
12. Ibid., November 15, 1878.
13. *New York Times*, November 16, 1878.
14. Elias, *Forgotten Merchant Prince*, pp. 159–160.
15. *New York Times*, November 15, 1878.
16. Ibid.
17. Ibid., November 16, 1878.

Chapter 8: Closing In on the Ghouls

1. *New York Herald*, November 8, 1878.
2. Lewis, *Assassination of Lincoln*, p. 283.
3. *Chicago Tribune*, November 17, 1878.
4. *New York Times*, November 17, 1878.
5. *Chicago Tribune*, November 17, 1878.

6. *New York Times*, November 16, 1878.
7. Ibid., November 17, 1878.
8. *The Evening Telegram* (New York), November 20, 1878.
9. *New York Herald*, November 17, 1878.
10. *New York Times*, November 20, 1878.
11. *New York Sun*, November 17, 1878.
12. *New York Times*, November 17, 1878.
13. Ibid., November 17, 1878.
14. *New York Herald*, November 9, 1878.
15. Ibid., November 16, 1878.
16. Ibid., November 17, 1878.
17. *New York Sun*, November 17, 1878.
18. *New York Times*, November 17, 1878.
19. *New York Sun*, November 17, 1878.
20. *New York Times*, November 17, 1878.
21. Ibid., November 19, 1878.
22. *New York Herald*, November 18, 1878.
23. Edward Robb Ellis, *The Epic of New York City* (New York: Old Town Books, 1990), pp. 358–359.
24. *New York Herald*, November 19, 1878.
25. Herbert Asbury, *The Gangs of New York* (New York: Capricorn Books, 1970), p. 219. Leslie came from a good Ohio family and had a well-rounded education, but after the Civil War, he went to New York and launched a career of crime. He became known as a genius among bank robbers. New York City Police Superintendent George W. Walling credited Leslie and his gang with 80 percent of the bank robberies in the United States from 1865 until he was murdered in 1884.
26. *New York Evening Post*, November 9, 1878.
27. *The Evening Telegram*, August 2, 1878.
28. Edward Crapsey, *The Nether Side of New York* (Montclair, NJ: Patterson Smith, 1969), p. 116.
29. Mott, *American Journalism*, p. 423.
30. *New York Sun*, August 24, 1879.
31. Crapsey, *Nether Side of New York*, p. 7.
32. *St. Paul Pioneer*, April 19, 1867.
33. *Albany Argus* in the *Bismarck* (Dakota Territory) *Tribune*, May 24, 1876.
34. *New York Evening Express*, November 19, 1878.
35. *New York Times*, November 19, 1878
36. *New York Evening Express*, November 19, 1878.

258   Notes

37. Ibid., November 18, 1878.
38. *New York Herald*, November 17, 1878.
39. Ibid.
40. Ibid., November 19, 1878.
41. Ibid., November 17, 1878.
42. Andy Logan, "That Was New York," p. 84.

Chapter 9: The Mystery Deepens

1. *New York Herald*, November 17, 1878.
2. *New York Times*, November 19, 1878.
3. Lardner and Reppetto, *NYPD, A City and Its Police*, pp. 72–73.
4. James F. Richardson, *The New York Police, Colonial Times to 1901* (New York: Oxford University Press, 1970), pp. 210–211.
5. *New York Herald*, November 19, 1878.
6. *New York Herald*, November 19, 1878; *New York Times*, November 19, 1878.
7. *New York Sun*, November 8, 1878.
8. *New York Herald*, November 21, 1878.
9. Ibid., November 18, 1878.
10. *New York Times*, November 19, 1878.
11. *New York Sun*, November 18, 1878.
12. *New York Herald*, November 19, 1878.
13. *New York Times*, November 20, 1878.
14. *New York Herald*, November 20, 1878.
15. Ibid.
16. *Minutes of the Court of General Sessions*, part I (New York City Department of Records and Information Services, Municipal Archives), p. 360.
17. *New York Herald*, November 20, 1878.
18. *The Evening Telegram*, November 20, 1878.
19. *New York Times*, November 20, 1878.

Chapter 10: Grave Robber Christian Again

1. *New York Times*, November 21, 1878.
2. *New York Evening Post*, November 20, 1878.
3. *New York Times*, November 21, 1878.
4. *New York Sun*, November 22, 1878.
5. *New York Times*, November 22, 1878.
6. Ibid., November 21, 1878.

7. *The Evening Telegram* (New York), November 22, 1878.
8. *New York Times*, November 21, 1878.
9. *New York Evening Post*, November 22, 1878.
10. *Chicago Tribune*, November 22, 1878.
11. *New York Times*, November 23, 1878.
12. Ibid., November 22, 1878.
13. Ibid., November 23, 1878.
14. *New York Herald*, November 22, 1878.
15. *New York Evening Post*, November 20, 1878.
16. *New York Herald*, November 22, 1878.
17. *New York Evening Post*, November 21, 1878; the boardinghouse was also referred to as "Kimball's" and the proprietress as "Mrs. Kimball."
18. *New York Times*, November 24, 1878; *New York Herald*, November 24, 1878.
19. *New York Sun*, November 24, 1878.
20. *New York Herald*, November 22, 1878.
21. Ibid., November 23, 1878.
22. *New York Evening Post*, November 23, 1878.
23. *New York Evening Express*, November 23, 1878.
24. *New York Sun*, November 23, 1878.
25. *The Evening Telegram*, November 21, 1878.
26. *New York Herald*, November 23 and 24, 1878.
27. *Washington Post*, November 23, 1878.
28. Ibid., December 2 and 3, 1878.
29. *The Evening Telegram*, November 30, 1878.
30. *New York Times*, November 25, 1878.
31. *New York Herald*, November 25, 1878.

Chapter 11: The Investigation Winds Down

1. *New York Tribune*, November 26, 1878.
2. *New York Weekly Tribune*, November 27, 1878.
3. *New York Herald*, November 28, 1878.
4. *New York Times*, December 3, 1878.
5. Ibid.
6. *Oil City Derrick* in the *Dakota Pantagraph*, December 4, 1878.
7. *New York Tribune*, November 20, 1878.
8. *New York Herald*, December 2, 1878.
9. Riis, *Making of an American*, p. 221.
10. *New York Sun*, November 24, 1878.

11. *New York Times*, August 27, 1896.
12. *New York Herald*, December 10, 1878.
13. *New York Herald*, December 11, 1878.
14. Ibid., December 12, 1878.
15. Ibid., December 13, 1878.
16. Ibid.
17. *New York World*, August 22, 1881.
18. *Chicago Tribune*, December 6, 1878.
19. Ibid., December 30, 1878.

Chapter 12: First Contact with the Ghouls

1. *New York Times*, March 17, 1878.
2. *New York Sun*, April 6, 1879.
3. Ibid., June 19, 1879.
4. Ibid., July 6, 1879.
5. *New York Tribune*, August 8, 1879.
6. *Philadelphia Inquirer*, November 15, 1878.
7. *New York Times*, August 14, 1879.
8. *New York Herald* in the *Rochelle* (Illinois) *Register*, August 23, 1879; *New York Sun*, August 14, 1879.
9. *New York Evening Post*, November 14, 1878.
10. *New York Herald*, November 17, 1878.
11. *New York Herald* in the *Rochelle* (Illinois) *Register*, August 23, 1879.
12. *New York Times*, August 14, 1879.
13. *New York Herald* in the *Rochelle* (Illinois) *Register*, August 23, 1879.
14. *New York Times*, August 14, 1879.
15. Seyfried, *Founding of Garden City*, p. 39.
16. *New York Sun*, August 17, 1879.
17. Ibid.
18. *New York Times*, August 14, 1879.
19. *New York Sun*, August 17, 1879.
20. Ibid.
21. *New York Tribune*, August 16, 1879.
22. *New York Herald* in the *Rochelle* (Illinois) *Register*, August 23, 1879; *New York Sun*, August 17, 1879.
23. *New York Sun*, January 16, 1879.
24. Ibid., January 17, 1879.
25. Ibid., January 18, 1879.
26. Ibid., January 19, 1879.

27. James, "Corpse of A. T. Stewart," p. 58.
28. *New York Tribune*, January 17 and 27, 1879.
29. *New York World*, April 19, 1890.
30. *New York Tribune*, August 19, 1879.
31. Ibid., August 20, 1879.
32. Ibid., August 14, 1879.
33. *New York Telegram* in the *Rochelle* (Illinois) *Register*, August 23, 1879.
34. Howard G. Baetzhold, "Of Detectives and Their Derring-Do: The Genesis of Mark Twain's 'The Stolen White Elephant,'" in *Studies in American Humor*, pp. 183–194.
35. Artist Unknown, "A Great Advertising Dodge," *Puck*, August 27, 1879, p. 393.
36. *New York Sun*, August 17, 1879.
37. *New York World*, August 18, 1879.
38. *New York Tribune*, January 17, 1879.

Chapter 13: The Dream of Mr. Bryson

1. *New York Times*, August 22, 1881.
2. *New York Evening Telegram*, August 25, 1881.
3. *New York Times*, August 22, 1881; *New York Herald*, August 21, 1881.
4. *New York Herald*, August 21, 1881.
5. *New York Times*, August 21, 1881.
6. Carolee Inskeep, *The Graveyard Shift, A Family Historian's Guide to New York City Cemeteries* (Orem, Utah: Ancestry Publications, 2000), p. 47; *New York Times*, May 30, 1866.
7. *New York Times*, August 22, 1881.
8. *New York Sun*, August 22, 1881.
9. *New York Times*, August 21, 1881.
10. Ibid.
11. Ibid., August 22, 1881.
12. *New York Herald*, August 21, 1881.
13. Ibid.
14. Ibid., August 22, 1881.
15. Ibid.
16. *New York Tribune*, August 22, 1881.
17. *New York Sun*, August 22, 1881.
18. *Brooklyn Daily Eagle*, August 24, 1881.
19. *New York Times*, August 22, 1881.
20. *Brooklyn Daily Eagle*, August 24, 1881.

21. *New York Sun*, August 22, 1881.
22. *New York Evening Post*, August 22, 1881.
23. Ibid., August 24, 1881.
24. Ibid.
25. *New York Times*, August 25, 1881.
26. *New York Evening Post*, August 30, 1881.
27. *Brooklyn Daily Eagle*, August 24, 1881.
28. *New York World*, August 22, 1881.

Chapter 14: A Footnote to a Grave Robbery

1. Mott, *American Journalism*, p. 431.
2. Douglas, *Golden Age of the Newspaper*, pp. 95–105.
3. Mott, *American Journalism*, pp. 436–438.
4. Elias, *Forgotten Merchant Prince*, p. 197.
5. Ibid., pp. 195–196.
6. *New York World*, April 19, 1890.
7. Sanborn, *Reminiscences of Richard Lathers*, p. 44.
8. *The Nation*, April 20, 1882.
9. *New York World*, April 14, 1890.
10. Ibid., April 15, 1890.
11. Ibid., April 16, 1890.
12. Resseguie, *Decline and Fall*, p. 260.
13. *New York World*, April 16, 1890.
14. Ibid., April 17, 1890.
15. Logan, "That Was New York," p. 84.
16. Elias, *Forgotten Merchant Prince*, p. 146.
17. *New York World*, April 18, 1890.
18. Ibid., April 15, 1890.
19. Ibid., April 18, 1890.
20. A. T. Stewart Papers, New York Public Library, Box 3, Carrie Stevens to A. T. Stewart, December 7, 1871.
21. A. T. Stewart Papers, New York Public Library, Box 1, Hattie Nerval to A. T. Stewart, January 24, 1871.
22. *New York Times*, January 21, 1866.
23. Ibid., February 4, 1866.
24. Elias, *Forgotten Merchant Prince*, p. 158.
25. *New York Times*, May 1, 1890.
26. *New York World*, May 1, 1890.
27. Ibid., May 2, 1890.

28. Ibid., May 7, 1890.
29. Ibid., May 9, 1890.
30. Ibid., May 11, 1890.
31. Mott, *American Journalism*, p. 440.
32. *New York World*, August 27, 1899.

Chapter 15: Was Stewart's Body Recovered?

1. *New York Sun*, March 3, 1879.
2. Ibid.
3. *New York World*, April 19, 1890.
4. *New York Sun*, August 23, 1881.
5. Sievers, *Harrison Horror*, p. 50.
6. *New York Letter* in the *Rochelle* (Illinois) *Register*, February 12, 1881.
7. *New York Times*, April 7, 1884.
8. *New York World*, October 26, 1886.
9. Ibid.
10. *New York Times*, October 24, 1884.
11. Ibid.
12. Ibid., December 9, 1884.
13. Ibid., October 30, 1887.
14. James, "Corpse of A. T. Stewart," p. 60.
15. *New York Times*, October 30, 1887.
16. Author Unknown, "An Early Account of A. T. Stewart and the Cathedral," Manuscript, Archives of The Cathedral of the Incarnation.
17. Asbury, *Gangs of New York*, pp. 222–223.
18. *North Countryman*, May 7, 1836.
19. *New York Times*, October 26 and 27, 1886.
20. Ibid., October 28, 1886.
21. *New York Sun*, October 26, 1886.
22. *New York World*, October 26, 1886.
23. Ibid., September 3, 1899.
24. *New York Times*, August 30, 1895.
25. *New York Herald*, August 25, 1899.
26. *New York Times*, August 27, 1896.
27. Ibid., August 25, 1899.
28. Inskeep, *Graveyard Shift*, p. 79.
29. *New York World*, August 29, 1899.
30. Ibid., August 27, 1899.

31. Author Unknown, "An Early Account of A. T. Stewart and the Cathedral."
32. James, "Corpse of A. T. Stewart," p. 61.
33. Elias, *Forgotten Merchant Prince*, p. 150.
34. Logan, "That Was New York," p. 106.
35. Harry Resseguie, Letter to Mildred Smith, April 6, 1961.
36. Sanborn, *Reminiscences of Richard Lathers*, p. 48.
37. *New York World*, April 19, 1890.
38. *New York Times*, July 15, 1956.
39. Reynolds, "Merchant Prince and the Grave Robbers," *New York Daily News*, August 12, 1956.

Index

"A Company," letters from, 79, 97, 100–101
Alexander and Greene law firm, 232
Allekton, 69, 74–76, 123, 147, 156
Amity Street Baptist Church, 99–101, 248
Anstey, Herbert, 245
Astor, Helen, 137
Astor, John Jacob, 2, 7
Astor, William B., 2, 15, 20, 137
A. T. Stewart and Company, 10, 15, 24, 156; decline and failure, 43, 46, 212–213, 237; Jewish merchants, 239
attitudes toward death and burial, 19–20, 26–27, 53, 91, 119–120, 160, 199

Banker, Ellen, 46
Banker, James H., 46
Bartholow, Dr. Robert, 65–66
Bell, David, 3, 4

Bell, James, 4
Bell, Mary, 4
Belmont, August, 27, 139
Bennett, James Gordon, 80–81, 102, 210
Bennett, James Gordon, Jr., 80–81
Bierstadt, Albert, 22
Blodgett, William T., 224
Blood, Dr. C. L., 149, 153–155
Body Snatcher's League, 244
Bonheur, Rosa, "The Horse Fair" painting, 22
Boyd, Ben, 59–60
Brooklyn Daily Eagle, 208
Brown, Billy, 60–61
Brown, Maud, 77
Brown, Percy, 77, 156–157
Bryson, Mr., 191, 193
Burke, William, 118, 121–123, 129, 152, 169; in court, 139–145
Butler, Prescott Hall (nephew of Mrs. Stewart), 232

Byrne, Thomas (police captain), 139, 152; background, 140; investigates Stewart grave robbery, 141, 143

Campbell boardinghouse, 145, 148–149, 152–154; landlady, 145–146, 148, 153–154
Canada, 107, 112, 152, 165, 176–179, 181–183, 186–187, 188, 233
"Canada Mack," 156–157
Carlisle, Dr. Erwin C., 90
Carney, Dr. Sidney H., 183
Cathedral of the Incarnation, 18, 175, 212, 217, 234; "alarm system" in crypt, 240, 242; church archives, 232; Stewart Crypt, 44–45, 164, 173–174, 184, 236; Stewart's bones supposedly placed in crypt, 231, 241–242, 245; visitors, 175–176
Chicago Tribune, 59, 83–84, 115, 151
Christian, George A., 67, 76, 77, 107, 123, 154–155, 243; alias Dr. Douglas, 147–149, 152–155; never found, 169, 226; reputation as a grave robber, 156, 165; as suspect in Lincoln tomb break-in, 147; as suspect in Stewart case, 123, 147–150, 157–158
Civil War, 21, 62, 169, 241; Battle of Bull Run, 35, 140; construction of the Stewart mansion, 95; draft riots in 1863, 35, 92; Joseph Pulitzer serves, 210; Pinkerton agents, 117; Southern conspiracy to desecrate Stewart's grave, 111; spiritualists, 134; Stewart profiteering, 12–14
Clair, Henry, 163
clairvoyants, 99, 110; Stewart mystery, 133–137, 169, 243
Clay, Henry, grave of, 115
Clinch, Jacob, 6
Clinch, Susanna (Banker), 6
Clover, Phil K., 67
Cooper, Peter, 26, 47, 240
Cowen, Bernard, 246–248
Creamer, Thomas J., 107–108
Cross, Kate, 159
Crow, Dr., 156–158, 165
Cypress Hills Cemetery, 192–195, 225–227; digging for Stewart's body, 192, 202–207; history of, 198

Dagner, James, 206
Daily Eagle. See Brooklyn Daily Eagle
Daily News, recalls Stewart mystery in 1956, 247–248
Dana, Charles A., 221
Devin, Augustus, 63, 66–67
Dickens, Charles, 7, 125
Dilks, George W. (police inspector), 35, 72, 165–166, 189; interview, 119; letters, 112
doctors' riot of 1788, 39–41
Douglas, Stephen O., 13
Dr. "A," 146, 147–148
Dr. "Douglas." *See* Christian, George A.

East Fourteenth street boardinghouse. *See* Campbell boardinghouse

Eaton, George, 64
Ely, H. O., 229–230
Evans, Dr. George, 148–149, 155
Evarts, Southmayd, and Choatt law firm, 183
Evarts, William M., 26, 126

Field, Cyrus W., 12
Field, Marshall, 12
Fisk, Jim, 16, 29, 110
Fleging, Adam, 241–242
Forrest, Terrence H., 247
Fox, George P., 100
French, Edwin, 89–90
French, Julius E., 89–91
Fuller, J. M., 193–195; digs for Stewart's body, 202–207, 225; interviews, 196–198; letters to Hilton, 197, 201; superstitions, 205–206; visit from Cor, 207–208; visits Cypress Hills Cemetery, 198–200
Fuller's New York Detective Bureau, 192–193, 194

Gangs of New York, The, 232
Garden City, 17–18, 20, 43, 44, 84, 232; Mrs. Stewart interred in crypt, 236; Stewart crypt, 93, 131, 142, 173–174, 184–185, 191, 200–201, 203, 224; Stewart's bones allegedly placed in crypt, 231, 242
Gould, Jay, 16, 126
Grace Episcopal Church, 138–139, 247–248
Graham, James F., 219, 221–222
Graham, John, 106–107
Grand Union Hotel, 2, 113, 186

Grant, Ulysses S., 14–15, 27, 77, 215
grave robbing: in the 1870s, 31, 39, 63, 68, 89, 156, 226, 243; in the 1880s, 244; bodies for dissection, 51–52, 64–67, 77, 160; decrease in grave robbing, 226; in Illinois, 171–172; in Ohio, 43, 52, 58, 63, 89–91, 156, 226; methods of grave robbers, 54–58; penalty in New York, 141; vow of secrecy, 243–244
Great Iron Store, 8, 9, 212, 248; destroyed by fire in 1956, 245–246
Greeley, Horace, 15, 81, 102, 168, 189, 240
Greenwood Cemetery, 185, 240
guarding graves, 71, 89, 166–167, 173, 224, 226, 229

Hall, Abraham Oakey, 16, 115
Hamill, George W., 33–34, 41, 45–46, 185, 190, 223, 243; exonerated, 98, 101
Harper's New Monthly Magazine, 4
Harrison, Carter, 63, 64
Harrison, General Benjamin, 63, 65–67
Harrison, Henry G., 44
Harrison, John, 63, 64
Harrison, John Scott, plot to steal his body, 63–67, 156
Harrison, William Henry, 63
Hatch, Dr., alias Douglas, alias Howard, 153–157
Hickok, Wild Bill, 67
Hilton, Albert B., 238
Hilton, Henry, 15, 83, 191; anti-Semitism, 112–113, 169,

188, 239; associated with Tweed, 46–47, 215; attacked by the *World*, 209, 213–216 220–222; blackmail of Mrs. Stewart, 216, 220; Cathedral of the Incarnation, 235; contacts J. M. Fuller, 198, 201–202; contacts Patrick H. Jones, 180–181; death in 1899, 222, 239–240; deception of Mrs. Stewart, 176, 184–186; digging at Cypress Hills, 202, 206–207; early years, 46–48, 240; funeral and burial, 240–241; influence over Stewart, 214–216; interviews in the *Herald*, 103, 129, 142, 186, 189; interviews in the *Times*, 84, 98, 103, 129, 144–145; keeps silent about Stewart's body, 226, 237, 239–240, 245; lambasted by Romaine, 182; lampooned by Mark Twain, 188; letters to, 108–113, 130–131, 228; libel, 219, 221–222; mismanages Stewart estate, 169, 212–213, 237–239; Mrs. Stewart's funeral, 236; obituary, 222, 240, 241; offer of reward, 71–72, 111–112, 122, 144, 183, 187, 228; power of attorney, 212, 239; public opinion of, 210–212, 240; relationship with Stewart, 47–49, 211–213, 221; secret negotiations, 224–225, 227, 233, 237; spiritualists and clairvoyants, 136–137; Stewart crypt at Garden City, 173, 175; Stewart grave robbery, 34, 41–42, 44, 49, 70–76, 79, 87–89, 91–93, 99–102, 119, 129, 142, 150, 159, 200–202, 239; Stewart's funeral, 22–23, 26–27

Hilton, Henry G., 237
Hilton, Hughes and Company, 237–238. *See also* A. T. Stewart and Company
Hinsdale, W. R., 224
Hughes, Jack, 59–62
Hughes, John, 237

Jesuits, blamed for Stewart grave robbery, 109
Jews: blamed for Stewart grave robbery, 112; Hilton bias, 113, 169, 188, 239
Jones, Patrick H., 176, 185–186, 224–226, 243; abandons the case, 187; correspondence with Romaine, 177–183; interviews, 176, 181, 184; letter to the *Sun*, 189; negotiates with Romaine, 232; sees Hilton, 180–181; sees Walling, 179; in the *World*, 189

Kealy, Captain (chief of detectives), 108, 119, 159
Keeton, Charles, interview with grave robber, 55–56
Kelly, Michael "Hackman," 105–106, 226, 243; in Canada, 152; disappearance of, 122, 152; killed in Arizona, 169, 228; in New

Jersey, 165–166; under suspicion, 107–108, 157
Koenig, Bernard, 99

Lathers, Richard, 213; believed Stewart's body not found, 245
Leslie, George Leonidas, 125
Libbey, William, 41, 42–44, 73, 75, 129; benefits from Stewart estate, 213; Mrs. Stewart's funeral, 236
Lincoln, Abraham, 6, 13, 192, 221; plot to rob his grave, 58–63, 115, 147, 151, 227
Lincoln, Mary Todd, 13
Lincoln, Robert, 59–60
Long Island, 17, 192, 207, 212, 217, 224, 236; historians, 245; story of burial of Stewart's body, 248

Mahoney, aka Louis Mahon, 114; 141–142
Making of an American, The, 89
Marble Palace, 7, 8, 12, 13, 212; disturbance of cemetery property while under construction, 248; "secret passage," 242
Maxwell, Alexander, 95–96
May, William H., 151; 152, 156, 169
McCargile, Chicago Chief of Police, 227–228
McCarty, Thomas, 75, 76
McCullagh, John H. (police captain), 73, 95, 151
Middleton, C. N., 74–76, 107, 123, 147
Minor, Dr. John C., 186

Morgan, Justice, 139, 141–143
Murray, William (police inspector), 35, 144, 159, 202

National Police Gazette, 55, 218
Newark Standard, 220–221
New Jersey: search for Stewart's body, 72, 78, 108, 113–114, 208; Stewart's body reported found near Chatham, 140–141, 145; Stewart's body reported found near Shamony, 101; Stewart's body reported in Weehawken, 114, 119, 141–142
Newspapers, bias and reckless reporting, 209, 225
Newton boardinghouse, 74, 103–104
New York City: brothels, 218; criminal activity, 70, 83–84, 94, 118, 124–126, 127–129; decadent city, 128, 219; early descriptions, 7, 19, 127; first automobiles, 237–238; grave robbery excitement, 113; high society, 21, 22, 24, 27, 137–139, 237, 247; Hilton spectacle, 210–213; loss of interest in Stewart case, 169, 191, 222, 226, 243; newspaper reporting, 79–82; Police Department, 33, 83, 87, 92, 100, 152, 205, 223–225, 243; technological advances, 123–124; tenement houses, 125
New Yorker, 241–242
New York Evening Express, 89, 156
New York Evening News, 101–102
New York Evening Post, 32, 42, 72, 75, 154, 155; Fuller

investigation, 208; Hackman Kelly, 105; interview at Stewart residence, 85
New York Evening Telegram, 92–94, 159; Hackman Kelly, 105; interview of Burke and Vreeland, 144
New York Herald, 37, 44, 102, 160–161, 163, 183; Allekton "clew," 74–76; conspiracy theory, 158; construction of Marble Palace, 248; copy at crime scene, 33, 114, 168; critical of police, 93, 94, 168; critical of Walling's book, 232; digging at Cypress Hills Cemetery, 203; Dr. "A" ad, 146; editorial, 132; George A. Christian, 123, 147, 153–155; Hackman Kelly, 105–107; Hilton's personal ads, 181, 187; history, 80–81; interview of Burke's relatives, 121; interview of Fuller, 196; interview of Hilton, 103, 129, 142, 186, 189; interview of Walling, 93–94; Jones' personal ad, 178–179; letters from "A Company," 79, 97, 100; letters from the public, 99, 100, 109, 124, 130–131, 133, 135–136; rivalry with the *Times*, 142, 165; Virginia articles, 169–170
New York Morning Herald, 80. *See also New York Herald*
New York Sun, 72, 80, 102, 122, 183, 221; Fuller investigation, 208; George A. Christian, 156; Hackman Kelly, 105; Hilton interview, 100, 150; Hilton's deception of Mrs. Stewart, 184–185; New Jersey solution, 142; obituary of Mrs. Stewart, 236; reports Stewart's body recovered, 224–225
New York Times, 14, 16, 81, 88, 121, 183, 189, 191, 228; admonishes the poor, 125–126; arrest of Vreeland and Burke, 118, 122, 139, 143; construction of Marble Palace, 248; critical of Hilton, 113; debunks Walling's story of recovery, 231–232; editorial, 159–160; failure of Stewart's enterprise, 239; George A. Christian, 147, 152, 154; Hackman Kelly, 105–106; history, 102; interview of Fuller, 196–198; interview of Inspector Dilks, 119; interviews of Hilton, 84–85, 98, 103, 129, 144–145; interviews of Patrick H. Jones, 176, 181, 184; letters from the public, 164; mystery suspect, 145–146; obituary of Hilton, 240–241; obituary of Mrs. Stewart, 236; Ohio grave robbery, 89–91; reports Stewart's body found, 101–102, 114, 115, 149–150, 174; rivalry with the *Herald*, 142, 165; search in 1879, 173; search in Cypress Hills cemetery, 192, 196, 199, 203; Stewart grave robbery, 32, 38–39, 42, 74, 87, 92, 93,

163, 170; Stewart's funeral, 24, 26; theory of the crime, 144; unsolved mystery, 246
New York Tribune 102, 130, 164, 176, 183; Hackman Kelly, 107; Hilton deception, 185–186; history, 81; Jacob Riis, 88–89, 168–169; Reid editorial, 126
New York Weekly Tribune, 44, 81, 85
New York World, 4, 48; attacks Hilton, 209, 212–216, 220–222; attacks Stewart, 216–219, 236–237; attacks the *Sun*, 221; critical of Walling's book, 232; declares Stewart's body not recovered, 237; declares Stewart's body recovered, 189; discredits Jones and Romaine, 189; Fuller investigation, 208; obituary of Hilton, 241; obituary of Mrs. Stewart, 236–237; purchased by Pulitzer, 210; sued for libel, 219
Niblo's Garden Theatre, 2, 20, 127
Nichols, Sidney P. (police commissioner), 34, 73, 79
North Countryman, 233
Note from "Cor" to J. M. Fuller, 195

Pach, Gustavus, 22
Panic of 1873, 10, 81, 123
Parker, Francis, 33, 41, 45, 98
Perrys Mills, 233
Phelps, Robert S., 228–230
Philadelphia: cemeteries, 166; excitement over Stewart case, 113

Pinkerton, Allen, 117, 188
Pinkerton, Robert, 117
Pinkerton Detective Agency, 78–79, 117, 148–149; lampooned by Mark Twain, 188; looking for Hackman Kelly, 166
Poe, Edgar Allan, 32, 120, 231
poor people of New York, 16, 83, 88, 95, 123–129, 194
Puck Magazine, Stewart and Hilton cartoon, 188–189
Pulitzer, Joseph, 48, 209; attacks Hilton, 213–216, 220–222, 237; attacks Stewart, 216–219; attacks the *Sun*, 221; background, 210; death in 1911, 222; sued for libel, 219–220, 222

Raymond, Henry, 102
Recollections of New York Chief of Police, 230–232
Reid, Whitelaw, 81, 126, 167–168
Relyen, Peter, 165–166
Resseguie, Harry, 245
Resurrectionists, 51–53
Reynolds, Ruth, story of Stewart grave robbery, 246
Riis, Jacob, 88–89, 168–169
Rogers, Dr. David L., 52
Rogers Horseless Wagons, 237–238
Romaine, Henry G., 176, 185–187, 195, 224–226, 232, 243; in the *World*, 189, 237; letters to Patrick H. Jones, 177–183; negotiates with Jones, 232; rejects Hilton's offer and disappears, 183; reveals terms for release of body, 181; sends coffin nameplate to Jones,

180; tells Jones to see Mrs. Stewart, 182
Roosevelt, James T., 15
Runcie, John, 199, 202
Russell, Horace (assistant district attorney), 92, 149
Russick, Bernard, 78
Rylance, Dr. J. H., 37, 45, 164, 178; interview in the *Sun*, 185; sermon at St. Mark's, 82–83
Rylance, Mrs., 164

St. Mark's Episcopal Church, 6, 70–71,103, 137, 164, 174; attracting the curious, 88; George A. Christian, 148–149; history of the Church, 36; search for the body, 72, 74, 98, 109, 223–224; Stewart grave robbery, 31–33, 118, 120, 131, 145, 155, 208, 247; Stewart's funeral, 22–28, 125; Stewart's mother interred, 217
Saratoga Springs, 2, 113, 201, 235, 238, 239
Seligman, Joseph, 113
Shafer, Ira, 44
Siegel, Henry, 12
Sook, John, 183
Spiritualists, 99; beliefs 133–134; Stewart mystery, 135–137, 169
Spring Forest Cemetery, 229
Staples, Horace, 242
Staten Island, 88
Stewart, Alexander T.: arrives in New York, 4; attacked by the *World*, 216–219; birth, 3; body not recovered, 226–227, 245; body thought to be in Canada, 176–179, 182–183; business practices; 9–12, 42, 125, 217, 239; business skills, 4–6; bust of, 246; called the Merchant Prince, 1, 12, 17, 20, 22, 29, 43, 45, 119, 130, 195, 217, 228; coffin nameplate, 33, 180; criticized in a sermon, 83; cursed by two Irishmen, 247–248; death in 1876, 19; descriptions, 2, 79, 111, 218; early life, 2–3; first store, 4; funeral, 22–28, 125, 212; Garden City, 17–18; ghost, 110; grave robbery, 31–39, 42, 52, 120–122, 146, 151, 153–154, 158–159, 208, 212, 221, 245–246; Hilton inheritance, 216; Hilton intrigue, 45–48, 215–216; letters from women, 218; libel suits, 218; mansion on Fifth Avenue, 20–22, 95–96, 242; marriage, 6; "The Modern Un-Pharoah," 11; photographs, 131; relationship with Hilton, 211–214, 221–222; robbers of his grave, 192, 220, 225, 241, 243; Romaine letters, 177–183; Romaine's terms for release of body, 181; rumors and stories of recovery of his body, 84–85, 197, 224, 231–233, 241–242, 246; search for his body in 1878, 70–77, 81, 87–89, 97–104, 108–109, 113–114, 129, 131, 163, 167, 241; search for his body in

1879, 173–190, 223; search for his body in 1881, 192–207; search for his body in New Jersey, 72, 78, 101, 113–114, 119, 140–142, 145, 208; search for his body in Virginia, 169–170; Secretary of the Treasury, 13–15, 215; snubbed by high society, 21, 24, 139; story of burial at Amityville, 248; superstitions, 6, 48, 96; support for Andrew Johnson, 14; support for Grant, 14; support for Horace Greeley, 15; support for Lincoln, 13; suspects charged with theft of his body, 143; *Times* editorial, 159–160; unsolved mystery, 191, 222; "war Democrat," 13; will and codicils, 216; working women's hotel, 17, 18; *World* believed body recovered, 189

Stewart, Cornelia, 20, 22, 83, 97, 101, 207; background, 6; believed husband's body recovered, 150, 173, 184, 189, 224–225; death in 1886, 213–214, 235, 242; deceived by Hilton 184–187, 216, 220; funeral, 236; gets involved in the case, 183–185; gives Hilton power of attorney, 212; husband's funeral, 28; letters from the public, 109–110, 130–131; plan to recover the body, 230–234; Quoted in the *Sun*, 184; reward offered 71–72, 132; Romaine letter, 178, 182; suffering, 69–70, 85, 131, 164–165, 213, 234–235; told of grave robbery, 49; will, 243

Stewart, John, 157–158
Stewart, John Turney, 6
Stewart, May, 6
Stiner, Joseph H., 143
"Stolen White Elephant, The," 188
"Story of a Great Advertising Dodge, The," 188
Stuart, Gilbert, picture of George Washington, 22
Stuyvesant, Peter, 23, 36
Swegles, Lewis C., 59–61. *See also* Sweigels, Lewis C.
Sweigels, Lewis C., 227–228

Talmage, Reverend T. DeWitt, 120–121, 167
Thompson, Miss, 148, 153–155
Tilden, Samuel J., 26, 62
torpedo gun to stop grave robbers, 67
Townsend, Dr. Samuel P., 21
Train, George Francis, 167
Turney, John, 3
Twain, Mark, satire of Stewart case, 187–188
Tweed, William "Boss," 16, 46, 47, 124, 240
Tweed ring, 46, 115, 215, 216, 221, 241

Vanderbilt, Commodore. *See* Vanderbilt, Cornelius
Vanderbilt, Cornelius, 2, 13, 20, 24, 71; belief in spiritualism, 134; ghost of, 110
Vanderbilt, William H., 27

Virginia, search for Stewart's body, 169–170
Vreeland, Henry ("Hank"), alias Whalen, Wheeler, and Wilson, 118, 121–123, 129, 152; in court, 139–144; released from jail, 169

Walling, George W. (police superintendent), 77–78, 156, 243–245; background, 92; interview in *Herald*, 93–94; in New Jersey, 113–114; press criticizes book, 232; *Recollections of New York Chief of Police*, 230; sees Patrick H. Jones, 179–180; Stewart's body not recovered, 176; Stewart's body recovered, 230–232

Wanamaker, John, 12
Wanamaker Store, 245. *See also* Stewart's Great Iron Store
Washington Chronicle, 220
Washington DC detectives, 76, 77, 156–158
Washington Post, 157–158
Washington Resurrectionist, 76, 147, 226. *See also* Christian, George A.
Wickham, William H., 27
Wickman boardinghouse, 103–104, 107–108
workingwomen's hotel, 17, 18
Wright, Mrs. (sister of William Burke), 118, 122

Yellow Journalism, 169, 211

Zelinski, H., 108

About the Author

WAYNE FANEBUST is an attorney and freelance writer based in South Dakota. His books include *Echoes of November, The Life and Times of Senator R. F. Pettigrew of South Dakota* and other titles on Dakota history, politics, and biography.